LAW AND PERFORMANCE

A VOLUME IN
The Amherst Series in Law,
Jurisprudence, and Social Thought

EDITED BY
Austin Sarat
Martha Merrill Umphrey
Lawrence Douglas

LAW AND PERFORMANCE

Edited by

Austin Sarat
Lawrence Douglas
Martha Merrill Umphrey

University of Massachusetts Press
Amherst and Boston

Printed in the United States of America

ISBN 978-1-62534-355-0 (paper); 354-3 (hardcover)

Designed by Jack Harrison
Set in Scala
Printed and bound by Maple Press, Inc.

Cover design by Sally Nichols
Cover art: Plate 412, *Lower the curtain, the farce is ended (Baissez le rideau, la farce est jouée)*, by Honoré Daumier, from the journal *La Caricature*, volume no. 201.

Library of Congress Cataloging-in-Publication Data

Names: Sarat, Austin, editor. | Douglas, Lawrence, editor. | Umphrey, Martha Merrill, editor.
Title: Law and performance / edited by Austin Sarat, Lawrence Douglas, Martha Merrill Umphrey.
Description: Amherst : University of Massachusetts Press, 2018. | Series: The Amherst series in law, jurisprudence, and social thought | Includes bibliographical references and index. |
Identifiers: LCCN 2017050261 (print) | LCCN 2017052142 (ebook) | ISBN 9781613765968 (e-book) | ISBN 9781613765975 (e-book) | ISBN 9781625343543 (hardcover) | ISBN 9781625343550 (pbk.)
Subjects: LCSH: Sociological jurisprudence. | Performance art. | Law and art.
Classification: LCC K376 (ebook) | LCC K376 .L3554 2018 (print) | DDC 340/.115—dc23
LC record available at https://lccn.loc.gov/2017050261

British Library Cataloguing-in-Publication Data
A catalog record for this book is available from the British Library.

For my son Ben
(A.S.)

Contents

Acknowledgments

We are grateful to our Amherst College colleagues David Delaney and Adam Sitze for their intellectual companionship. We thank our students in Amherst College's Department of Law, Jurisprudence, and Social Thought for their interest in the issues addressed in this book. Finally, we would like to express our appreciation for generous financial support provided by Amherst College's Corliss Lamont Fund.

LAW AND PERFORMANCE

INTRODUCTION

Law and/as Performance

MARTHA MERRILL UMPHREY, AUSTIN SARAT,

AND LAWRENCE DOUGLAS

One can find traces of a conversation between law and performance scattered across the pages of scholarship in law and the humanities. This volume brings together the contemporary contours of that conversation, which has intensified in the last few decades with the flourishing of performance studies alongside a growing law-and-humanities movement. Drawing on these rich and variegated fields, the essays presented in this volume propose a kind of three-dimensional, kinetic way of thinking about what law is and what it does or refrains from doing. Taken together, they offer a theory of law that is fundamentally dialogic, dynamic, and political in unpredictable ways, and challenge us to consider the place that contingency, repetition, spectacle, and audience play in the constitution of legality, justice, and legal subjectivity. Our contributors attend to the varied ways that law is imagined and enacted and take seriously the impact of performance and performativity in shaping the cultural life of law and its uptake by different audiences.

Recent scholarship exploring the relation between law and performance builds upon debates in both fields about the nature and contours of their objects of inquiry. Implicitly, conceiving law through the lens of performance invokes legal realist claims about the nature of law as law-in-action (as opposed to law on the books); that is, we assume that the meaning of law is articulated in its doing, in ways that are situated and embodied rather than abstracted into formal rules and principles inert in the pages of statute books and judicial opinions.[1] Of course, law and literature scholars have emphasized the ways in which legal language is not inert but quite alive—indeterminate, narratively and rhetorically structured, historicized, and ideologically saturated.[2] Their inquiries have raised a set of critical questions about legal meaning and representation that remain of central and continuing relevance. And yet, through the lens of performance it becomes clear that focusing on law-as-text—as writing alone—elides, erases, or represses certain aspects of law that bring it into being in the moment of its articulation and thereafter. A statute written on the page is applied in the street, the booking room, an attorney's office, and the courtroom. Judicial opinions transmitted to the world as text are subsequently taken up, rearticulated, reworked, or rejected in an active process not just of textual interpretation but public enunciation to an engaged audience.

As Sanford Levinson and Jack Balkin have suggested in their work on law and music, "The basic idea is that law, music, and drama . . . are similar . . . insofar as they involve the transformation of ink on a page—call it a statute, a score, a script—into complex social action."[3] Both law and music involve "the acting out of texts rather than the texts themselves."[4] "To be sure," they argue, "one can read the texts of the law as collected in statute books and the like, but in that guise they are only in a state of limbo. They await their performance by legal actors and actresses or, to shift the metaphor, by virtuosos of the law who can interpret melodic lines in the law in ways overlooked by previous players."[5] In that sense a musical score, a theatrical script, or a law is both itself and not yet itself; it is only fully realized in its performance.[6]

Law and performance scholarship takes up that insight, specifying the dynamics through which legal action is ritualized, demands recognition, asserts control, attempts enforcement, generates knowledge, and engenders resistance in modalities that are both contingent and patterned. This kind of analysis directs attention less to text than to embodiment, context, role, action, and uptake. On this view, law is enacted in the performance of punishment (in the chapter by Julie Stone Peters), in the theatrics of the courtroom (Ryan Hartigan), in social rituals of legal reenactments (Ann Pellegrini and Karen Shimakawa); and it is contested and critiqued in theatrical productions (Catherine M. Cole), photographs and art installations (Lara D. Nielsen), and the literary and musical sounds that react to and counter legal violence (Joshua Chambers-Letson).

Like law, performance has been conceived in ways that are variegated and unstable. Fundamentally, it is closely linked with the idea of theatricality, a term that itself contains a number of different meanings.[7] Since antiquity, theatricality has been associated with mimesis (usually understood as some form of imitation that is sometimes criticized and other times embraced).[8] Given its imitative relationship to the real, it is often equated with artifice and counterfeit.[9] As Diana Taylor suggests, theatricality "flaunts its artifice, its constructedness . . . it highlights the mechanics of spectacle."[10] The broader concept of performance resonates with this imitative, constructed understanding of theatricality. Taylor offers a specific catalog of objects, both artistic and anthropological, for performance studies scholarship: "The many practices and events—dance, theatre, ritual, political rallies, funerals—that involve theatrical, rehearsed, or conventional/event-appropriate behaviors."[11] And in emphasizing the importance noted by Taylor of rehearsal and convention, Richard Schechner defines performance as "restored" or "twice-behaved behavior." "Restored behavior," he argues "is the main characteristic of performance. . . . Performance means: never for the first time. It means: for the second to the nth time. Performance is 'twice-behaved behavior.'"[12]

At the same time, historically the idea of theatricality has also been understood through the idea of *theatrum mundi,* an assertion of the commensurability of life and stage, which Davis and Postlewait argue "suggests that human beings are required to act out their social identities in daily life."[13] This broader conceptualization of imitation and role in theater studies literature provides the conduit connecting performance studies with anthropological and sociological theories of human activity. On this view, performance can be understood as a methodological lens enabling scholars to analyze a wide variety of events as performance,[14] embodying "a broad, multidimensional concept that is used to interpret human activities, from folk cultures and social ceremonies to gender identities and political actions."[15] Sociologist Erving Goffman, for example, considers performance to be constitutive of everyday social relations, "all the activity of an individual which occurs during a period marked by his continuous presence before a particular set of observers and which has some influence on the observers."[16] For Goffman, people perform when, wittingly or unwittingly, they take on a role for an audience.

From that perspective, it is but a short leap to connect performance with the idea of performativity, a concept derived from work in linguistics, philosophy, and rhetoric. Building on J. L. Austin's theory of the performative as a speech act (an enunciation such as "Guilty!" that itself, under felicitous conditions, does things in the world),[17] Judith Butler, for example, has argued that social identity is fundamentally a matter not of inner nature but of role and repetition, citation and iteration. On this view, we become what we "are" because we are made through discourse into specific, normalized versions of identity.[18] "Performativity" thus becomes a way to conceive of performance as extending before and beyond discrete instances of what Barbara Kirschenblatt-Gimblett calls "embodied practice and event,"[19] instead signifying a set of ongoing practices that disguise rather than highlight their constructedness.

These varying definitions of performance make their ways into law, highlighting the importance of embodiment, affect, and orientation to audience on the one hand, and on the other the constitution and reconstitution of law and legal subjectivity through rehearsal and reiteration. One obvious domain of law particularly saturated with both of these dimensions of performance is the trial, a self-consciously theatrical event that enacts a doing of law with every verdict.[20] Trials have long been likened to the stage, as public spectacles with performers playing roles and acting out dramas in front of audiences. In 1924, for example, Sir Edward Parry wrote,

> Even to-day when we think of a trial or a lawsuit we picture it to ourselves in terms of drama, applauding the hero or heroine, execrating the villain of the piece, chuckling at the comedian in the witness-box and expressing approval of the modest demeanour [*sic*] of the small-part man who walks on to the dim bench and gives the necessary cues to the great actors in the limelight. And as we read the report of a law case we recall the familiar scenery of a court house, the traditional costumes of the characters and that dramatic setting which we inwardly approve of as essential to the earliest administration of justice.[21]

For Parry, trials are the performances that lie *behind* legal texts, creating the prior conditions that produce and legitimate case law.

Parry imagines himself as part of an audience, responding to the actions of players taking on specific and conventional roles that are understood to be constructed by the rituals and legal scripts of the adversarial system. Whether embodied in a jury or the public more generally, trials bring together edification and entertainment as audiences witness two parties in a case doing battle in front of a judge over the facts and meanings of past events.[22] Those past events are not simply transcribed in a written record; they are reconstructed and reenacted through carefully crafted and rehearsed argument and the constrained but vivid presentation of evidence. Like theater, trials simultaneously conjure another place and time even as they act on their audiences in the present.[23] Advocates play roles, tell stories, and appeal to both reason and emotion in order to persuade audiences that their rendering of the past is more accurate, their arguments more compelling, and their desired outcomes more just.

In *A Theory of the Trial* Robert Burns offers a careful analysis specifically of the jury's live encounter with performance in court, arguing that it gives trials an urgency that persuades not logically but histrionically.

> The "enactment" of the trial provides the material for a dramatic sensibility on the jury's part, a "primitive and direct" awareness "before predication," as Aristotle put it, of the actions and performances displayed before it. . . . The trial requires that all the evidence come before the jury in the form of performances which, in this "primitive" but profound way, ring true or false.[24]

What matters, argues Burns, is not so much the deliberative nature of the jury, but the fact of immediate encounter with complicated, self-reflexive, competing narratives—an encounter that, in its intensity and distinctiveness, provokes a kind of intuitive response to the particular fact situation. The trial's performance orientation generates the conditions for that provocation—the electricity of watching a witness or an argument, from an immediate perspective, without knowing the outcome ahead of time.[25] Shifting allegiances produced by the adversarial format, compelling evidence, authoritative rulings from the bench, the rhetorical force of argument—all can produce a visceral affective context for judgment.[26] As Julie Stone Peters suggests, "Performance makes authority visual, palpable, bodily (accessible to the senses)."[27]

At the same time, legal performances in courtrooms, whatever an individual trial's underlying fact situation, are structured by already-given rules and role expectations, suffused with legal concepts and their discursive frameworks reiterated in trials across time and space, and structured (at least in the Anglo-American trial system) by a rigid adversarial format.[28] Hence, while individual trials, unlike theatrical scripts, are partially constituted by contingency (making them akin to improvisation, as Sara Ramshaw might suggest), trials as performances also exhibit a "performativity" in which "law" and the legal subjects who come before it are fabricated and staged through the "a reenactment and reexperiencing of a set of meanings already socially established" in prior trials.[29] Reiteration gives the trial its recognizable form, shaped by ritual (oyez! oyez!), role, procedure, instructions on applying already articulated law, and pronouncements of judgment. That form defines the terms by which conflicts are resolved and at least potentially legitimated by their various audiences.

This last point implicates the political dimensions of legal performances in trials, which under most circumstances are staged to legitimate state authority. In extreme versions of this staging, show trials are conducted in the manner of pedagogical events, placing a broader community at the center rather than the periphery of the legal process.[30] Justice is meted out to impress certain norms upon and into the local community and to demonstrate the power of the state. Presented as spectacles of justice, the theatricality of the show trial's setting and dramaturgy underscores the grand scale of adjudication in play, not only to individual defendants, but when politics and historical memory come to be judged as part of larger projects of nation-building and state legitimation.[31] Yet even trials without overt political agendas perform state authority: officials direct and regulate the adjudicative process, judges maintain a decorum respectful of hierarchies in the room; rules and procedures govern the terms of discourse and disputation, enforced by threats of citation for contempt of court. One can see the effects of this state dramaturgy most clearly in those rare cases in which the courtroom is rendered carnivalesque, when defendants and witnesses parody or subvert the processes designed to contain them.[32]

While trials might be the most recognizable legal site of state performance and performativity, this focus on audience, affect, and iterability suffuses other juridical scenes as well. Consider, for example, the moment of arrest. Police perform a role with specific signifiers of authority (uniform, badge, gun) designed to affect those being policed, to generate deference and fear in some, confidence and comfort in others. They are trained in procedure, constrained by the scope of particular laws, and required to say certain lines ("you have the right . . .") that, "twice performed," gain authority through authorization and repetition. And, in today's highly mediatized and racially fraught world, their audiences are plural and profoundly affected by the violent nature of arrest, performed again and again, then recorded and screened to larger audiences.

In both cases, legal performativity stages and is in fundamental ways complicit with the imposition of state authority. And yet attending not just to law's performances, but to the performances of those subject to law, opens up a set of questions about the shapes and forms of legal subordination and, as L. M. Bogad suggests, "creative responses to restriction."[33] As Julie Stone Peters has argued, there is a politics to legal performance and performativity, but one that is difficult to predict. She suggests that performance invites counter-performance and contest and can be an agent of liberation from, or at least resistance to, authority. "Theatre," she argues, "is law's twisted mirror, its funhouse double: ever-present, substantiating, mocking, reinforcing, undermining."[34] Some art and political theater directly addresses and contests authority;[35] in other contexts, performance employs irony, misdirection, and subtle expressiveness as a mode of critique.[36] Such counter-performances, whether they take place in a theater, a photograph, or role-playing in everyday life, can illuminate the epistemologies and operations of legal authority by revealing what has remained unseen or has been silenced by state power. Performance thus offers a lens through which we can theorize law from the perspective of its audiences and the critiques that resonate back to and through the juridical realm.

The chapters in this volume take up these problematics of legal performance and counter-performance in wide-ranging ways. Here we encounter performance in the heart of law, performances of law's cultural traces, performance as disruptive of law, and performance against law and its silences. Peters, Hartigan, and Pellegrini and Shimakawa focus primarily on scenes staging legal authority in legal and nonlegal settings, while Cole, Nielsen, and Chambers-Letson explore the ways in which artists have confronted state power through their own creative work.

Julie Stone Peters's chapter, "Penitentiary Performances: Spectators, Affecting Scenes, and Terrible Apparitions in the Nineteenth-Century Model Prison," offers a history of punishment as public spectacle. In it she argues (contra Foucault) that the spectacular performance of punishment, far from waning with the end of public executions in the eighteenth century, was central to penal regimes through the early twentieth century. Crowds of spectators visited penitentiaries to watch various kinds of penal performances; indeed, prisons functioned as tourist destinations and performance spaces that offered "edification, opportunities for philanthropic action, and spectacular pleasures." Jeremy Bentham himself called for just this sort of Panopticon, one that shames prisoners.[37]

In England and the United States, thousands yearly bought tickets to see melodramatic and gothic scenes of misery and despair, witnessing the suffering of the imprisoned and condemned up close. Prison officials embraced this tourist industry, in effect directing penal performances such as the highly choreographed lockstep for their audiences. Peters offers a reading of images depicting the lockstep, interpreting it as both an example of discipline in the Foucauldian sense and as a theatrical production rife with symbolism for its audience: prisoners were forbidden to return their audience's gaze, performing the temptation to look and its overcoming. Similarly, she argues, penitentiaries produced the spectacle of labor (the treadmill, the crank, the shot drill) that was in practical terms useless beyond audience consumption, restaging the crime of "unproductivity" or laziness.

Ironically, Peters ultimately suggests, these stagings failed both in disciplining convicts (who looked back anyway) and uplifting spectators. For the audience, the lockstep and treadmill generated an uncanny feeling that disturbed as much as edified, rendering the prisoners ghostly to their eyes—even as guards continued to flog prisoners offstage in ways that belied the entire disciplinary and shaming project of these performances. Such indeterminacy, Peters argues, ultimately protected the ambivalent sensibilities of the spectators, who desired to see and not to see the violence of imprisonment. For them, ultimately, seeing was both doing and not doing, which rendered the project of penal theater hollow.

Ryan Hartigan takes up the theme of ambivalence around performance in a different context: the courtroom. In "'This Is a Trial, Not a Performance!': Staging the Time of Law," he explores the relationship between law, performance, and temporality in *Delgamuukw v. R,* an important 1987–1991 case out of British Columbia in which indigenous groups petitioned the court for legal recognition of their claims to a large swath of land in northwest British Columbia. At trial, the Gitksan and Wet'suwet'en petitioners offered performances—dances and oral histories—as expert testimony concerning their ownership of the land from "time immemorial."[38] The court, while dismissing their evidence as "performance," allowed it into the record only to discredit it as epistemologically unreliable. Because the trial judge invoked the logic of the legal doctrine "terra nullius," which depends upon a portrayal of indigenous peoples as lacking the institutions of civilized society and in particular of failing to occupy and use land continuously, this discrediting of indigenous oral history inevitably doomed their case.

Noting the judge's dismissal of certain kinds of theatrical performance in court, Hartigan argues that the trial itself *is* a performance—that the judge manages the shape and politics of the spectacle by selecting, presenting, and privileging certain "embodied processes" while also disguising those operations. In this case, the court favored one form of time—linear, evolutionary, borne of Enlightenment colonialist practice—over another, more continuous and capacious form of time displayed in the trial's indigenous performances. Yet the court also displayed, Hartigan suggests, a profound anxiety around the problem of difference, embodied in the judge's exclamation: "This is a trial, not a performance!" Such a statement is itself performative, he claims, in the sense that it creates a self-authorizing distinction and then enacts it. Hartigan critiques the politics infusing that anxiety, which embeds the court "within the historical forms of life that it structures" even as it purports to be detached from them. Ultimately, the Canadian Supreme Court rejected the trial court's analysis, expanding evidentiary categories to include performance and oral history as Aboriginal common law. This more capacious approach to temporality and difference offers, Hartigan concludes, the possibility of exposing and reappraising law's performative structurings of the world it governs.

If Peters's contribution illuminates the ambiguous efficacy of penal theater and Hartigan's the anxieties over authorization that lie at the heart of courtroom performance, Ann Pellegrini and Karen Shimakawa theorize the paradoxes of legal reenactment. Their chapter, "Reenactability," examines the ways in which contemporary performances of historical trials that legitimized racial oppression generate a kind of reparative pleasure out of prior abjection. J. L. Austin's dismissal of theatrical speech as parasitic ("hollow and void") on performatives offers Pellegrini and Shimakawa a metaphor, the parasite/host relation, with which to take up the mock trial as a not-quite-legal form. Focusing in particular on reenactments performed by the Asian American Bar Association of New York, they argue that these "legal" performances offer both pedagogy, educating audiences about past injustice, and pleasure, in spite of recreating the scene of past injury.

Pellegrini and Shimakawa suggest that, like camp performance, reenactments engage in off-kilter, anachronistic quotation by actors playing roles and the pleasures of this kind of camp disrupt old racial conventions by creating a performative shield to deflect insults without "refusal to refuse negativity." Camp transforms injury; it is, in Eve Sedgwick's terms, performative repair, a reembodying of histories of exclusion and abjection. Reenactments of cases such as the Vincent Chin murder trial, the *Yasui* case legitimizing curfews against Asian Americans during wartime, and others produce and generate ontological discomfort that helps contemporary audiences manage encounters with difference. In both authorizing and imperiling law, these mock trials pose questions about the ethics and politics of memory and history in legal performance. They also, Pellegrini and Shimakawa argue, tell us something about the nature of legal misrecognition, the capacity of law to recognize and redress harm, and the ways in which the shards of past legal violence can be transformed into material usable in the present and future.

Our final three chapters introduce us to creative work that performs responses to state indifference, silencing, and subjugation. Catherine M. Cole turns to theater itself to pry open the internal affective dynamics of arrest and their differentiation within structures of racism. In "Statements before and after Arrests: Performing at Law's Edge in Apartheid South Africa," she offers a reading of South African playwright Athol Fugard's 1972 play *Statements after an Arrest Under the Immorality Act*. Fugard produced the play under conditions of intense state policing of the colour line, and it concerns the state's Immorality Act, which prohibited "illicit carnal intercourse between Europeans and natives."

In the play, Errol, a coloured Anglican missionary, and Frieda, a white librarian, are having a clandestine affair in Frieda's library. They are discovered making love by a policeman halfway through the play, caught in the officer's blinding flashlight and camera flashes. Cole focuses on this moment of arrest—the moment at which law hails and seizes someone, performatively interpellating them into a particular kind of legal subjectivity—and Errol and Frieda's experience of it. The arrest stages a scene of subjection that fractures the play aesthetically and politically. In the first half, their affair offers some sanctuary together from their separate and separated worlds; in the second, they unravel, responding to their capture in differing, racialized ways. Errol, in particular, experiences what Cole calls a "drama of unbecoming." He metaphorically is dismembered and in that process becomes one who refuses or disrupts the dual performativity of the subject and the law. In Judith Butler's terms, he is a man willing not to be, desubjectivizing himself in his monologues, and in so doing—in becoming pure will—exposes the limits of legal power.

The play, Cole suggests, makes the audience complicit in the arrest—as witness, spy, or accomplice in the interrogations. Yet she also notes the irony of the startling simultaneity between two aspects of theater mainly kept separate: the presentness of the production (its ontic quality) and its reference to the world beyond (its mimetic quality): in apartheid South Africa the law prohibited mixed-raced audiences. Hence the audience was *inside* the anxious racial problematic of the play itself; the play performatively generated the immorality it portrayed and hailed the law through its "statement."

In "Freedom with Silence: Cryptoanalytics and the *Differend* in the Afterlives of Legal Things," Lara D. Nielsen asks: How does performance respond to epistemological violence—a violence of dispossession and suffering? Focusing on Mexico and artists' responses to its war on drugs,

Nielsen explores the poetics of law's remains—the disposable and left-over fragments of people and their lives that persist through the work of four artists who approach problems of justice indirectly, using silence as a resource to respond to legal and extralegal violence.

Nielsen begins with the photographic form of the mugshot, used by small town mayor María Santos Gorrostieta Salazar to display herself as a woman injured by drug cartels. Her images "enact an archive" that authorizes, even demands, legal verification. It offers a kind of historical effervescence that questions the silences of law around the violence that surrounds her. Next Nielsen turns to a play/film, *Backyard*, about the biopolitics of border economics in Juárez, Mexico, where the murder of an indigenous woman emanates from both interpersonal violence (she is killed senselessly by an indigenous compatriot) and the state, which has produced space hierarchically along the border in ways that structure subjugation.

Nielsen then analyzes an installation by artist Teresa Margolles comprising the real forensic evidence fragments from morgues (blood, bodily effluvia, wash water, autopsy thread) collected after the autopsies of those executed in Mexico's "narcoscape." These uncanny scenes, she argues, ultimately subvert colonial empathy in a poetics of the missing, of statelessness. Nielsen concludes with Natalia Almada's 2011 documentary, *El Velador/The Nightwatchman*, about a Sinaloa cemetery's night watchman and those he watches in a monumental cemetery growing swiftly. The night watchman listens to those who visit and watches as grave after new grave is dug. The film's quiet repetition stands in for the silence generated by violence, the eloquence of Lyotard's *differend*—the site of absolute incommensurability.[39]

These artists, Nielsen suggests, offer strategies for responding to Mexico's narcoscapes, generated by its war on drugs and the silences it produces. Their works provide their audience different versions of silences—silences which are themselves encrypted proof, beyond legal certification. "Here," Nielsen argues, "the police, the state, the border, the morgue, the cemetery, and social media present archivizing sites that are as bound up with the protocols of legal regulation as they discard its rituals of verifiability." They are, in Avital Ronell's telling phrase, the "testamentary whimpers"[40] emerging out of law's own silences.

If Nielsen concentrates on the ways in which forensic evidence can fill in state-generated silence, Joshua Chambers-Letson captures the political power of the insurgent scream. In his chapter "Twelve Notes on Ferguson: Black Performance and Police Power," we are offered what amounts to a myth about performance, and indeed a performance itself in essay form. Chambers-Letson charts a landscape of screams in African American literature and music, the ways in which they disrupt law as they engage in their own world-making. He likens Nina Simone, and Frederick Douglass's Aunt Hester to Clytemnestra from *The Oresteia*—a character who engaged in justified violence, killing her husband to avenge his sacrifice of her daughter, but who was in the end abandoned by law when Athena's judgment favored her son Orestes over her champions, the Furies.[41] In his rendering, Clytemnestra becomes Walter Benjamin's angel of history, watching tragedies meld into a single catastrophe behind her as she inexorably moves forward.[42]

Listen to the screams, Chambers-Letson enjoins us as readers. Offering a compendium of law's refusals to listen to the cries of African Americans across two centuries, from slavery and Jim Crow through the 2014 killing of Michael Brown in Ferguson, Missouri, Chambers-Letson argues that law's historical relation to white supremacy and racial capitalism inclines it toward gagging insurgent speech acts, like screams. Yet the screams continue—in uprisings, in hip-hop, and most dramatically in Nina Simone's 1964 Carnegie Hall rendition of a Kurt Weill song, "Pirate Jenny," sung after the bombing of the Sixteenth Street Baptist Church in Birmingham, Alabama. Chambers-Letson's narration of Simone's performance comes as near as any writing can to transporting us, as readers, back to the scene of her performance, her "aesthetic insurgency" against her white audience. How her biting rendition of the song affected that audience we do not know; but now, in this moment, Chambers-Letson says, we are beginning to listen.

Chambers-Letson's vivid description of Nina Simone's powerful political act implicitly poses a difficult epistemological problem for scholars of law and performance: How does one approach and analyze an event, however iterable, whose affective landscape is contextual and ephemeral? The liveness of performance, its contingencies and its reception, are difficult to reconstruct *post hoc*. How could we know what Renaissance music really sounded like and how it was understood, or how florid nineteenth-century courtroom rhetoric moved jurors toward judgment? Yet this interpretive problem—asking how meaning is generated dialogically, in between legal act and audience—is central to the cultural analysis of law, whether performance or text.

As Diana Taylor notes, "By taking performance seriously as a system of learning, storing, and transmitting knowledge, performance studies allows us to expand what we understand by 'knowledge'"[43]—in this case knowledge about law and its effects. We understand better what law is by exploring how it is staged. In focusing our gaze on embodiment and affect, audience and reception, contingency and reiteration, our contributors enable us to see law's multidimensional modes of enunciation and transmission, and the ways in which legal power is continuously enacted and reenacted, reinforced and contested. And as Elin Diamond suggests, in attending to performance's investment in both repetition and presence, and the unstable, creative space in between, we can begin to "assert the possibility of materializing something that exceeds our knowledge, that alters the shape of sites and imagines other as yet unsuspected modes of being."[44]

NOTES

1. On legal realism, see William Fisher, Morton Horwitz, and Thomas Reed, *American Legal Realism* (Oxford: Oxford University Press, 1993).

2. See, among many works, Guyora Binder and Robert Weisburg, *Literary Criticisms of Law* (Princeton, NJ: Princeton University Press, 2000); Peter Brooks, *Troubling Confessions: Speaking Guilt in Law and Literature* (Chicago: University of Chicago Press, 2001); Peter Brooks and Paul Gewirtz, eds., *Law's Stories: Narrative and Rhetoric in the Law* (New Haven, CT: Yale University Press, 1998); Sanford Levinson and Steven Mailloux, eds., *Interpreting Law and Literature: A Hermeneutic Reader* (Evanston, IL: Northwestern University Press, 1988); Richard H. Weisberg, *Poethics, and Other Strategies of Law and Literature* (New York: Columbia University Press, 1992); James Boyd White, *Heracles' Bow: Essays on the Rhetoric and Poetics of the Law* (Madison: University of Wisconsin Press, 1985); James Boyd White, *Acts of Hope: Creating Authority in Literature, Law and Politics* (Chicago: University of Chicago Press, 1994).

3. Sanford Levinson and Jack Balkin, "Interpreting Law and Music: Performance Notes on 'The Banjo Serenader and 'The Lying Crowd of Jews,'" *Cardozo Law Review* 20 (1999): 1513.

4. Sanford Levinson and Jack Balkin, "Law as Performance," in *Law and Literature*, ed. Michael Freeman and Andrew D. E. Lewis (Oxford: Oxford University Press, 1999), 729.

5. Sanford Levinson and Jack Balkin, "Law, Music, and Other Performing Arts," 139 *U. Pa. L. Rev.* 1597 (1991): 57. http://www.yale.edu/lawweb/jbalkin/articles/lawmusic.pdf (accessed July 14, 2016).

6. In her recent essay Sara Ramshaw takes the law-music analogy further, likening law to musical improvisation. Improvisation, she argues, is "the aporetic negotiation between text and performance, singularity and generality, the pre-existent and the new. . . . [It] shares with law an impossible openness to the unpredictable and uncertain other. However, to be recognized *as* improvisation, it must obey certain pre-existent structures or 'laws.'" Sara Ramshaw, "The Paradox of Performative Immediacy: Law, Music, Improvisation," *Law, Culture and the Humanities* 12:1 (2016): 8, 12.

7. As Tracy C. Davis and Thomas Postlewait pose the question, "Does dramatic performance refer beyond itself to the world or does it serve to make explicit the theatrical aspects of presentation?" Tracy C. Davis and Thomas Postlewait, eds., *Theatricality* (Cambridge: Cambridge University Press, 2003), 13.

8. See ibid., 4–8. See also Erich Auerbach, *Mimesis: The Representation of Reality in Western Literature* (Princeton, NJ: Princeton University Press, 2003); Michael Taussig, *Mimesis and Alterity* (New York: Routledge, 1992).

9. Davis and Postlewait, *Theatricality*, 17. Art historian Michael Fried, for example, defines theatricality as a consciousness of viewing that sacrifices absorption for the sake of the beholder's applause. Michael Fried, *Absorption and Theatricality: Painting and Beholder in the Age of Diderot* (Berkeley: University of California Press, 2000), 100.

10. Diana Taylor, *The Archive and the Repertoire* (Durham, NC: Duke University Press, 2003), 13.

11. Ibid., 3. Both Taylor's introduction and Julie Stone Peters's article offer extended overviews of the term's many definitions. See Julie Stone Peters, "Legal Performance Good and Bad," *Law, Culture and the Humanities* 4 (2008): 179–200.

12. Richard Schechner, *Between Theater and Anthropology* (Philadelphia: University of Pennsylvania Press, 1985), 36.

13. Davis and Postlewait, *Theatricality*, 10.

14. Taylor, *The Archive and the Repertoire*, 3.

15. Davis and Postlewait, *Theatricality*, 31.

16. Erving Goffmann, *The Presentation of Self in Everyday Life* (New York: Doubleday, 1959), 22.

17. J. L. Austin, *How to Do Things with Words* (Cambridge, MA: Harvard University Press, 1975).

18. See Judith Butler: *Gender Trouble: Feminism and the Subversion of Identity* (New York: Routledge, 1990); *Bodies That Matter: On the Discursive Limits of Sex* (New York: Routledge, 1993); *Excitable Speech: A Politics of the Performative* (New York: Routledge, 1997). This emphasis on iteration is derived from Jacques Derrida's analysis of J. L. Austin's concept of the performative, and in particular Derrida's critique of Austin's dismissal of theater as an "impure" performative speech act because of its artifice. See Jacques Derrida, "Signature Event Context," in *Limited Inc.*, trans. Samuel Weber and Jeffrey Mehlman (Evanston, IL: Northwestern University Press, 1988).

19. Barbara Kirschenblatt-Gimblett, "Performance Studies," in *The Performance Studies Reader*, 3rd. ed., ed. Henry Bial and Sara Brady (London: Routledge, 2016), 25.

20. Catherine M. Cole has elaborated on these claims in the somewhat different context of South Africa's Truth and Reconciliation Commission proceedings, exploring "how the commission used restored behavior, expressive embodiment, storytelling and retelling; how it called into being different audiences and arenas of witnessing; how it functioned as a ritual for addressing a massive breach in the social fabric; how it drew upon existing genealogies of performance, particularly as the disempowered came into contact with the law in judicial or quasi-judicial arenas; how, in sum, the TRC served as a literal and figurative stage for South Africa's political transition." Catherine M. Cole, *Performing South Africa's Truth Commission: Stages of Transition* (Bloomington: Indiana University Press, 2010), xvi.

21. Sir Edward Parry, *The Drama of the Law* (London: Ernst Benn Ltd., 1924), 7–8.

22. Of course, we do not follow routine trials with the same attention we give to spectacular trials, a fact suggesting that their entertainment value lies in more than the pleasures of contest. Certain trials have, since the printing of murder trial narratives in the late eighteenth century, captured the public gaze. Some have concerned political corruption and rebellion; some have exposed the underbelly of the "respectable" classes; some

have dramatized conflict born of social segregation and stratification; some have laid bare the most violent and anti-normative human tendencies. On the history of gothic narratives about murder in particular, see Karen Haltunnen, *Murder Made Foul: The Killer and the American Gothic Imagination* (Cambridge, MA: Harvard University Press, 1998). On spectacular trials generally, see Robert Hariman, ed., *Popular Trials: Rhetoric, Mass Media, and the Law* (Tuscaloosa: University of Alabama Press, 1990).

23. As Rebecca Schneider suggests, "In theater, representing something occurs simultaneously with making/doing on stage. . . . Both are true—real *and* faux, action *and* representation—and this both/and is the beloved and often discussed conundrum of theatricality in which the represented bumps uncomfortably (and ultimately undecideably) against the affective, bodily instrument of the real." Rebecca Schneider, *Performing Remains: Art and War in Times of Theatrical Reenactment* (London: Routledge, 2011), 42.

24. Robert Burns, *A Theory of the Trial* (Princeton, NJ: Princeton University Press, 2001), 139–40 (footnotes omitted).

25. As Peggy Phelan has argued, "Performance's only life is in the present. Performance cannot be saved, recorded, documented, or otherwise participate in the circulation of representations *of* representations: once it does so, it becomes something other than performance." Peggy Phelan, *Unmarked: The Politics of Performance* (London: Routledge, 1993), 146. While this view is somewhat at odds with performance studies scholars who stress the iterative nature of performance, it does suggest that performance has particular effects in the moment that affect its reception.

26. Milner Ball describes this dynamic as imparting an important poetic or metaphoric element to trials. "What the advocate seeks . . . is," he suggests, "the passage from the materials of fact and law (the text) by means of courtroom presentation (the performance) to a persuasive statement of what ought to be done in a given situation (the metaphor)." Milner Ball, "The Play's the Thing: An Unscientific Reflection on Courts under the Rubric of Theater," *Stanford Law Review* 28 (1975): 91. In the context of mapping new methodological strategies in cultural-legal history, Ariela Gross has suggested three ways in which treating trials as performances allows us to attend to what might loosely be understood as the cultural dimension of trials: it draws our eye toward the actual audiences for trials and the ways in which information is presented to and consumed by them; it helps us to understand trials as public performances that exert certain kinds of moral and psychological effects on various communities; and it conceives trials as fora for the performance of certain kinds of identities, and as arenas for the representation of selves. Ariela Gross, "Beyond Black and White: Cultural Approaches to Race and Slavery," *Columbia Law Review* 101 (April 2001): 651–54.

27. Peters, "Legal Performance Good and Bad," 180.

28. In that sense, trial performances are a kind of ritual that, Clifford Geertz argues, "not only brings out the temporal and collective dimensions of such action and its inherently public nature with particular sharpness; it brings out also its power to transmute not just opinions but . . . the people who hold them." Clifford Geertz, "Blurred Genres: The Refiguration of Social Thought," *Local Knowledge: Further Essays in Interpretive Anthropology* (New York: Basic Books, 1983), 29.

29. Judith Butler, *Gender Trouble*, 140. On this point see Martha Merrill Umphrey, "Law in Drag: Trials and Legal Performativity," *Columbia Journal of Gender and Law* 21, no. 2 (2011): 114–29. As Peters articulates the point, "Indeed . . . law is the ultimate performative institution: producing the frameworks of subjecthood and subjectivity through discursive acts." Peters, "Legal Performance Good and Bad," 181.

30. On show trials, see Judith Sklar, *Legalism: Law, Morals, and Political Trials* (Cambridge, MA: Harvard University Press, 1986); Hannah Arendt, *Eichmann in Jerusalem: A Report on the Banality of Evil* (New York: Penguin, 1994); Robert Hariman, *Popular Trials.*

31. In noting the theatricality of the Eichmann trial, Hannah Arendt writes that "the show Ben-Gurion had had in mind to begin with did take place, or, rather, the 'lessons' he thought should be taught to Jew and Gentiles, to Israelis and Arabs, in short, to the whole world." Arendt, *Eichmann in Jerusalem*, 9. For an insightful consideration of high-profile trials generally, see Ferguson, *The Trial in American Life* (Chicago: University of Chicago Press, 2007), part 1.

32. See, for example, Tom Hayden, Ron Sossi, and Frank Condon, *Voices of the Chicago Eight: A Generation on Trial* (San Francisco: City Lights Books, 2008); Peter Goodrich, "Let Us Compare Mythologies: The Question of the Legal Other," in *Languages of Law: From Logics of Memory to Nomadic Masks* (London: Weidenfeld & Nicolson, 1990).

33. L. M. Bogad, *Tactical Performance: The Theory and Practice of Serious Play* (New York: Routledge, 2016), 2. As Bogad describes artists engaged in explicitly political "tactical performance" acts, "They do not make the rules of the game, but can deliberately misinterpret or subvert them. They scavenge, filch, and repurpose the dominant players' words and tropes for cultural sabotage, subvertisement, and social-movement organizing" (5).

34. Peters, "Legal Performance Good and Bad," 198. As Jon Erickson suggests, "Much of theatrical performance engages in ethical judgments that can be appropriated for a political purpose by its audience." Jon Erickson, "Defining Political Performance with Foucault and Habermas: Strategic and Communicative Action," in *Theatricality*, 183. Diana Taylor emphasizes the ways in which theatricality is suffused with politics. "Theatricality," she suggests, "strives for efficaciousness, not authenticity. It connotes a conscious, controlled, and, thus, always political dimension." Taylor, *The Archive and the Repertoire*, 13. See also Peggy Phelan, *Unmarked: The Politics of Performance* (New York: Routledge, 1993); Lisbeth Goodman with Jane de Gay, eds., *The Routledge Reader in Politics and Performance* (New York: Routledge, 2000); Elin Diamond, ed., *Performance & Cultural Politics* (New York: Routledge, 1996); Taylor, *The Archive and the Repertoire*, 15.

35. The classic text on political theater is Augusto Boal, *Theatre of the Oppressed*, trans. Charles A. and Maria-Odilia Leal McBride (New York: Theatre Communications Group, 1985).

36. As Dwight Conquergood has argued, "Subordinated people do not have the privilege of explicitness," but meaning can nevertheless be expressed forcefully through "intonation, silence, body tension, arched eyebrows, blank stares, and other protective arts of communication." Dwight Conquergood, "Performance Studies: Interventions and Radical Research," *TDR* 46, no. 2 (Summer 2002): 146.

37. Michel Foucault, *Discipline and Punish: The Birth of the Penitentiary* (New York: Pantheon, 1977).

38. In Diana Taylor's terms, Hartigan argues, these performances are more akin to "repertoire" (embodied culture) than "archive" (written culture).

39. See Jean-François Lyotard, *The Differend: Phrases in Dispute* (Minneapolis: University of Minnesota Press, 1988).

40. Avital Ronell, "The Testamentary Whimper," *South Atlantic Quarterly* 102, no. 2/3 (Spring/Summer 2004): 489–99.

41. Aeschylus, *The Oresteia: Agamemnon, The Libation Bearers, The Eumenides*, trans. Robert Fagles (New York: Penguin, 1984).

42. See Walter Benjamin, "Theses on the Philosophy of History," in *Illuminations: Essays and Reflections* (New York: Schocken, 1969).

43. Taylor, *The Archive and the Repertoire*, 16.

44. More fully, Diamond argues, "Indeed, postmodern notions of performance embrace what Plato condemned in theatrical representation—its non-originality—and gesture toward an epistemology grounded not on the distinction between truthful

models and fictional representations but on different ways of knowing and doing that are constitutively heterogeneous, contingent, and risky. Thus while a performance embeds traces of other performances, it also produces experiences whose interpretation only partially depends on previous experience. This creates the terminology of 're' in discussions of performance, as in *re*embody, *re*inscribe, *re*configure, *re*signify. 'Re' acknowledges the preexisting discursive field, the repetition—and the desire to repeat—within the performative present, while 'embody,' 'configure,' 'inscribe,' and 'signify' assert the possibility of materializing something that exceeds our knowledge, that alters the shape of sites and imagines other as yet unsuspected modes of being. Of course, what alters the shape of sites and imagines into existence other modes of being is anathema to those who would police social borders and identities." Diamond, *Performance & Cultural Politics*, 1–2.

CHAPTER 1

Penitentiary Performances

Spectators, Affecting Scenes, and Terrible Apparitions in the Nineteenth-Century Model Prison

Julie Stone Peters

> *Multum ex scenâ,* I will venture to say, speaking of the penal. . . . To say, *Multum ex scenâ,* is to say, lose no occasion of speaking to the eye. In a well-composed committee of penal law, I know not a more essential personage than the manager of a theatre.
>
> —Jeremy Bentham, *The Panopticon* (1791)

In the course of describing *The Panopticon* (1791), the perfect prison he has designed, Jeremy Bentham briefly reflects on the staging of punishment during the Spanish Inquisition, musing:

> [Its] authors, . . . whatever enormities . . . may be laid to their charge, must at least be allowed to have had some knowledge of *stage effect*. Unjust as was their penal system in its application and barbarous in its degree, the skill they displayed in making the most of it in point of impression, their solemn processions, their emblematic dresses, their terrific scenery, deserve rather to be admired and imitated than condemned.[1]

Recognizing the importance of "stage effect" in punishment—the powerful "impression" made by "solemn processions," "emblematic dresses," "terrific scenery"—Bentham offers a revision of one of Sir Francis Bacon's maxims:

> *Nihil ex scenâ* [*nothing from the theatre*], says Lord Bacon, speaking of procedure in the civil branch of the law: *Multum ex scenâ* [*much from the theatre*], I will venture to say, speaking of the penal. The disagreement is but verbal: *Scena,* in the language of the noble philosopher, means *lying:* in mine, *scena*

is but *scenery*. To say, *Multum ex scenâ*, is to say, lose no occasion of speaking to the eye. In a well-composed committee of penal law, I know not a more essential personage than the manager of a theatre. (174)[2]

The Historiography of the Performance of Punishment

Bentham's plan for the Panopticon is, of course, a *locus classicus* for historians studying the remarkable transformation in practices of punishment that took place between the sixteenth and nineteenth centuries: the disappearance of such dramatic and varied public punishments as breaking at the wheel, drawing and quartering, burning at the stake, branding, the pillory (and so on). Accompanying these changes, prisons, penitentiaries, and reformatories multiplied, and many previously violent physical penalties were replaced with prison sentences or transportation overseas. By the 1840s, historians argue, the modern prison system had come into being. Scholars disagree about why the change took place.[3] But they tend to agree on one thing: sometime in the late eighteenth or nineteenth century, the prison supplanted the spectacular performance of punishment that had characterized penal regimes since at least the late middle ages. Punishment was now hidden from the public eye. The era of penal spectacle was over.[4] Under the influence of such views (and the long shadow of Foucault), it now seems to go without saying that the spectacular performance of punishment went the way of the *ancien régime* and was, in the nineteenth century, replaced by a regime of insidious, invisible discipline.[5]

Nineteenth-century penal power unquestionably often worked in distinctly untheatrical ways (through, for instance, solitary confinement, transportation, fines, and more). But, as I hope to show (here and elsewhere), the spectacular, theatrical performance of punishment—far from disappearing in the nineteenth century—was at the heart of penal regimes, including prison regimes, until well into the twentieth century. In a separate study, I will examine the ongoing public performance of execution and flogging (which continued even when these were most under attack in the nineteenth and early twentieth centuries) and the role of dramatic and theatrical theory in the reconceptualization of punishment. As I will show, theatrical aesthetics helped crystallize ideas about what was special about performance (in penal regimes and elsewhere): its visible expressiveness, multi-sensory intensity, symbolic capacity, clarity, immediacy, animation, temporal and spatial delimitation, exemplarity, power to shame, ability to create communal bonds and to reinforce social norms, and cathartic potential. During this period, the ongoing public performance of execution and flogging became a critical locus for examining anthropological and affective issues: the status of the human, the nature of perception, the experience of pain, the translation of bodily sensation into knowledge, and more. Rather than doing away with public performance as a penal tool, nineteenth- and early twentieth-century legislators, prison administrators, and others transformed its meaning, spaces, and modes of expression, forms, styles, audiences, and ideologies, reworking penal performance for "modern" spectators. This means that to argue that the public performance of punishment disappeared around 1800 or 1840 or 1880 is not merely to get the dates wrong: it is to miss a crucially transformative period in the modern history of punishment.

In the essay that follows, I look not at public execution and flogging but at the nineteenth-century Anglo-American prison. In some places in the nineteenth century, prisons could in fact be fairly isolated, but in North America and Britain (as I will show), and in many other parts of the world, model penitentiaries functioned as tourist destinations and performance spaces: staging exhibitions of prison regimentation and the mechanics of reform for the many spectators who thronged to these sites in search of edification, opportunities for philanthropic action, and spectacular pleasures.[6] This essay attempts both to describe the performances staged there and to say something about what they meant. In an epilogue, I reflect on the meaning of this history for the reemergence of the prison as tourist destination and performance space in the twenty-first-century reality show.

These arguments are themselves part of a longer historical study of legal performance. In that study (as here), I use the word "performance" in a narrower sense than that in which it is often used in contemporary criticism.[7] Poststructuralist-inflected discussions of "performativity" have taught us to see all doing, being, behaving, or producing (indeed, pretty much everything) as a kind of performance. My use of the word, on the contrary, references a distinction between "performance" and everyday life that the word often conjures in ordinary discourse, a distinction strongly inflected by the historically theatrical associations of the word. The performances I study are not theater proper: to call them "theater" would be to suggest, misleadingly, that they bear the same institutional framework as performances that take place in the settings we normally call "theaters." At the same time, unlike everyday life, the performances I study are, on the whole, overtly and conspicuously (often intentionally, sometimes embarrassingly) theatrical. In these, there is no need to expose a covert performativity (gender, race . . .) masquerading as the natural: theatricality is generally out there for all to see. Using the word "performance" in this sense does not mean that I wish to redefine it, or narrow its critical usage. It merely means that this narrower usage allows me to see things about legal acts, events, and practices that the broader usage might obscure. If the objects I look at are "performances" in this sense, it is historical nomenclature and imagery that guide me (at least in the first instance): legal acts, events, and practices may be "dramas," "spectacles," "shows," "entertainments," or "exhibitions," "staged" or "acted" or "performed" in "scenes" for "spectators"; images may represent legal scenes on stages, framed by theatrical curtains, in circuses or as parades or marches or exhibits, gazed upon by a crowd of spectators. Each of these words or icons, of course, has its own valence, with its own set of historical associations (associations I often try to capture in my usage). But together they form a constellation that my discussion of legal performance evokes and describes.

Texts and images that portray legal acts, events, and practices in theatrical terms (explicitly or implicitly) tend to highlight three features: they highlight the fact that they are performed for spectators (in delimited spaces and time periods); they highlight the fact that they use visual, aural, animate, and bodily effects for purposes of expression or representation; and (harder to pinpoint) they highlight the fact that they seem to have an air of phenomenological duality—that is, while real, they also somehow feel like imitations or repetitions or quotations, self-consciously produced, masking something else, not quite fully real. In short, such legal acts, events, and practices may seem to be produced (as Bentham puts it) by "the manager of a theatre."

The Theater of the Panopticon

Bentham's Panopticon has, of course, become familiar to most scholars of the humanities through Foucault's reading of it in *Discipline and Punish,* in which it signals the death of the old theater of punishment and the birth of a regime of covert discipline.[8] In Foucault's description of Bentham's Panopticon, it is a prison that has at last rid itself of "those compact, swarming, howling masses that were [once] to be found in places of confinement" (200). It has become a place "closed upon itself" (205), "rigorously closed" (207). "The crowd [has been] abolished," and the prisoner placed in "a sequestered and observed solitude" (201).[9]

Bentham would have been surprised by Foucault's rendering of his Panopticon. For in the Panopticon as Bentham actually describes it, the spectators—a bustling, curious, audience full of desires and passions—are visibly, audibly, palpably present, and very much subjects in their own right. In order for the guard to be able to see into the cells, Bentham explains, there must be a considerable space between guard tower and cells. "What . . . shall we do with this vacuity[?]" asks Bentham. His answer: "Fill it with company[!] . . . Why not as well as to the Asylum, the Magdalen and the Lock Hospital, in London? The scene would be more picturesque: the occasion not less interesting and affecting" (169–70). That is, the Panopticon is to be filled with sightseers of the kind who regularly visited the "Bedlam" Hospital madhouse, the Magdalen Hospital for Penitent Prostitutes, and the Lock Hospital and Asylum (for those with venereal disease) in order to enjoy the spectacle of the reformed prostitutes or mad inmates and their antics.[10] Spectators, most of whom (Bentham explains) will probably come "merely [to] satisf[y] . . . general curiosity" (29), will find that "the scene" offers a "great and constant fund of entertainment": a "very various," and "not altogether . . . unamusing one" (24). They may be moved by "the affecting prospect" of prisoners "detained in durance" (29). They will find, in any case, scenes deeply "interesting to human feelings" (29). The Panopticon is not to be like the chaotic space of the eighteenth-century prison: the raucous criminal subculture and marketplace of debauchery that John Howard had described in horrifying detail in *The State of the Prisons in England and Wales* (1777).[11] Instead, it is to be more like the contemporary theater, portraying "picturesque," "interesting," and "affecting" scenes.

These three terms might be taken as keywords for describing the aims of the period's drama, and particularly of three of its main genres: the sentimental drama, gothic, and melodrama (the latter two just coming into focus in the 1790s). Melodrama and gothic shared a repertoire of techniques: organization around the scenic picture (often an emotional tableau in which picturesque qualities highlighted "human feelings"); chiaroscuro effects (the pictorial representation of light and darkness standing in for moral light and darkness); the deliberate production of fear and horror that would invariably be relieved by a last-minute reprieve. All three genres were serious, but almost always skirted tragedy for a satisfying ending in which justice triumphed.

One might see in Bentham's trio of terms not just a description, but a narrative of the experience of theatrical reception (common to many theatrical genres, but particularly pointed in these three genres): the spectator was first to be drawn by the aesthetic (the "picturesque"), was then to become interested in the lives of the characters (the "interesting"), and was eventually to become emotionally involved (in "the affecting"). Together, the aesthetic, the intellectual, and the affective effected a process of judgment that ultimately produced moral knowledge.

Sensitive to the "picturesque," "interesting," and "affecting" scenes of the Panopticon, Bentham's spectators do not visit the prison, then, merely as instrumental extensions of the police power (as in Foucault's vision). They are there as affective subjects whose judgments are formed by watching scenes "interesting to human feelings." The spectators are, certainly, to act as a kind of general judiciary ("witnesses and judges" [29]): "I take for granted as a matter of course, that . . . the doors of these establishments will be, as, without very special reasons to the contrary, the doors of all public establishments ought to be, thrown wide open to the body of the curious at large:—the great *open committee* of the tribunal of the world" (30).[12] But the nature of this "committee" is suggested in Bentham's use here of language that tracks the conventional eighteenth-century identification of theater as a "great tribunal" ("the stage [is] the great tribunal of mankind," declares Arthur Murphy's prologue to Robert Jephson's tragedy *Braganza* [1775]).[13] The Panopticon's audience is to be a committee whose judgment is inseparable from aesthetic and affective experience, like that of eighteenth-century theatrical spectators.

In a text published the same year as *The Panopticon,* Bentham explicitly references law's likeness to theater in order to explain the importance of making legal institutions public. "Publicity is the very soul of justice," he writes. "It is the . . . surest of all guards against improbity. . . . It is through publicity alone that justice becomes the mother of security. By publicity, the temple of justice is converted into a school of the first order, where the most important branches of morality are enforced, by the most impressive means:—into a theatre, where the sports of the imagination g[i]ve place to the more interesting exhibitions of real life."[14] We have here something of a surplus of institutions—temples, courts, schools, theaters—but Bentham articulates a clear set of relationships. The "temple of justice" (in which law is as sacred as religion) must be a school that teaches the precepts of morality. But the best kind of "school of morality" is a theater (as critics often said in the eighteenth century)[15] because theaters use "the most impressive means" to teach their precepts. Legal institutions must learn to exploit the "impressive means" of theater: that is, they should act like theaters.

While the theater is a model for legal institutions, the passage also insists that the theater of law has an advantage over the theater proper: "the exhibitions of real life" that one sees in courtrooms and prisons are actually *more* interesting than theatrical scenes (which are mere "sports of the imagination"). This claim should recall a famous passage in Edmund Burke's *Philosophical Enquiry into the . . . Sublime and Beautiful* (1757), in which Burke offered a challenge to his readers:

> Chuse a day on which to represent the most sublime and affecting tragedy . . . ; appoint the most favourite actors; spare no cost upon the scenes and decorations; . . . and when you have collected your audience, just at the moment when their minds are erect with expectation, let it be reported that a [criminal] is on the point of being executed in the adjoining square; in a moment the emptiness of the theatre would demonstrate the comparative weakness of the imitative arts.[16]

Bentham's Panopticon may excise the violence of public executions, but it capitalizes on the appeal of the reality show. In contrast to the theater's comparatively feeble "sports of the imagination," the Panopticon promises to "displa[y] the more interesting exhibitions of real life."

Apparently, Bentham anticipated objections to his plan for making the prison into a theater for exhibiting real convicts, for he presents a dialogue with an "intelligent friend" in which he defends the theater of the Panopticon: "All this may be very well, said an intelligent friend, in the way of example:—but how stands it upon the footing of Reformation? Might it not have ultimately a corruptive effect upon the persons thus exhibited, shaming them, indeed and distressing them at first, but by degrees hardening them, and at length rendering them insensible? Would it not, in short, . . . be a sort of perpetual pillory?" (172).

Bentham has three answers. First, exhibiting prisoners as an example for spectators is far more important than reforming them because "the number of the yet innocent" is so much greater than the number of the "convicted guilty" (172). That is, the Panopticon's primary purpose is not the reformation of the relatively small number of prisoners, but the creation of a spectacle that will deter the great number of "yet innocent" spectators from crime. Second, the prisoners in the Panopticon have committed crimes "of a deeper dye" than people normally "consigned to the pillory," and thus they require a "punishment more severe" (172): exhibiting them will serve as that punishment. Third (in a point somewhat in tension with the second point), during the trial, each prisoner was already "exhibited in a manner equally public, and in circumstances reflecting a much greater measure of humiliation and shame, . . . stand[ing] forth [as] the sole hero of the melancholy drama," with "the eyes of the whole audience . . . fixed upon him alone." In "an exhibition like that here proposed" (that is, the Panopticon), on the other hand, "the attention of the spectators [is] divided among [the] many," so the prisoner is no longer the solitary object of their gaze (173). As important, during the trial, the "hero of the melancholy drama . . . is held forth to view with the marks of guilt fresh upon his head," whereas, in the Panopticon, "he does not appear till a progress more or less considerable may be presumed to have been made in the career of penitence, and the idea of guilt has been covered by expiation" (173). That is, a period of expiation has intervened between the "melancholy drama" of the trial and the prisoner's exhibition in the Panopticon, allowing the Panopticon to display the now penitent prisoner in a "picturesque" and "affecting" scene.

Bentham certainly knew all of the Enlightenment critiques of the public performance of punishment. Ignoring such critiques, his responses to his "intelligent friend" actually reiterate (in updated form) the classic *justifications* for the public performance of punishment. In these responses, one can find, first, the argument that punishment must be publicly performed so that it may serve as a deterrent to spectators (the "yet innocent"), who might otherwise become criminals. One can find the argument that punishment must be publicly performed because shaming is an essential element of punishment, often more severe (and thus more efficacious) than physical pain. Finally, one can find the argument that punishment must be publicly performed in order to expiate the crime: in the trial, the crime is revealed to the public; through punishment, the criminal publicly atones for the crime, and the community is healed. Instead of rejecting these ideas (as so many of his contemporaries did), Bentham attempts to modernize them, detaching them from the scene of violence and transferring them to a newly "picturesque" and "affecting" theater of deterrence, shaming, and expiation.

In case these ideas do not offer a sufficient rejoinder to critiques of the performance of punishment, Bentham has one further answer to his "intelligent friend," a creative idea that suggests his ambivalence about shaming but his utter determination to make the Panopticon a performance space: "Should these answers be thought not to have disproved the mischief, nothing can be simpler than the remedy. A mask affords it at once" (173). That is, all the prisoners exhibited in the Panopticon should wear masks. Bentham does not seem to mean this as a joke (nor did his interpreters take it as one, as we will see):

> Guilt will thus be pilloried in the abstract, without the exposure of the guilty. With regard to the sufferer, the sting of shame will be sheathed, and with regard to the spectators, the salutary impression, instead of being weakened, will be heightened, by this imagery. The scene . . . will be decorated by—why mince the word?—by a masquerade: a masquerade, indeed, but of what kind? not a gay and dangerous, but a serious, affecting, and instructive one. A Spanish *[a]uto-da-fe* has still more in it of the theatre:—and what is the objection there? That the spectacle is light or ludicrous? No: but rather that it is too serious and too horrible. (173)

This decorative masquerade makes a "salutary impression" on the spectators because, Bentham suggests, it is not the individual criminal but the crime "in the abstract" that is pilloried. Thus, the spectators will more easily be able to apply to themselves the lesson about the wages of crime that they see performed in the Panopticon.

If the Panopticon is to be a masquerade, it will not be a "light" or "ludicrous" or "gay" one, as masquerades sometimes are. Here we can see Bentham subtly invoking Enlightenment critiques of execution crowds in order to make a point about the use and misuse of penal performance. What was hideous about the Spanish *auto-da-fé* was that, while it was "dangerous" and "horrible," it was also callously "gay." In this it treated the spectacle of punishment much as contemporary English executions crowds did. The clergyman William Dodd, writing a poem called *Thoughts in Prison* while awaiting execution for forgery in London's Newgate in 1777, described such crowds as "giddy," "cruel," and "unimpress'd" by "the sad spectacle."[17] Like the theater of execution at Tyburn (or the "serious and . . . horrible" Spanish *auto-da-fé*), the Panopticon—Bentham insists—will "lose no occasion of speaking to the eye." Like them, it will exploit all the arts of the theater manager in the production of "stage effect." But the spectacle offered in the Panopticon will not, like Tyburn or the *auto-da-fé,* be "gay" while issuing in "horr[or]." Instead, like sentimental drama, melodrama, and gothic, it will be "serious," but will soften its "serious[ness]" with the "picturesque" and the "affecting." That is, it will be serious but not, ultimately, tragic.

Prison Sightseeing: Spectators in the Model Penitentiary

Dodd's *Thoughts in Prison* was published the same year that Howard published *The State of Prisons,* and their portraits of the prison are much the same (if in different genres): "Hark—what a rattling din!" exclaims Dodd:

> . . . On every side
> The congregated chains clank frightful:—Throngs
> Tumultuous press around, to view, to gaze . . .
> Rough voices rage discordant ; dreadful shrieks ! . . .
> . . . Roaring bursts / Of loud obstreperous laughter,
> . . . vex / E'en the dull ear of Midnight![18]

Momentarily imagining himself instead in the prison of his dreams, a space of silence and solitude far from Newgate's madding crowd, he apostrophizes:

> Hail, sacred Solitude! . . . Ev'n now I view
> The revel-rout dispers'd ;
> [All] silent! . . . / Hush'd in calm order![19]

Such desiderata inspired not only theoretical schemes like Bentham's but an energetic program of reforming prisons and constructing model penitentiaries in the decades following the publication of *The Panopticon*.[20] One of the main objects of the new prisons was to separate prisoners from one another—either through complete isolation or enforced silence—not only so that prisoners like Dodd could have their "sacred Solitude," but also so that prisons would no longer act as criminal subcultures and training grounds for young criminals.[21]

If prisoners were to be separated from one another, however, the new penitentiaries were hardly to be places of "sacred Solitude," but were, in fact, to be places more like Bentham's Panopticon: "fill[ed] with company," "thrown wide open to the body of the curious at large." This was partly the result of the attention drawn to the prison problem by reformers themselves. One nineteenth-century critic of prison tourism, looking back, described the flood of sightseers into Newgate in 1817, following the publication of an article on the work there of prison Good Samaritan Elizabeth Fry: "already numerous," the visitors to Newgate "increased and multiplied." On the two "public mornings" in the week, "parties of inspection" streamed through Newgate. "Fashionable philanthropists, benevolent aristocrats, members of parliament, cabinet ministers, royal dukes and duchesses, flocked to the philanthropic show."[22]

Recognizing the extent of the prison tourism industry in the nineteenth century, it is impossible to sustain the generally held view that, with the birth of the modern prison, prisoners were segregated from the rest of society and became invisible to the public.[23] As Janet Miron has shown, nineteenth-century prison tourism was not just an occasional event but grew into a vast enterprise over the course of the century, with tens of thousands of people visiting penitentiaries every year.[24] Since prison visits generally required official permission in Britain, the number of visitors was smaller there than in North America. But sightseers nonetheless regularly visited British "Model Prison[s]" such as Pentonville (designed as a modified Panopticon and opened in 1842).[25] And in North America, by midcentury one could speak of an industry. Nearly 1,600 people visited Kingston Penitentiary in Ontario 1847.[26] Over 6,000 people visited the Massachusetts State Prison in 1846.[27] Philadelphia's Eastern State Penitentiary received about 8,000 visitors per year in the 1850s, and well over 11,000 per year in the 1860s and early 1870s.[28] In 1866, almost 13,000 people visited New York's State Prison at Auburn (a number that, according to one observer, included only those who were there because of "curiosity" and did not count family, friends, and official visitors).[29] Early in the twentieth century, the former chaplain of New York City's House of Detention ("the Tombs") estimated that the prison received on average 50,000 visitors per year.[30]

To handle the large number of visitors and earn revenue, prisons sold admission tickets. In their encyclopedic report on North American prisons, published in 1867, the prison reformers Enoch Cobb Wines and Timothy Dwight complained of this practice: "In the great majority of American prisons, an entrance fee of twenty-five cents is charged, which gives the custom still more the air of a public exhibition, and makes the state a showman for a few paltry coppers."[31] But it was hard to combat the practice, because in many places the sale of admission tickets provided substantially more income than prison labor (between $1,000 and $15,000 per year, the equivalent of hundreds of thousands of dollars today).[32]

The vast majority of those who "flocked to the philanthropic show" were, as these numbers suggest, not journalists or professional reformers but the kind of spectators whom Bentham had envisioned in the Panopticon: "the body of the curious at large," seeking "the gratification of their own particular curiosity" (29–30). Tour guides began to list penitentiaries as "must sees" alongside museums, zoological gardens, and asylums. J. C. Myers's *Sketches on a Tour through the Northern and Eastern States, the Canadas and Nova Scotia* (1849) particularly recommends Auburn: "a small fee will procure admittance, and the scenes presented to view return a rich equivalent for the pittance required."[33] A headline in the *New York Times* for July 8, 1866, gives a sense of the mood of much of such sightseeing, jauntily reporting on "BLACKWELL'S ISLAND. A Summer-day's Tour . . . The Penitentiary, the Almshouse, the Work-house . . .":

> Let those whose philanthropy or curiosity suggests a visit to Blackwell's Island be prudent, above all things, in the selection of their weather. Better postpone the visit for a quarter of a century, even at the risk of allowing your philanthropy to evaporate and your curiosity to die, than to permit yourself to be carried by your enthusiasm and the boat over to the Island on a July day about noon, with the thermometer at ninety-five in the shade.[34]

Another visitor to the penitentiary on Blackwell's Island describes the end of the touring party: "Our ramblings finished, a sumptuous repast was set forth in the house of Mr Keen [the warden], and festivity reigned undisturbed. Humor and hilarity became the order of the day, . . . and at a seasonable hour the party were ferried over, and dispersed to their several homes, highly gratified with the day's entertainment."[35]

At some prisons, the "day's entertainment" might include seeing celebrities, or at least trying to see them. Robina and Kathleen Lizars traveled to New York to see William Lyon Mackenzie, imprisoned for his leadership of a rebellion against the British in Ontario in 1837, who told them that "the iron doors" of his Rochester Prison "were freely opened to those who wished to see a real live Canadian rebel."[36] In London, a prison visitor enthused that among the "array of . . . prisoners" to be seen in Newgate were "R——A——, and other *distinguished* individuals."[37] Another visitor described an attempt to see Henrietta Robinson, the "Veiled Murderess," in Sing Sing: "It is impossible to obtain the slightest glimpse of her countenance. . . . The sight of a strange face . . . causes her to hide herself instantly from the gaze of the curious."[38] The writer Susanna Moodie, who visited Kingston Penitentiary in 1853, was somewhat embarrassed by fact that she was more interested in seeing the convicts than the noble edifice, as she wrote in one of her memoirs, but she overcame her embarrassment, "and my wishes were completely gratified."[39]

Gratifying the spectator's wishes, the "day's entertainment" at the prison responded to what has sometimes been seen as an insatiable demand for spectacular pleasures in the nineteenth century (served by the proliferation of theaters, music halls, circuses, zoos, peep shows, stereoscopes, "animated pictures" . . . the list goes on). We have already seen that the "picturesque," "interesting," and "affecting" scenes that

Bentham promised in the Panopticon were very like those offered by late eighteenth- and nineteenth-century drama. Scenes set in prisons were, of course, stock elements of the popular stage, decorated with all the paraphernalia of the gothic (dungeons, chains, sometimes ghosts). Many who visited prisons clearly went there in search of such scenes. "What is this dismal fronted pile of bastard Egyptian, like an enchanter's palace in a melodrama?" Dickens asks the readers of his *American Notes,* having invited them to follow him through the streets of New York: "—a famous prison, called The Tombs. Shall we go in?"[40]

One 1834 article entitled "Scenes in Prison" recounts a visit to Newgate —an "indescribably and irresistibly affecting" "picture [of] unmitigated wretchedness" among the "horrours" [*sic*] and "miseries"—that was just the kind of thing sightseers hoped to find when they toured such prisons. The scene is set in the prison chapel, where the chaplain will be delivering a "condemned sermon": a sermon intended to prepare those under a death sentence for what is to come. In the center of the pew reserved for the condemned "stood a large table, covered with black, on which was placed a coffin, and other emblems of death." Those "under a sentence of death, but not yet ordered for execution, first entered the chapel," a "sad . . . assemblage," whose "dejected aspect, neglected dress, and rattling chains, were sufficient to appal [*sic*] every beholder." They were followed by "two devoted victims," the "unfortunate M——M——" (an "ill-fated young woman") and "a man of the name of J——," who are to be executed in three days. J—— "seemed to sustain his situation with manly fortitude and decent resignation," but the congregation was weeping, and "the unhappy female" herself "was drowned in tears and overwhelmed with wo [*sic*]." This very wet scene comes to a conclusion when the chaplain, "Doctor F——, with a tremulous hand, and a feeling approximating to parental tenderness, led the unfortunate M——M—— out of the chapel, . . . followed by the other prisoners, who with sighs, groans, and hideous aspects, the clang of iron bolts, manacles, and fetters, closed the dismal procession." Several days later, the visitor who witnessed the scene hears "St. Paul's and St. Sepulchre's clocks" striking eight: "the prison bell ceased to toll—and two fellow beings were launched into eternity!"[41] Closure comes not in attendance at the scene of the hanging (that would be merely grotesque), but in a sublime moment in which the curtains have closed, the bells are heard, eternity lies ahead, and the rest is silence.

In their vast survey of London prisons, *The Criminal Prisons of London and Scenes of Prison Life* (1862), Henry Mayhew and John Binny warn against the tendency to imagine the real prison in melodramatic or gothic terms. The jailer at Pentonville Prison, for instance, is not the "ferocious-looking prison-officia[l] ordinarily represented on the stage" (a "kind of human Cerberus—a creature that looks as surly and sullen as an officer of the Inquisition, and with a bunch of huge keys, . . . whose jangle, as he moves, reminds one of the clink of fetters"). Rather, he is "a gentleman with a half military air, who . . . is usually marked by an almost tender consideration for those placed under his charge."[42] But most accounts of prison visits during the period attempt not to challenge but to confirm melodramatic and gothic expectations, in scenes very like what one might see represented on the stage: visions of "miseries," with human-Cerberus jailers, convicts dragging their "iron bolts, manacles, and fetters" with "sighs, groans, and hideous aspects," "ill-fated young wom[e]n," heroes of "manly fortitude," and weeping spectators in an "irresistibly affecting" scene. The social reformer Jane Ellice, visiting Auburn in 1838, was pleased to find it just like "the scene in 'Fidelio,' where *S[c]hroeder[-] Devri[en]t* [singing the role of Leonore] said in her pretty broken English 'Let the *Preesoners* breathe the fresh air; to see them shut up *penetrates* the *inmost recesses of my heart.*'"[43]

If it was nice to experience oneself as one's favorite heroic character, such scenes were, at the same time, *better* than theater because they were real. "It is hardly possible," writes the Newgate visitor, "to give the reader an adequate idea of this affecting ceremony. . . . No theatrical imitation or mimic exhibition of such a scene can give an adequate idea of the genuine one. . . . No mimic representation can be compared to the terrible reality of such a scene! heightened as it is by all its horrid accompaniments." Here, we can see an assertion of the superiority of the "genuine" over the "theatrical imitation" or "mimic exhibition" similar to that we have already seen in Bentham and Burke. That is, "dismal [prison] spectacle[s]" on stage are not really adequate: one must see the real thing, in all of its "terrible reality," to have the proper affective experience, and thus to understand.

At the same time, "terrible reality" was not to be too terrible. "It used to be said that the heads and limbs of convicts should be exposed upon the city walls," wrote prison theorist Samuel Gridley Howe in 1846, "that their bones must be hung to bleach in chains,—that their faces must be exposed in the pillory,—that they must be executed before the multitude; and all for the poor people's terror and reformation!" "Civilized countries," he comments, are being "gradually driven, reluctantly enough, from such abominations."[44] *Pace* Burke, not everyone in "civilized countries" wanted to see "bones . . . hung to bleach in chains," "faces . . . exposed in the pillory," or executions. But nor were spectators quite ready to give up the spectacle of suffering. One continental legislator, discussing the possibility of moving executions behind prison walls in the 1850s, had argued that there must not be "too abrupt" a transition from open to restricted executions because people were accustomed to the spectacle of punishment, and would insist upon seeing it.[45] Scenes like that in Newgate served as a third way: one could avoid the old spectacle of horror without giving up the theater of punishment altogether. At the same time, visiting the penitentiary spoke not just to the popular *desire* that punishment be performed, but to the unique *value* of performance to penal regimes, which would be lost if punishment were taken out of the public eye. Even if executions were held in private, some kind of public performance, it was argued, was "necessary to serve as a warning."[46] The threat of punishment would become too abstract if the people were unable to see it in action. Only "ocular demonstration"[47] would make a vivid enough impression to prevent crime.

Thus, prison sightseeing not only offered some of the pleasures of theater (with the heightened savor of reality), but also continued to serve some of the traditional functions of penal performance: deterrence, the ceremonial processing of violence, catharsis. At the same time, it had several advantages over the old spectacle of punishment. First, prison sightseeing eliminated visible blood, violence, and bodily mutilation. It raised "horror" to an aesthetic principle (one that was pleasing because it was familiar from gothic genres) but it effectively did away with the "terrors" produced by the execution spectacle. Second, prison sightseeing replaced the chaotic execution scene with an orderly and highly curated tour led by a pleasant and well-informed guide. In his *Brief Account of the Construction, Management and Discipline of the New York State Prison at Auburn* (1826), Auburn's warden Gershom Powers describes what the prison tourist could expect: "The guard, at the front gate, admits, at the proper hours, all decent persons. . . . They are furnished with Tickets, at 25 cents, each person. . . . Visiters [*sic*] are conducted through the shops, north wing, and other departments, except that of the females and of the Hospital. They are treated politely, and all desired information cheerfully furnished them."[48] Third, as a necessary corollary to the orderly tour, prison sightseeing replaced the barbaric execution crowd that Dodd and others had described (the "obscene," "giddy," "madding, drunken, thoughtless, ruthless," "wild, blasphemous and cruel," multitude)[49] with a more polite class of spectator. To ensure proper spectator behavior, prisons had guidelines for the "government of spectators" (in the words of the Albany County Penitentiary's 1849 *Rules and Regulations*).[50] In almost all prisons, spectators were (according to Wines and Dwight) "admonished not to indulge in laughter, loud conversation, or boisterous conduct of any kind."[51] But politeness was also to be guaranteed by ticket prices. Powers notes in his *Brief Account* that the prison has recently decided to double its admission price to twenty-five cents, "not with a view to increase the revenue, but to operate as a check upon a certain class who overthronged the prison."[52] That is, prison tourism enacted a necessary class division: while the labor dislocations of the industrial revolution meant that the once-laboring classes were now the "criminal classes," making up most of the population behind bars, prison admission prices kept the laboring classes from entering as spectators. Thus, instead of "overthrong[ing]" the viewing space in an attempt to get a view of the spectacle, those of "a certain class" had become the spectacle.

A further advantage of prison sightseeing over the old spectacle of punishment was that, by attending the "philanthropic show" and paying the price of admission, spectators could not just *feel* humanitarian, but feel that they were doing something about it. In 1787, Benjamin Rush had offered a searing critique of the "abortive sympathy" that public executions produced in even the most benevolent of spectators: "By an immutable law of our nature, distress of all kinds, when seen, produces sympathy, and a disposition to relieve it. . . . Now, as the distress which the criminals suffer, is the effect of a law of the state, which cannot be resisted, the sympathy of the spectator is rendered abortive, and returns empty to the bosom in which it was awakened."[53] At an execution, one might be sympathetic but one was helpless to relieve suffering (an experience reinforced by reading novels, where the reader was similarly helpless to intervene).[54] Repeated experiences of such "abortive sympathy" trained empathetic spectators in moral passivity while rewarding them with the empty pleasures of sympathy in and for itself. Touring the model penitentiary, on the other hand, one was not standing idly by watching the unfortunate be flogged or hanged, but contributing to their reformation. Paying one's twenty-five cents, one was helping to fund a humane alternative to the cruel punishments of the past.

The fact that it might be inquisitiveness about the convicts' lives that led one to visit the prison did not vitiate one's philanthropy, according to the warden of the juvenile reformatory at Isle-Aux-Noix, Quebec: "The community cannot evince a too deep curiosity in prying into the working of all public institutions. . . . Each individual has a close interest in the well-being of the whole, and should, therefore, be anxious in inquiring into the management of establishments to whose maintenance he contributes."[55] For Wines, one could not leave such "prying" to officials. "It is essentially necessary that the interiors of prisons be subjected to a perpetual and vigilant observation" by general visitors, because official inspections were "too perfunctory," and official reports "too one-sided."[56] The general visitor, on the other hand, would be curious enough to look closely, and without preconceived notions. Moreover, the kind of sympathy that Rush argued was "abortive" at public executions could, after a tour of the penitentiary, lead to action. Prisons might not offer "an agreeable spectacle," asserted the *North American Review* in 1866, but "what stirs within us at such sights as these may well lead us to consider how our prisons can be improved."[57]

Not everyone agreed that prison sightseeing served either spectators, prisoners, or the public good. Samuel Gridley Howe, for instance, cited typical defenses of prison tourism precisely in order to refute them. "We of Massachusetts," he wrote, "still cling to our prison exhibitions, as little doubting their excellence as our fathers doubted the excellence of the *cuttystool,* the pillory, or the whipping-post." But to "urg[e] that the spectacle is necessary to serve as a warning to others" is to be as barbaric as they were.[58] "As for the common argument, that such exhibitions are very useful, because the public eye prevents the officers from abusing their power; in the first place, they do not do so, . . . and in the second place, if they did prevent abuses, the government has no right to . . . adop[t] a method which is profitable to itself, but degrading to the prisoner, if another can be found."[59] Others shared Howe's view that prison tourism was "degrading to the prisoner," and worried that treating prisoners as an exhibit tended to harden them to shame. "A considerable revenue has been derived . . . by 'admission money' . . . from numerous visitors," writes Dorothea Dix in her *Remarks on Prisons and Prison Discipline* (1845): "This should not be allowed. . . . All who go to gratify a mere curiosity, 'to see the place, and to see how the prisoners look,' should be excluded. The effect of this indiscriminate exposure of the prisoner is bad, or . . . proves that he is so hardened in guilt, and so debased, that in being made a spectacle for the gratification of the thoughtless and the curious, he is willing his degradation should be as public as his life has been debased."[60] Henry Cordier, commissioner of the Wisconsin State Prison, interviewed in the 1860s, agreed: "The influence upon convicts of admitting general visitors cannot be otherwise than injurious. This being gazed upon again and again, as criminals, tends to destroy all sense of shame, if there be any left. It further tends to harden [the convicts'] feelings, and make them indifferent to public opinion. . . . I consider the custom of making convicts a kind of public show, a nuisance and a disgrace, and one that should be abolished very speedily."[61]

Staging the Model Prison: The Lockmarch and the Theater of Labor

Unlike Howe, Dix, and Cordier, however, most prison officials, legislators, and reformers enthusiastically embraced the culture of penitentiary spectatorship, and worked hard to produce performances for sightseers that would express both the aspirations and the successes of the model prison. Among the most prominent of the performances in the North American model penitentiary was the lockmarch (or lockstep, as it was often called): the single-file marching formation required of inmates when they went from one activity to the next. At each bell, explains Gershom Powers, describing the lockmarch in Auburn, the convicts "proceed, in military order, under the eye of the turnkeys, in solid columns, with the lockmarch," all heads turned fixedly toward the keeper. It offers "a beautiful example of what may be done by proper discipline."[62]

A kind of set piece at the center of the prison tour, the lockmarch was intended to express in particularly vivid (synecdochic, choreographic) form what the prison could achieve. The regimentation and control it demonstrated could look quite a lot like the kind of "discipline" that Foucault describes. The convicts formed "solid columns" and proceeded in "military order." It was part of a regime at once of schedules and of micro-power: voice, gestures, head positions were all subject to exacting regulation. At the same time, it was also like the rather showy regimentation of the nineteenth-century military (or, indeed, the carefully choreographed displays of the *corps de ballet,* which Joseph Roach has identified with military training at the turn of the nineteenth century):[63] focused on the body (not the soul), stylized, learned through rigorous physical training, more ceremonial than functional. Here, discipline consisted not of a daily schedule but of a precisely mandated choreography.

In *Secrets of the Mount-Pleasant State Prison Revealed and Exposed* (1839), James Brice, convicted for perjury to four years in Sing Sing (as Mount

Pleasant became known), protested the theatrical quality of the Sing Sing version of the lockmarch. Before his time in Sing Sing, he explains, "little did I dream that a part of the services required of the convict in the State prison was a mock military drill," in which "silly exercises, some of the keepers appeared to take as much pride as if they had been military cadets at West Point." "When parading and marching his company, [the keeper's] words [a]re, heads up, eyes inclined to the keeper. . . . During these marchings, the unfortunate prisoner is compelled to mark time, and . . . step with his left foot foremost, with his tub in his right hand, which he has used from Sunday morning until Monday morning; and this without music—neither fife, or drum, or bugle horn to animate the Sing-Sing soldier."[64] Brice stresses here the preposterously stagey quality of the performance: the make-believe military, the imaginary music, the pretending-to-be-a-cadet by marching, keeping time, and banging on a bathing tub in place of a real drum. This theatricality, however, is central to its real meaning: the lockmarch may function to discipline the prisoners, but it is expressively turned outward, toward its spectators. As much as it aims to produce "discipline, cleanliness, and [good] behaviour" (in the words of one sightseer who visited Auburn in 1844),[65] it also aims to perform these expressively. It may be part of the daily schedule and the routinized trajectory across the prison complex, but it also *represents* these in compressed form. The "mark[ing] time" that Brice describes seems a metaphor for "doing time" as an intentional action, a rendering of this intentional temporality in the delimited time and space of performance.

Looking at the precise choreography of the march through both prison accounts and images can help us understand its meaning better. In its classic form, which early nineteenth-century prison officials adapted from the military lockstep, prisoners were required to form a single file, and place their right hands on the right shoulders of the person in front of them. Keeping their left arms down, they were then required to step in unison, raising the right foot high. They were to keep their heads facing right and their eyes fixed on the guard who was, effectively, the conductor of the march. The single file, with eyes inclined to the keeper, represented a fundamental principle: prisoners were not to look to each other; silence, lack of eye contact, and single file represented the dissociation that was to prevent the replication of criminal subcultures. At the same time, the fact that prisoners were "lock[ed]" together, linked by hands on shoulders and moving in rhythmic unity, represented an alternative kind of social interdependency: one that was orderly, linear, and stayed on course.

Modeling your body after the prisoners who come before you, it seemed to say, you will go straight (you will become an upright citizen). Looking to the right, "head erect" (in the words of one tourist),[66] and stepping high with the right foot (significantly, the right, representing rectitude, *droit,* or law) expressed the aspirations of the prison: "discipline" was to raise the convicts up from physical and moral degradation. At the same time, the left foot (sometimes chained to the other prisoners' left feet) tended to shuffle. The "shuffle" was not merely an effect of chains, but an expressive effect: the prisoners' left feet (on the *sinister*—wrong or evil in Latin—side) shuffled along as a way of remembering their crimes, and as a guard against pride.[67]

An illustration of the Auburn lockmarch from about 1841 [fig. 1] shows a moment in which the prisoners have come to a resting position. Some representations of the lockmarch—for instance a photograph of the Auburn lockmarch from around 1910 [fig. 2]—show the prisoners' left hands locked under the left arms of the prisoners in front of them, implying that this is the place where the prisoner's evil hand was to be locked down. In the c. 1841 image, however, each prisoner's right arm

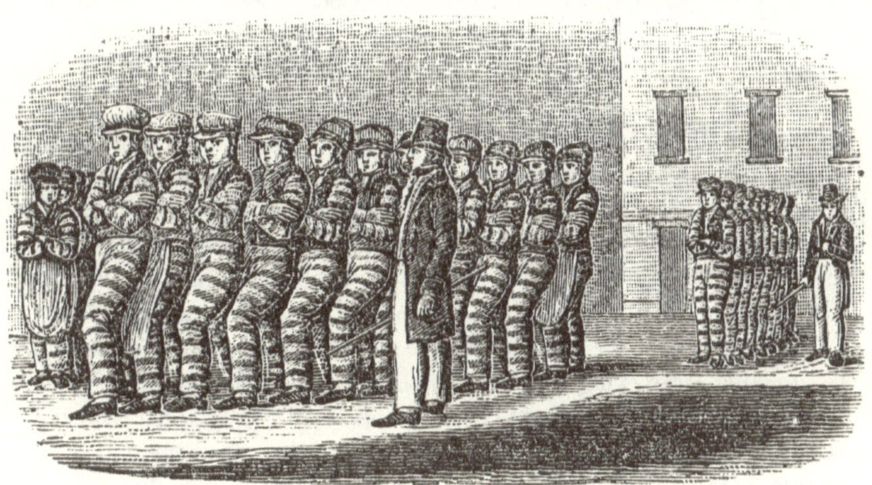

Prisoners at the State Prison at Auburn.

FIGURE 1. The lockmarch at the New York State Prison at Auburn, c. 1841. John Warner Barber, *Historical Collections of the State of New York* (1841). Courtesy of the Columbia University Rare Books Library.

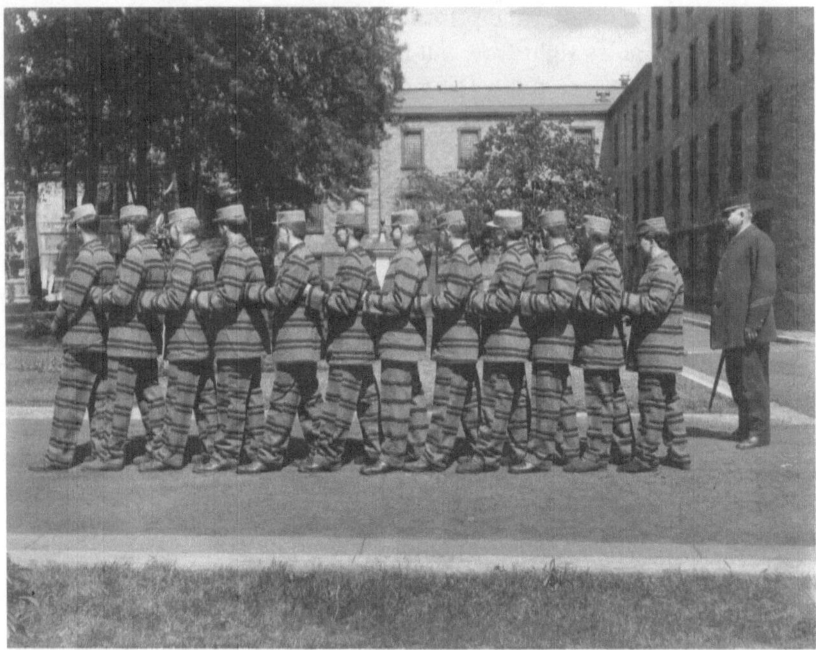

FIGURE 2. The lockmarch at the New York State Prison at Auburn, c. 1910. Courtesy of the Cayuga County Historian's Office.

locks down his *own* left arm completely, implying that he has transferred the law (or right), through the socialization of the march, into lessons of individual self-restraint. The illustrator reinforces this idea by placing a pool of shadow beside the prisoners, as if they have somehow stepped out of the shadow into the light in which they now stand. The guard in the fore of the image stands, significantly, between them and darkness. The guard in the rear, positioned next to the back line of prisoners, expresses this meaning somewhat differently: modeling the left hand's proper position for the prisoners, he holds his stick—in which cor*rect*ional power is vested —in his right. The "right" (*droit,* law), the scene seems to say, is backed by force. At the same time, both guards hold their sticks in abeyance, pointed downward rather than at the prisoners. The sticks back the scene: they guarantee the prisoners' discipline. But because the prisoners are self-disciplining (the guards' stance implies), the sticks will not be used. The image, in other words, shows the guards performing not violence but the *renunciation* of violence. This is because (the image implies) the model penitentiary renders violence unnecessary.

The choreography of the lockmarch seems to replicate, in stylized form, the ideal of surveillance in the nineteenth-century prison, while also complicating the narrative familiar from Foucault. For, of course, the guard is not invisible in the lockmarch—nor, let it be said, in almost any nineteenth-century photograph or drawing of a prison (including those replicated in *Discipline and Punish*). On the contrary, the guard is almost always perched on a raised (and sometimes quite theatrical) platform: if the guard can subject all the prisoners to surveillance, the guard is also on display. In the lockmarch, the prisoners must look at nothing *but* the guard, who is (effectively) part of the show. They may not, on the other hand, look at the spectators. This prohibition was strictly enforced, both in Auburn and elsewhere: a tourist named John Armour Jr. reported of his visit to Kingston Penitentiary, "If [the inmates] turn round their head when visitors go past them, they are flogged."[68] The lockmarch's rigid head position reinforces the prohibition against looking. If the prisoners keep their heads facing right, as they are ordered to do, they cannot, in fact, see the spectators. The c. 1910 photograph demonstrates this somewhat theatrically: the prisoners all look away from the photographer (aka spectator), clearly ordered to do so in a display of the correct lockmarch head position (surely some would otherwise be looking at the photographer, whose presence must have been quite interesting).

The lockmarch performed a boundary between prisoners and spectators. Other prison regulations reinforced this boundary. On their tour through Auburn, explains Powers, visitors "are to speak to no convict, nor excite him to look up, by stopping to gaze at him, or by signs."[69] This "fourth wall" between the polite spectators and those they come to see—a boundary whose rules sustain the pretense that the prisoners are completely absorbed in their world and cannot see the spectators—produces something like what Michael Fried (in his classic analysis of eighteenth- and nineteenth-century painting) termed "absorption" in contrast to "theatricality."[70] We might think of the lockmarch as, effectively, quoting absorption in stylized form, by directing the prisoner's gaze away from the spectator, and by forbidding the spectator from interacting with the prisoner. At the same time, however, translating absorption from painting into performance utterly alters it. The key paradox of "absorption" in theater is that it is artificial. For a performance to show absorption, there must be spectators, and the performers must be aware of the spectators' presence but pretend not to see them. In performance, absorption is a ruse. The prisoners are necessarily viscerally aware of the presence of spectators: they clearly feel their gaze. Not looking is surely difficult.

But they do not look because looking is prohibited: they are under strict orders not to "turn [their] head[s] to gaze at them." And, indeed, it is precisely *because* the spectators are present and visible that the prisoners turn their heads away. One of the things, then, that the lockmarch—and the images that represent it—perform is the *temptation* of looking, and the triumph over temptation. They say, "You are watching us, and we are tempted to look back, but we will not." That is, in addition to performing the fictions of reformation through discipline—rectitude without pride, the detachment from criminal social structures and the reattachment to orderly interdependency, the self-restraint that makes state-sponsored legal violence unnecessary—the lockmarch also performs the fictions of absorption, the invisible spectator, the unidirectional gaze, and the transcendence of sensual temptation, figured in the averted eye.

If the lockmarch performed the aspirations of the American penitentiary, three new penal labor practices invented in the nineteenth century—the treadmill, crank, and shot drill—performed the aspirations of the British penitentiary, where they predominated (although they were

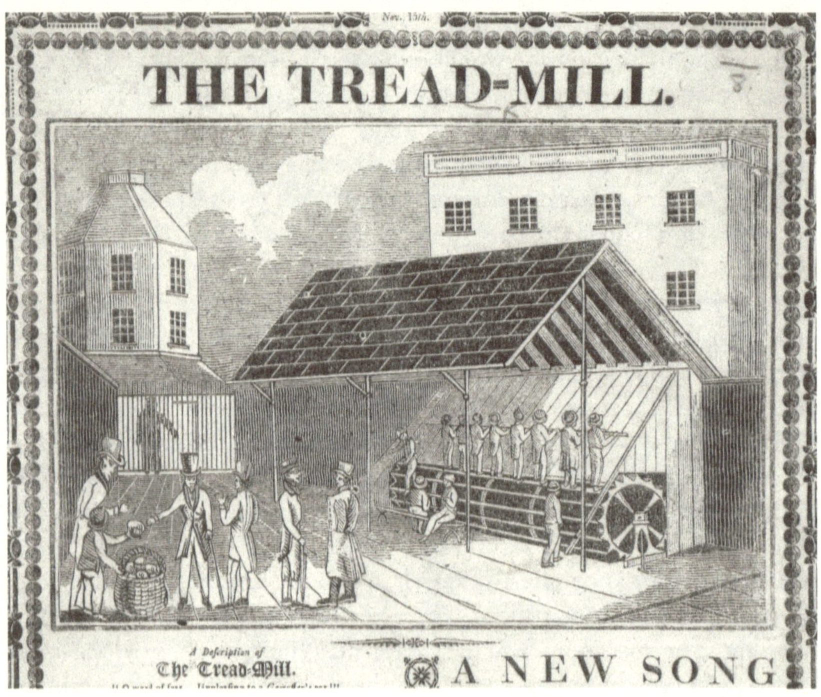

FIGURE 3. *The Tread-Mill* (broadside c. 1822). Courtesy of the British Library.

also used in North America and elsewhere). In all three, convicts performed labor, or, rather, something that looked like labor and acted like labor but was not really labor, or at least did not produce anything. In all three, a warden had to carefully choreograph the maneuvers of a group of inmates, who were required to move—sometimes in unison, sometimes in counterpoint—to a specific rhythm and timing. Thus, as showpieces of the British model prison, performances of the treadmill, crank, and shot drill were similar to lockmarch performances in several ways: they involved stylized, kinetic, rhythmic, almost dance-like movements; they served a more representational than useful function (representing the penitentiary's broader aspirations in the localized time and space of performance); and thus they had something of the "mock" quality that Brice identified in the Sing Sing bathtub march.

The treadmill (or "tread-wheel") [fig. 3], which was installed in almost every English prison and several U.S. prisons between the 1820s and the end of the century, was a giant cylinder, which prisoners (sometimes two dozen at a time or more) would rotate by stepping continually upward, as if "ascending an endless flight of steps" (in the words of one enthusiastic proponent).[71] To avoid falling off ("sinking with the wheel"),[72] all of the prisoners had to step at the same pace, rotating the wheel every thirty seconds or so. In some places, working the treadmill was referred to as "dancing" ("[I had] to dance the treadmill morning and evening"; one woman "could not dance the mill at all").[73] Describing the treadmill in Coldbath Fields, Mayhew and Binny note that it was originally invented

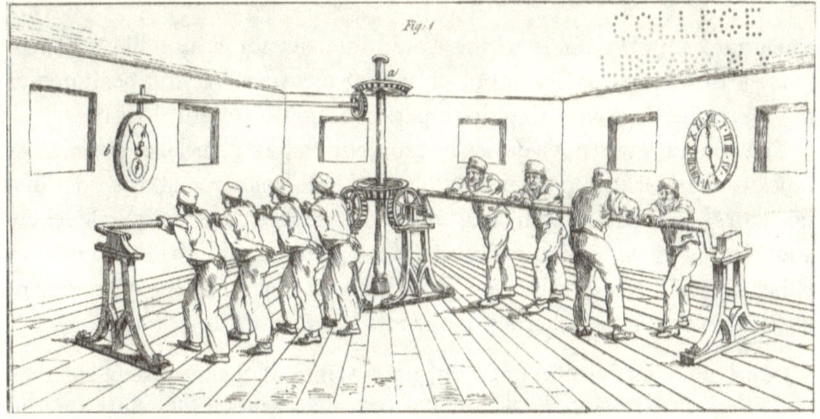

FIGURE 4. The Crank in Sir John Hippisley's *Prison Labour* (1823). Courtesy of the Columbia University Libraries.

"merely to . . . keep [the prisoners] from louting about the jail," and "with but few exceptions, [it] has never been applied, even to this day, to any useful purpose."[74] The emblem of this inutility stood above the treadmill: the "tread-wheel fan,"[75] a windmill-like apparatus that, instead of using wind power to help turn the wheel, used wind power to provide resistance and therefore make the work harder (hence the prisoners' name for treadmill labor: "grinding the wind").[76]

After numerous treadmill injuries, a country magistrate, Sir John Cox Hippisley, devised the hand-crank-mill, or "crank" [fig. 4], as a safer alternative. It was later adapted to individual use, but Hippisley designed it to be used by several groups of inmates at a time, each group rotating a long crank connected to a central shaft. Any number of additional cranks could be added to this shaft, each with its own set of prisoners, each regulated in such a way that the prisoners would have to move it at a particular speed and complete a particular number of rotations (10,000 in the Middlesex House of Correction in Coldbath Fields in the 1850s).[77] Hippisley's description of the crank suggests that the coordination of prisoners on the device required careful choreography: "The *position of the* men may be varied at pleasure," he explains, referring to his sketch:

> [T]hus, on one side of the sketch the men are shewn with their *right hands* only in action, and the right feet advanced; while on the other, the *left feet* are advanced, and *both hands* in action. One man is likewise shewn with his face towards the others; and the whole may thus be disposed, *alternately*, by which the labour also may be occasionally increased or diminished. . . . Any one or more of the cranks may . . . be *thrown out of gear, at pleasure, by which the work will be rendered more severe upon those that remain*.[78]

The guard running the machine would thus act something like a dance-master, throwing one crank out of gear at pleasure, varying positions of the men, and then watching them perform their different rhythms.

The shot drill was not a device but something like a hard labor version of mock military drills. Prisoners would stand in formation on three sides of a field, three feet apart (looking like "chess-men set out on a board" in Mayhew and Binny's view),[79] with pyramids of 24-pound cannonballs ("shot") on either side of them. The warden, from high on a stand on the other side of the field, would shout orders. In Mayhew and Binny's description:

> "*One*!" shouted the officer on duty, and instantly all the men, stooping, took up their heavy shot. "Two!" was scarcely uttered when the entire column advanced sideways, three yards. . . . On hearing "*Three*!" they every one bent down and placed the iron ball on the earth, and at "*Four*!" they shifted back

> empty-handed to their original stations. . . . Before re-commencing, the warder harangued the troop. "Mind, men, when I say *One!* every man stoop and carry his shot to the right. Now, *One!* Two! Heels close together every time you take up and put down." And the prisoners were off again, see-sawing backwards and forwards.[80]

The performance usually lasted for several hours.

Historians have argued that capitalist interests, as much as humanitarian, motivated the replacement of corporal punishment with the labor regime of the modern prison, and it is doubtless true that capitalists in search of cheap labor sources profited from prison labor regimes. However, such regimes were almost all ultimately more costly than lucrative for the state.[81] And the treadmill, crank, and shot drill were (of course) deliberately so. Prisons often had not one treadmill or crank but many: Coldbath Fields had no fewer than six treadmills running when Mayhew and Binny visited in the 1850s.[82] By then, according to them, treadmills had been "introduced into most of the houses of correction in the kingdom."[83] The fact that inventors, builders, wardens, prison administrations, and taxpayers were willing to spend so much time, money, creative thinking, and (above all) prisoner labor hours on machines and labor that did not actually produce anything is quite astonishing, and all the more so in an age in which a major complaint about prisons is that they were not self-supporting. The official justification was that the treadmill, crank, and shot drill trained lazy convicts in habits of work.[84] But *productive* labor in the prison was theoretically just as good at training lazy convicts in habits of work. This makes it puzzling that official parliamentary and prison reports from the period regularly seem to brag about the performance of "strictly penal," "non-productive work, such as tread-wheel, crank, and shot-drill," or (in the words of another report) "unproductive labour" in their prisons.[85] One explanation for this pride in the "strictly penal" nature of such labor is that productive labor was felt to be insufficiently punitive. A somewhat different explanation is offered by George Laval Chesterton, governor of the Coldbath Fields Prison from 1829 to 1854, in an anecdote about the invention of the treadmill, an anecdote that he claimed to have received from the inventor's "own lips."

According to Chesterton, an English civil engineer, the aptly named Sir William Cubitt, was visiting the prison one day. At the prison entrance, Cubitt crossed paths with an inspecting magistrate. The inmates (Cubitt told Chesterton) "were seen lounging idly about," arranged

> in repulsive groups, . . . and the whole aspect indicated a demoralizing waste of strength and time . . .

> "I wish to God, Mr. Cubitt," said the justice, "you could suggest to us some mode of employing those fellows! Could nothing like a wheel become available?"
>
> An instantaneous idea flashed through the mind of Mr. Cubitt, who whispered to himself, "the wheel elongated!" . . . And by such a casual incident did the treadwheel start into existence, and soon came into general adoption in the prisons of the country as the type of hard labour.[86]

Here, it is a moment of spectatorship—the sight of the "repulsive" groups, the "demoralizing waste" represented in the scene's "whole aspect"—that triggers the flash of revelation and the vision of the treadwheel ("the wheel elongated!"). The purpose of the treadwheel, in other words, is to transform this repulsive scene into something more "picturesque." The kind of scene that Cubitt wants to see is not one of "idl[e] lounging," with its "demoralizing waste of strength and time," but a scene of labor. It might strike us as ironic that, to rectify a "demoralizing waste of strength and time," Cubitt invented a machine precisely calculated to waste strength and time. It might, that is, until we realize that it is not the waste of strength and time in itself that troubles Cubitt, but the *spectacle* of waste: what he sees; its "aspect." The "treadwheel," in other words, exacerbates the "demoralizing waste of strength and time" rather than solving it, but it does solve the problem of repulsive *spectatorship*.

This small parable of the centrality of spectatorship to punishment in the nineteenth-century prison suggests the importance of the theatrical function of "unproductive labour"—its production of a *spectacle* of labor. And, indeed, such "unproductive labour" was one of the main tourist spectacles in certain prisons. In his *History of the Tread-Mill* (1824), James Hardie (a former drunk who ended up in the almshouse and then found god and discipline) complains of the fact that "the convicts on the Tread-Mill [are] a constant gazing stock." When he served as gatekeeper at Bellevue Penitentiary, he writes, "the crowds of people . . . were almost incredible. During the holidays, in the last Easter and Whitsun-weeks, they daily exceeded 1000. [Many] seemed fully as deserving of a place on the Tread-Mill as any of those, who were on it."[87]

Scenes of prisoners performing on the treadmill, crank, or shot drill offered a vivid alternative to the scene of inmates "lounging idly about" arranged "in *repulsive groups*, . . . the *whole aspect* indicat[ing]" (to Cubitt and many like him) "a *demoralizing waste* of strength and time." While offering relief that one did not, oneself, have to "dance" the treadmill, they also represented vividly humane alternatives to the spectacle of the bleeding and suffering body. Such scenes stood "against [the] multiplicity of sanguinary punishments" such as execution and flogging, wrote Hardie. Watching the treadmill, one could consider oneself a "frien[d] of humanity."[88] (It was not meant to be obvious that the treadmill could cause serious injuries and even death.)[89] At the same time, watching such scenes was supposed to offer a model of the benefit of performing labor in and of itself, regardless of productivity. Like the lockmarch, such scenes stood against sentimental claims that the prisoner (or industrial worker, for that matter) was merely "unfortunate." They performed for spectators the principle that past laziness would not be rewarded, but labor might eventually set you free.

Such "unproductive labour" devices arguably had a further symbolic function. The crime of indolence, which forced labor addressed, was about parasitism: "vagrants and rogues" fattened on the labor of others. The treadmill, crank, and shot drill corrected parasitism: convicts were to learn to work for their bread (in work that mimicked the efficiency of the new industrial economy). But indolence was also about lack of productivity: "vagrants and rogues" were not merely unproductive members of society; they were aggressively unproductive. The phrase "unproductive expenditure," coined by Georges Bataille to challenge classical political economy's emphasis on rational economic behavior,[90] has sometimes been taken to describe the performance of resistance to the relentless demand for labor productivity that acts in the service of capital accumulation. Whether or not we see it in these terms, we might imagine that nineteenth-century legislators and prison officials perceived criminal activities, which could be highly energetic but did not contribute to the official economy, as a kind of unproductive expenditure, or "unproductive labour." In this light, the treadmill, crank, and shot drill, while punishing and correcting the failure to work, also, somewhat paradoxically, *represented* criminal lack of productivity. On the treadmill or crank or in shot drill, convicts could *reproduce* their criminal lack of productivity in symbolic form. That is, just as early modern spectacular punishments had offered a symbolic, theatrical restaging of the crime in the punishment itself, so the spectacle of the treadmill, crank, and shot drill offered a symbolic, theatrical restaging of the crime of non-productivity. As in early modern torture, the crime was reproduced, but *as punishment*. We might think of this reproduction, in both contexts, as a kind of attempt to transform misconduct through symbolic performance: staging unproductive expenditure could be a way of taking control of it, and, instead of excising it, reprocessing it as submission to the labor machine. That is, the treadmill, crank, and shot drill pantomimed useful and useless labor simultaneously.

Acting Out, Sad Spectacles, and Terrible Apparitions in the Model Prison

These performances were not, however, really successes. Prisoners did not follow the scripts. Prohibited from staring (especially in the lockmarch), they stared. Powers chastises the "want of decorum" in the City Prison, where spectators "were met by the bold staring of the prisoners," who "left their work to gaze at them, . . . which indicated an unsubdued and audacious spirit, in the culprits," adding smugly, "This is never seen at Auburn."[91] And yet, in the image labeled "Prisoners at the State Prison at Auburn" [fig. 1], the convicts boldly defy the rules of the lockmarch by staring at the artist-spectator, with a look halfway between suspicion and hostility.

Forced to perform fake labor on the treadmill, the prisoners instead performed fake injuries, creating "foxes," or artificial sores, according to Chesterton, "and then, by an adroit fall, or an intentional contact with the revolving treadwheel, . . . writh[ing] and gesticulat[ing] to give colour to their deception."[92] Forced to perform the lockmarch, they turned it against the silent system. When Francis Lieber visited the Philadelphia Penitentiary in 1831, he was surprised that a prisoner he had never seen before not only knew his name, but was able to recount everything Lieber had done on a visit to Sing Sing (though the prisoner had never been there). "But how did you come to know all that?" asked Lieber. The prisoner responded, "Such things are known in a day or two all over the prison. We pass it along in the lock step."[93] Trained to perform, they performed: order visible to spectators and guards; codes visible only to other prisoners. This was decidedly not what prison officials had in mind.

One visitor to Sing Sing (perhaps having read *The Panopticon*) described the prison as "a system of espionage," where an "invisible eye watches [the prisoners'] actions every minute."[94] But the "invisible eye" seems to have failed to see through the most obvious prisoner artifices. Wines and Dwight report that no guard noticed when one female "tourist," paying her quarter each time she visited the prison, "adroitly dropped, . . . piece by piece, . . . a complete disguise, including false whiskers and moustache" for her "convict acquaintance."[95] And the "invisible eye" was often embarrassingly visible and audible. Brice describes with hilarity the Sing

Sing guards' delusion that they could spy on the prisoners without the prisoners' knowledge. The guards "would come in softly and take off their boots or shoes, and put on a pair of moccasins so as to make no noise, and thus take the men by surprise. Thus they would proceed along the galleries as silent as death. . . . But [they] always had the misfortune to find me looking [them] directly in the face." Surveillance techniques were "supposed to be a profound secret among the keepers and guard," but Brice "understood the planetary system of the prison." It was the guards who *"didn't understand the secrets!"*[96]

If the lockmarch, treadmill, crank, shot drill, and other such performances did not succeed in training prisoners to behave, neither did they give spectators what they wanted, or even succeed in impressing them with their message of moral uplift through rectitude and industry. When Jane Ellice visited Auburn (in 1838), she arrived just as the prisoners were performing the lockmarch, "marching in order (arms folded & each leaning on the back of the one before him)." While she tried to imagine herself in the role of Leonore in *Fidelio,* decrying the plight of the prisoners in "pretty broken English," the scene itself was not very pretty: "They all looked so *ghastly* & wretched. . . . It was a sad, sad sight & the silence . . . most oppressive."[97] A tourist named Gideon Davidson thought that the "convicts silently marching, . . . with a slow lock step, erect posture, keeping exact time . . . all give to the spectator somewhat similar feelings to those excited by a military funeral; and to the convicts, impressions not entirely dissimilar to those of culprits when marching to the gallows."[98] Mayhew and Binny compare the prisoners on the treadmill to squirrels on a wheel, or "the acrobat we have seen at a circus, perched on the cask that he causes to revolve under his feet," and are depressed by "the saddening spectacles" of these punishments, "which have been disguised under the name of *industrial* machines."[99] Watching a silent scene in a model workshop, they find it not an uplifting vision of "calm order" but an eerie "dumb show":

> To behold those whom we have seen full of life and emotion—some wondrous piece of breathing and speaking organism, reduced to the inanimateness of the statue, is assuredly the most appalling and depressing sight we can look upon. . . . The movements of the [prisoners] seem as noiseless, and therefore unearthly, as spectres. Nor does the sense of our being surrounded by some five hundred criminals—men of the wildest passions, and almost brute instincts, all toiling in dumb show and without a single syllable escaping from their lips—in any way detract from the *goblin* character of the sight. . . . What gall and bitterness, and suppressed fury, must be rankling in every bosom there, at the sense of having their tongues thus *virtually cut out.*[100]

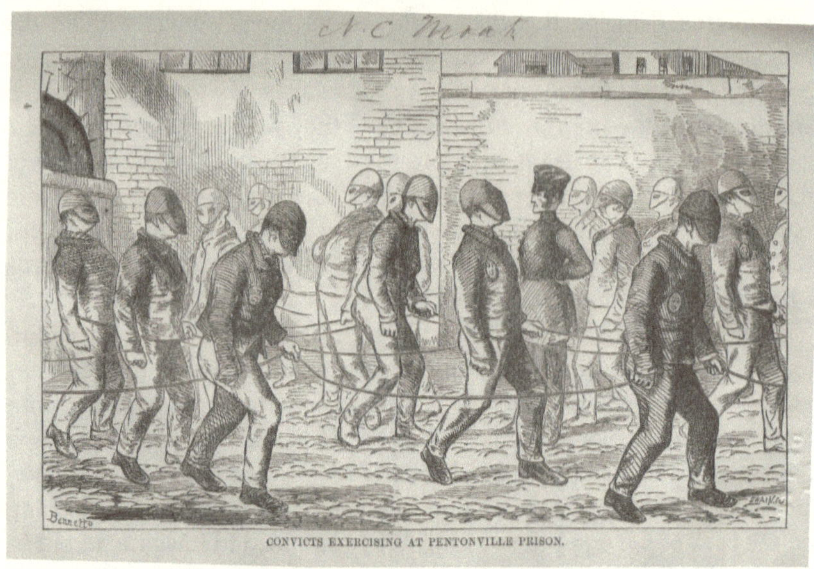

FIGURE 5. Prisoners wearing masks in Pentonville Prison. Henry Mayhew and John Binny, *The Criminal Prisons of London and Scenes of Prison Life* (1862). Courtesy of the Cornell University Law Library.

This is not the picturesque and instructive scene that Bentham had in mind.

Worst of all were the masks. When Mayhew and Binny visited Pentonville, they found that the prison had implemented Bentham's suggestion that the convicts wear masks: brown cloth caps, whose peaks hung down to "cover the face like a mask" [fig. 5]. This "masquerading," according to Mayhew and Binny, was "originally designed" to prevent the convicts from being "seen in their shame." But, they comment, since many outsiders see the convicts without these masks, they have become completely "theatrical in character." Wearing these masks in the exercise yard, they write, "the eyes alone" appear "through the two holes cut in the front, . . . like phosphoric lights shining through the sockets of a skull."

> This gives to the prisoners a half-spectral look, [so that] the costume of the men seems like the outward vestment to some wandering soul rather than that of a human being; for the eyes, glistening through the apertures in the mask, give one the notion of a spirit peeping out behind it, so that there is something positively terrible in the idea that these are men whose crimes have caused their very features to be hidden from the world.[101]

Part of what was wrong with performances of the lockmarch, or treadmill, crank, and shot drill, or displays of prisoners exercising in Pentonville, was a narrative problem. The scenes were anticlimactic: nothing happened. They did not contain dramas of sin, penitence, and sacrifice, nor did they allow spectators to participate in heroic moments of resistance (of the kind that could drive execution crowds to wild applause). They did not offer shared emotion (with prisoners and spectators alike "drowned in tears and overwhelmed with wo"). They did not offer the pleasures of individuated sympathy (as melodrama did), for the prisoners' faces were covered or turned away. They might show "horrours" ("the clang of iron bolts, manacles, and fetters"), but they did not perform climax, catharsis, or the promise of the world to come. They did not destroy the forces of evil, avenge the ghost, or release the protagonist from imprisonment in the dungeon. Here, there was not redemption, but obliteration. Mayhew and Binny try to find in this "screening of the faces" a "kind of tragic solemnity."[102] But the "phosphoric lights shining through the sockets of a skull" have nothing of tragedy. For tragedy (as Bentham suggested) requires a protagonist "stand[ing] forth [as] the sole hero of the melancholy drama." Here, instead, there are only ghosts. The punishment for the prisoners' crimes is erasure.

The descriptions of these performances as "oppressive," "saddening," "appalling," "depressing," "ghastly," or "spectral," however, share not just a sense of narrative disappointment, but also an uneasy sense that something is not right. That sense partly comes from the fact that these performances so obviously act out a lie: the lie that the model penitentiary has renounced "sanguinary punishments," and now teaches rectitude and labor with the stick held in abeyance. Locked up in Sing Sing, marching to the rhythm of the bathing tub, Brice has a good sense of humor ("I felt full of laughter [at this] unnecessary, foolish and barbarous exercise").[103] But it is not all that funny. Away from the eyes of spectators, the keeper, Joseph Perry, "marche[s] his company with a rawhide in his hand, . . . of which he [i]s not sparing to the unfortunate sufferers under his command. . . . In this all important exercise, if they are not punctual and attentive, they are caned, or flogged with the cat, (a most cruel instrument of torture)."[104] At Auburn, in the same year that Powers published his *Brief Account,* a prisoner named Rachel Welch (whom one of the guards had gotten pregnant) died after a guard beat her a little too severely.[105] In 1834 in the Eastern State Penitentiary, one inmate had an iron bar secured around his head so tightly that he died instantly from the suffusion of blood to his brain.[106]

In 1858, a "negro" named More (first name not recorded) was killed in a "shower-bath": a device in which the prisoner was placed in stocks inside a box and then water-boarded.[107] The 1858 *Harper's* article exposing More's death gives an illustrated account of the kinds of corporal punishment that, in addition to flogging, were currently being used in Auburn and other state prisons: the "pulley" (pulleys, connected to rings attached to the wrists and one ankle of the prisoner, were lifted so that the prisoner's whole weight would rest on one leg); "bucking" (a prisoner's hands were fastened and placed over the bent knees, and a stick was thrust under the knees above the arms); and the "yoke" (a bar was fastened behind the prisoner's arms, bearing down heavily on the neck and effectively crucifying him).[108] These were the punishments officially mandated by prison rules or allowed at the discretion of guards. In addition, there were the routine spontaneous punishments, not mandated but tolerated by the prison.[109] And there was the still more lethal brutality of unchecked disease and starvation, which made a prison sentence a death sentence.

In the Panopticon, writes Foucault, "There is no need for arms, physical violence, material constraints. Just a gaze."[110] This sanitized image—the image propagated by the prison manuals, architectural designs, and prison reformers' texts that were Foucault's sources—is maintained by no one who has actually studied the nineteenth-century prison. It may well be that flogging, along with shower-baths and use of the pulley, bucking, and the yoke, decreased over the course of the nineteenth century and continued to decrease in the twentieth, as perceptions of what kind of violence was acceptable (and how much) changed. But throughout the nineteenth century and still in the twentieth, reports of prison guards' routine violence, of serious injuries, and prison deaths emerged with numbing regularity. In the nineteenth century, this was an open secret. When spectators came upon whips or manacles—those "insignia of degradation" sometimes displayed on prison walls,[111] suddenly looming up before their eyes like a repressed nightmare as they turned a corner on a guided tour—they found them sinister. A representative of the Prison Discipline Society, visiting Auburn in 1839 and trying to process the "cow-hides and cat-o'nine-tails" he saw there, decided that they were "in bad taste."[112] Everyone knew that the lockmarch, the treadwheel, crank, and shot drill, the silence and averted gaze were enforced only by liberal use of the cat. Everyone knew that, instead of replacing the violence that one could no longer bear to see, the prison hid it behind doors. The panoptical "gaze" was not in any way a *replacement* for violence (spectacular or otherwise). It was in fact contingent on a spectacular scene, one that served as a theatrical front (not a deceptive one but, like theater's, an openly illusionary one) for the reality of the prison (offstage).

Austin Sarat has described the spectator's "sadistic" participatory pleasure in the state's violence at executions, which (as he suggests) is often, in the modern period, an embarrassed sadism, one quickly repressed or disavowed, replaced by claims about sympathy, humanitarianism, and the reduction of pain.[113] While the theater of executions and the theater of the prisons were quite different, they did have similarities. Those who attended executions primarily to rail against the barbarity of the spectacle and the vulgarity of the crowd, as Dickens did when he went to see the hanging of Frederick and Marie Manning in 1849,[114] or those who went to prisons hoping to hear the "sighs, groans, and hideous aspects, the clang of iron bolts, manacles, and fetters" while doing their philanthropic duty (like the visitor to the Newgate chapel), surely felt some conjunction of sadistic participatory pleasure and disavowal.

However, in the prison (unlike at the scene of execution), this conjunction of sadistic participatory pleasure and disavowal depended on a split between the visible and the invisible. Onstage there was, ideally, the picturesque, or affecting, or at least instructive scene. Offstage there was flogging and the many instruments of pain. In offering performances of the lockmarch or labor devices, or even scenes like that in the Newgate chapel, prison officials drew the spectator's gaze from the violence behind doors in the prison, while permitting spectators to know that it was just offstage. The broadside with the image of the treadmill in figure 3 offers a cheerful morality tale about three gamesters sentenced to "the Mill" ("O word of fear, . . . Unpleasing to a Gamester's ear!").[115] But the shadowy figure behind the bars in the background hints that just beyond the scene of salutary labor lurks something more sinister. Like the architecture of the model penitentiary itself, onstage performances said, "Look here, not there," while hinting darkly at a "there." At the scene of execution, spectators were required to engage in their own process of splitting and disavowal. In the prison, architectural or scenic splitting and disavowal did the work *for* the spectator. In effect, prison theatricality helped to shield spectators from their own ambivalence: from the psychic split produced by the sadistic desire to see and the simultaneous desire not to see. At the same time, of course, the prison shielded itself.

At the risk of being vulgarly Freudian, we might, for a moment, analogize the spectator's experience of the model penitentiary to the Freudian dreamscape, understanding its public scenes as a kind of manifest dream content and behind-doors violence as a kind of latent dream content. In this theoretical frame, Ellice's or Mayhew and Binny's pervasive but hard-to-locate sense of "oppressi[on]," their sadness, the vague sense of "unearthl[iness]," their sense of the "*goblin* character" of the mute workers or the "half-spectral look" of the men in their masks with eyes "like phosphoric lights shining through the sockets of a skull" may be seen as symptoms: something is not right. And yet, like the "cow-hides and cat-o'nine-tails" hanging on the prison wall, these offered a bridge to the unconscious of the prison. For Ellice, Mayhew, Binny, and other sightseers dedicated to philanthropic spectatorship, the pleasures of the picturesque scene, or even a dose of gothic thrill such encounters with the unconscious of the prison were neither pleasurable nor edifying but (like most encounters with the unconscious) disturbing. Maybe it was better to stay home. Abort sympathy. Flee.

"'The dark places of the earth are full of cruelty,'" writes Wines, quoting Psalms, "and a prison is a very dark place."[116] In Pentonville, a jailer invites Mayhew and Binny to visit "the dark cells," a subterranean world of solitary cells in which prisoners subject to extra punishment are kept in complete darkness:

> "Would you like to step inside," asked the warder, "and see how dark it is when the door is closed?" . . . We entered the terrible place with a shudder, for there is something intensely horrible in absolute darkness. . . . And as the warder shut the door upon us—and we felt the cell walls shake and moan . . . like a tomb, as he did so—the utter darkness was, as Milton sublimely says—"*visible*." The eyes not only saw, but *felt* the absolute negation of their sense, . . . as if [we] were buried alive, deep down in the earth itself, [where] continual straining of the eye-balls . . . would end in conjuring up all kinds of terrible apparitions.[117]

Here, we are invited into the hellish underworld of the prison, a Miltonic "darkness visible" that also evokes the *ancien régime* Bastille. The scene is in some ways pure gothic (with all its pleasures), creating a *felt* darkness, with the capacity to conjure a phantasmagoria of "terrible apparitions." But at the same time it registers an "oppressive," "saddening," "depressing" sense that there is really, after all, no scenic, narrative, or ethical meaning to be found in the prison. The "absolute negation of [the] sense[s]" may intensify sensations and emotions (shuddering, moaning, horrors). But here anesthesia also serves as a figure for loss of meaning, invisibility, and erasure: the disappearance of the prisoner from public view, into the darkness. The apparitions conjured in the dark are like the goblins of Coldbath Fields or the masked prisoners moving eerily about the yard: mute skulls with sockets for eyes, more than half-spectral, "men whose crimes have caused their very features to be hidden from the world." No one is being granted the pleasures of the picturesque, edified by the visit, deterred from crime, taught the lessons of labor, or choreographically molded. Nor is there narrative closure: no one here will be magnificently "launched into eternity" as the church bells toll. Here, the prisoners will remain, subject to a violence not eradicated by enlightenment but merely pushed offstage. Here, they will remain, "buried alive, deep down in the earth itself," subject to a slow-motion death sentence.

Epilogue: Prison Performance in the Age of Reality TV

We might take the scene in "the tombs" as not only emblematizing the invisibility of those effectively buried there but also in some sense presaging the condition of the prison to come. In the twentieth century, penitentiaries were gradually closed to tourists, and prisoners did, in fact, largely recede into invisibility. Concerns like those of Samuel Gridley Howe, Dorothea Dix, or Henry Cordier certainly had something to do with it: many people came to feel that "making convicts a kind of public show" and "indiscriminate[ly] expos[ing]" them for the "mere gratification of the thoughtless and the curious" was wrong and could not continue. At the same time, police forces—increasingly visible and professional—shifted penal spectacle to preemptive rather than reactive deterrence. Perhaps more important, the proliferation of penal-themed spectacle in fiction film—cops and robbers, cowboys, Indians, and sheriffs, detectives and outlaws—satisfied some of the urges that had driven spectators to penitentiaries in the nineteenth century. Offering (on the whole) endings in which law triumphed, these conjoined the spectacular violence of executions and floggings with the apparent orderliness, legalism, and moral righteousness of the prison.

And yet, the spectacle of the real prison never disappeared altogether. Public prison rodeos, featuring inmates on bucking broncos (channeling violence into "safe" outlets), started to appear in the 1930s, around the same time that the last few states in the United States were definitively outlawing public executions and floggings.[118] Beginning in the 1970s, many former penitentiaries were turned into museums, full of gothic horrors representing the barbarism of the past. (The Buckingham Old Gaol Museum "dare[s] you [to] . . . see which tortured souls still inhabit the corridors and cells"; the Eastern State Penitentiary Museum offers "terror behind the walls: six haunted attractions . . . inside the cellblocks.")[119] At the same time, the prison documentary joined fictional media to create a new form of remote prison tourism, updated for the era of mass media, which is also, of course, the era of mass incarceration.

With the rise of "reality TV" in the early twenty-first century, television programs showing "life behind bars" have multiplied: *Beyond Scared Straight, Behind Bars: Rookie Year, Women Behind Bars, Hard Time, 60 Days In, Lockdown, Lockup,* several *Lockup* spinoffs, and such British series as *The Lock Up* and *Jailbreak* (to name just a few). Some of these have had huge successes: *Lockup,* for instance, is almost the longest-running reality show in television history, and one of the highest rated, at its height attracting nearly 300,000 viewers for a single episode.[120] From the viewpoint of the twenty-first century, one might say (in a different formulation of my initial claim): the spectacular, theatrical performance of punishment—far from disappearing in the nineteenth century—never fully disappeared and, in the twenty-first century, has had an astonishing resurgence.

A thoroughgoing analysis of such programs would require another essay, but what follows are some musings on what the culture of nineteenth-century prison performance might tell us about the meaning of twenty-first-century prison spectacle for law, and for culture generally. For one thing, despite all the differences between nineteenth- and twenty-first-century prison spectacle, and despite changes in aesthetic vocabularies, twenty-first-century spectators admit to an array of theatrical pleasures uncannily similar to those of their nineteenth-century forebears: the vicarious thrill of getting close to the violent drama of the prisoners' lives (hair-raisingly real, but seen from a safe distance); the shivers of horror at the scenes of misery; the relief and gratitude that that such misery is not one's own; and (not least) the sweet sympathy felt in viewing affecting scenes and moments of human pathos, ultimately crowned with a moral. "This is real life[!]" (but so entertaining: "Dear lockup, . . . U have entertained my wife and I for years now").[121] "It's sad to make a spectacle of the prisoners, but I can't help watching to satisfy my curiosity." "I love the show: [its] stories . . . pull at your heart strings." "The scenes are so touching." One scene "has stayed with me for years. Broke my heart." "This program is like watching a train wreck—I'm horrified, yet I can't turn away."[122] "This show . . . has helped me be grateful for the life that I have."

At the same time (say twenty-first-century spectators, like their nineteenth-century forebears), such pleasures are justified by their utility.

Not only do these programs "displa[y] the . . . exhibitions of real life," which are far more interesting than fiction (as Bentham writes). They deter crime (say fans), humanize those behind bars, allow the public to inspect prisons, and potentially serve prison reform. *Lockup* (says one fan) "deters violence" because it "deter[s] someone even thinking about . . . breaking the law." "Believe me if you watch enough lock up episodes . . . you will want to stay sweet and innocent!!!" At the same time that the scenes of prison life they show are "serious" and "affecting" (to use Bentham's language), they are also highly "instructive" (say their spectators): "This show served . . . as my 'homework' [and] continuing education." It "gets [the prisoners'] stories out there to the public." It "show[s] real people, and [shows] in a real way what [goes] on inside prison walls."

Just as advocates of prison reality shows sound much like their nineteenth-century predecessors, so do critics of these shows, citing their tendency to degrade their subjects, turning misery into an object of public spectacle, their profiteering from unpaid prisoners as performers, who are made to collude in their own exploitation, and their specious representation of prison life. Such shows, say twenty-first-century critics, are "prison porn," speaking to "prurient interests" to increase ratings.[123] They create a public spectacle of the most miserable.[124] They exploit prisoners for gain (in a situation of *de facto* coercion), increasing profits by using free performance labor (in fact, a form of slave labor).[125] One cannot say that participation is voluntary, for free consent depends upon freedom, which is precisely what the prisoners do not have.[126] They propagate two forms of nefarious ideology by splitting the "bad prisoner" from the "good prisoner." Social demonization represents the "bad prisoner" as an irredeemable psychopath, incapable of reform or reentry.[127] Neoliberal ideology represents the "good prisoner" as repentant, hard-working, self-improving, a paragon whose path to reentry and upward mobility will thus be unimpeded by race, class, or opportunity.[128] The distortions embedded in such ideologically saturated splitting, say critics, are exacerbated by the refusal of networks to expose the real politics and economics of prisons in the age of mass incarceration.

I suspect that most readers of this essay will sympathize with such critiques, as do I. And yet, denunciation of popular culture representations of this kind is so *de rigeur* among humanities academics that it would seem worth testing such critiques for their nuance and applicability simply on principle, even were there not some quite evident problems with them. But there are such problems. For one thing, while critics tend to treat prison reality programs as if they were all the same, in fact, they reflect a wide variety of documentary strategies, methodologies, and perspectives. For instance, *Behind Bars: Rookie Year* is filmed from the perspective of rookie corrections officers, learning to get tough on crime in a violent New Mexico jail. *Lockup,* claiming to be neutral, represents prisoners' and guards' stories from multiple perspectives, sometimes giving the prisoners video cameras ("inmate cams") to record their thoughts. In *60 Days In,* participants posing as prisoners expose crime and corruption (the first episode led not only to sanctions for some prisoners but to the firing of numerous correction officers).[129] A new reality show in the works, *Fresh Out the Feds,* has been launched by three former inmates, whose focus is the impact of mass incarceration on women and their families.[130]

As the above descriptions should suggest, many such programs are in fact quite critical of both conditions in particular prisons and the so-called justice system more broadly.[131] And critique of the prison system is, in fact, the lesson many spectators take away, even from such "neutral" programs as *Lockup:* "The Inmates have to purchase everything. Meaning toilet paper soap everything." "One roll of toilet paper per week?" "It's a NEED not a want to have TP." "What's messed up is the boxes the food comes in says not for human consumption." "It's funny how most people try to . . . separate themselves from [the] 'convict,' . . . saying things like you should be lucky to get food[.] Are you serious? . . . Food is not something that you should receive depending on your behavior. . . . The only thing that separates you from them on lock up is that you [haven't gotten] caught yet." "I spent all day yesterday watching. . . . Our Prison system should be illegal."

While it is tempting to mock nineteenth-century prison Good Samaritans and their twenty-first-century counterparts for "flock[ing] to the philanthropic show" in order to feel the pleasures of their own beneficence, such programs' criticism of the prison system and ability to rouse sympathy in fact create not just aspiring but actual prison activists and advocates. "Watching this show" has taught me "to have compassion for others," writes one *Lockup* fan, and "inspired me to hopefully one day . . . teach inmates who wish to obtain their GED." Another writes that the plight of prisoners in *Lockup* was the reason she majored in criminal justice and went on to work in prisons. Another writes that she has spent "[m]any weekend nights" watching *Lockup* and "planning how [to] change prisons."

It is certainly true that some spectators are venomously hostile toward prisoners, but the vast majority testify that such shows have given them a better understanding of the circumstances that contribute to incarceration and the misery of prison life. Spectators become involved with individual prisoners' lives in ways that can be weird (as in much reality fandom), but also break down barriers between those on the outside and those on the inside. Prisoners seem like virtual friends, part of a small friend group that includes other viewers: "Anyone else want to shake some sense into Manda Lynch?! Or swoop in and rescue her? I'm not sure which I want to do, but my God does she have bad taste in women!" And, on the death of one of the inmates, "Nooooooo." "Watching the show you felt like you knew [Ray] and the up[s] and down[s] [he] went through." "So sad to hear. . . . it seemed like Ray could never catch a decent break." "RIP brother!" "Click here to support Ray Slagle Memorial Expense Fund." (The funeral was, in fact, paid for by fans.)

Fan sites and online prison support communities suggest that there is not, in fact, a clear divide between spectator and spectacle (or, as critics might put it, gawker and gawked). Those posting on PrisonTalk.com, an online family support community, have a healthy skepticism about what is shown, some of it clearly "just for show."[132] But they nonetheless talk about how important *Lockup* is to them: first, it allows them to see conditions in better prisons and thus advocate for imprisoned family members ("tvs, weekend conjugal visits, . . . acs, . . . cigarettes, pet cats . . . That[']s right, i said pet cats[!]");[133] second, because it allows them to feel connected to the lives of those they have lost to prison ("I watch because its comforting just to get close to my BF but then he was ON the show!").[134] *Lockup* regularly produces spectators who become prison pen-pals, who sometimes become visitors, who sometimes become spouses, granted the right to conjugal visits.[135] Many spectators are in fact former inmates. "I love this show. As a former inmate, it was good to see the good and the bad aired." "Lived it for 27 years plenty of reruns in my memory bank." "The guy with the flames and tattoos on his neck I was locked up with him [in] Hutchinson Correctional Facility he was one of my cellys." "I'd like to thank the staff of Lockup for being in Cincinnati when I was . . . incarcerated there. For 7 Days I was belittled and taunted by the jail staff. Then the Lockup crew [came]. I don't think I could have lasted another 10 Days without them." Such comments make it hard to maintain the critique that (in the words of Mansfield Frazier) spectators of such shows are like those who "cag[e] animals and then pok[e] them with sticks for the[ir] amusement."[136]

Perhaps most important, such programs can give prisoners an otherwise inaccessible vehicle for protest and self-representation, whether or not they have "inmate cams." Footage is, of course, edited. Episodes are curated. Performance conventions and ideology clearly shape how prisoners perform on camera. What prisoners can say is necessarily constrained by the fear of retaliation from prison personnel. But *de facto* censorship (while bad) is not the same as coercion *to perform*. Prisoners seem to embrace the chance to be on camera because—like nineteenth-century prisoners who faked treadmill injuries, or those who used the lockmarch to pass messages, or William Lyon Mackenzie, who told visitors that the doors of his prison "were freely opened to those who wished to see a real live Canadian rebel"—they know how to exploit performance opportunities. To tell them they are deluded would be both insulting and false. And they would surely have withering remarks to make about scholars who hold such programs in contempt without having been behind bars.

Ultimately, such programs refuse to allow the incarceration regime to function *sub rosa*, swallowing prisoners in obscurity. As L. B. Eisen of the Brennan Center for Justice at NYU has commented, "I think it would be more disturbing if we had [millions of people] behind bars and nobody paid attention or wanted to know what it was like."[137] Or, in the words of one *Lockup* fan, "Many wan[t] criminals to just be forgotten about. . . . This show keeps them from just being invisible."

None of this is to suggest that such programs have the power to change the underlying problem of the prison system in the United States (and, to a lesser extent, in Britain and elsewhere): first, mass incarceration, increasingly entrenched in the United States (and increasingly racialized);[138] second, the creation of private for-profit prisons, whose main goals are minimizing costs by reducing services and maximizing profits by expanding the prison population and charging prisoners monopoly prices for basic goods.[139] Nor is it to suggest that these programs justly distribute value: prisoners get some air time; networks get air time, too, but also make millions of dollars annually from their captive populations (profits partly derived from zero labor costs), none of which go to the participants. And it is highly doubtful that these productions have deterred even a single crime.[140] One might argue that, like the nineteenth-century lockmarch or treadmill, twenty-first-century prison spectacle attempts to mask both conditions and underlying structural issues. And yet, it was not prison spectacle but the invisibility of prisons in the twentieth century that obscured the growth of mass incarceration and the resulting conditions. Making it possible for prisoners to participate as actors in our culture of media performance—with all its negatives—is crucial to keeping them visible. And visibility matters. For all the discomfort that shows like *Lockup* may produce, objecting that prisoners' performances are "prison porn," or the object of vulgar and depraved tastes, or that it is somehow unseemly for law to traffic in such things, smacks of warmed-over antitheatricality. With a good dose of utopianism about the power of performance and the ability of prisoners to act as managers of their own theater, one might still say, with Bentham, "In a well-composed committee of penal law, I know not a more essential personage than the manager of a theatre."

NOTES

1. Bentham first elaborated on his plan for a model prison in a very short text with plans (Jeremy Bentham, *Outline of the Plan of Construction of a Panopticon Penitentiary House* [n.p., 1790]), soon adding revisions and postscripts, and continuing to refine it over the next decades. Because it includes both the initial text and the postscripts, but still reflects Bentham's initial conception (as opposed to the changes he made in the nineteenth century), I am using the following edition: Jeremy Bentham, *Panopticon: or, the Inspection-House* (Dublin: Thomas Byrne, 1791), 173 (hereafter cited in the text). I thank Aurélie A. Roy for her invaluable research assistance.

2. It is worth noting that Bentham misquotes Bacon and radically changes his meaning. Bacon's phrase is actually: "*Nil habeat Forum ex scenâ*"; the court should have nothing to do with matters outside its purview. From the context, it is clear that he means that people should not bring "*Cases* of *Contradiction* . . . under fained parties," in other words, test cases. Bacon, "A Proposition to His Majesty . . . Touching the Compiling and Amendment of the Laws of England" (c. 1616), in Bacon, *Resuscitatio, or, Bringing into Publick Light Severall Pieces . . . Hitherto Sleeping* (1657), 278. I am grateful to Alan Stewart for helping me locate this passage.

3. To simplify, one group of scholars sees the cause of the change as the rise of manners (and a concomitant repression of violence, pain, death, sex, and the excretory functions), which manifests itself as, among other things, the "humanitarianism" that defeated the spectacle of suffering. The most prominent statement of this view is Pieter Spierenburg, *The Spectacle of Suffering: Executions and the Evolution of Repression; from a Preindustrial Metropolis to the European Experience* (Cambridge: Cambridge University Press, 1984). The other (heavily Marxist-inflected) group of scholars sees the cause of the change as the product of economic and class interests. One might identify with this group Georg Rusche and Otto Kirchheimer's seminal *Punishment and Social Structure* (New York: Columbia University Press, 1939), Dario Melossi and Massimo Pavarini's *The Prison and the Factory: Origins of the Penitentiary System*, trans. Glynis Cousin (1977; reprint London: Macmillan, 1981), Michael Ignatieff's *A Just Measure of Pain: The*

Penitentiary in the Industrial Revolution, 1750–1850 (New York: Pantheon Books, 1978), and (arguably) Michel Foucault's *Discipline and Punish: The Birth of the Prison* (1975; reprint, New York: Pantheon Books, 1977).

4. "By the end of the eighteenth and the beginning of the nineteenth century," writes Foucault, punishment "ceased to be a spectacle." "Theatrical representation" was pushed aside, and "replaced by a punishment that act[ed] in depth on the heart, the thoughts, the will, the inclinations." "Punishment [became] the most hidden part of the penal process" (8–9, 14, 16). Pieter Spierenburg similarly claims: "the spectacle of suffering was to survive" (202) until the nineteenth century. With the completion of the "privatization of repression" came a "closing of the curtains" (*Spectacle of Suffering*, 201–6). Or see Michael Ignatieff: "Between 1770 and 1840 [a] form of carceral discipline 'directed at the mind' replaced a cluster of punishments 'directed at the body'" (1). "Penitentiary discipline . . . played out in private, behind the walls of the institution," "contrasted sharply with the ritual of public punishment. . . . [D]efiance could not call on the support of a watching crowd . . . Discipline, therefore, was a new rite, one from which the public was locked out" (*Just Measure of Pain*, 105).

5. Despite the critiques of *Discipline and Punish* that have circulated since its first publication, Foucault remains the most widely cited authority on the history of punishment, and scholars in many fields continue to build their claims on his argument that a regime of invisible discipline replaced the early modern theater of punishment in the late eighteenth century. For a summary of critiques of *Discipline and Punish*, see David Garland, *Punishment and Modern Society: A Study in Social Theory* (Chicago: University of Chicago Press, 1993), 157–75 (and the book as a whole for an excellent review of the historiography of punishment generally).

6. In this essay I focus only on the Anglo-American world. More research is required to understand the culture of prison tourism elsewhere. In his study of prisons throughout the world, written in the 1870s, Enoch Cobb Wines refers to "a strong feeling against the admission into prisons of non-official visitors" in most places in Europe except the Netherlands, which may partly explain the absence of sources on prison tourism in places other than England and North America. Wines, *The State of Prisons and of Child-Saving Institutions in the Civilized World* (Cambridge, MA: J. Wilson and Son, 1880), 247. However, it is clear from the numerous unofficial visitors' descriptions of European and colonial prisons that there were many such visitors, if not quite the industry that developed in North America.

7. For a more complete discussion of my use of the word "performance," see my "Law as Performance: Historical Interpretation, Objects, Lexicons, and Other Methodological Problems," in *New Directions in Law and Literature*, ed. Elizabeth S. Anker and Bernadette Meyler (New York: Oxford University Press, 2017), 200–203, and throughout.

8. See Foucault, *Discipline*, 195–228, for his discussion of the Panopticon (references hereafter in the text).

9. While Foucault does discuss Bentham's idea that the prison should be open to spectators, he seems to imagine its viewership as a kind of seeing machine without subjectivity: abstract, faceless, invisible, insensible, indistinguishable from the Panopticon's instrumentality. And while the cells may be like "so many small theatres" (200), these are really more like the images that a surveillance camera might show. Foucault's Panopticon is not a theater but a specular instrument, an apparatus for the diffusion of power in the society of surveillance. The presence of the guard in the Panopticon's tower seems irrelevant, for Foucault, not just because (as Bentham argues) the prisoners must feel themselves to be under constant and omniscient surveillance, with or without an actual watcher, but because Foucault sees the spectator's experience as irrelevant; effectively, the spectator, even if physically present, is not there.

10. For an account of madhouse tourism, see Jonathan Andrews and Andrew Scull, *Customers and Patrons of the Mad-Trade: The Management of Lunacy in Eighteenth-Century London* (Berkeley: University of California Press, 2003).

11. John Howard, *The State of the Prisons in England and Wales: With Preliminary Observations, and an Account of Some Foreign Prisons* (London: T. Cadell and N. Conant, 1777).

12. See Foucault's reference to this passage in *Discipline and Punish*, 207.

13. Jephson, *Braganza, A Tragedy* (London: T. Evans; and T. Davies, 1775), v.

14. Jeremy Bentham, *Draught of a New Plan for the Organisation of the Judicial Establishment in France* ([London?]: n.p., 1790), 25–26.

15. See, for instance, Theophilus Cibber, *Cibber's Two Dissertations on the Theatres* (London: the Author, 1757): Cibber made "Theatre a School of Morality" ("To his most Ex—-t M—-," 29; pagination in the volume is non-consecutive).

16. Edmund Burke, *A Philosophical Enquiry into the Origin of Our Ideas of the Sublime and Beautiful*, ed. Adam Phillips (Oxford: Oxford University Press, 1990), 43.

17. William Dodd, *Thoughts in Prison* (London: Edward and Charles Dilly, 1777), 62–63.

18. Ibid., 58–59.

19. Ibid., 87.

20. For a description of Bentham's attempts to get his Panopticon built, see Ignatieff, *Just Measure*, 109–13. While reformers often distinguished "penitentiaries" from "prisons" (and the word "penitentiary" had a significance widely discussed in the scholarly literature on nineteenth-century prison reform), the words were often used interchangeably, and many of the institutions that exemplified the goals of the penitentiary most fully were called "prisons." Hence, I use the words somewhat interchangeably.

21. The two principal new prison systems developed in the United States and were then transferred back to the old world, each responding to this desideratum: the "separate" or "Philadelphia" system, in which prisoners were to live alone in cells and see no other prisoners; and the "silent" or "congregate" or "Auburn" system, in which prisoners were to work together in strictly enforced silence during the day and sleep alone in their cells at night.

22. Wines, *State of Prisons*, 17 (and see the letter on Fry's work in the *Morning Chronicle*, July 30, 1817, 3, column 4).

23. The idea of the prison as a "closed world"—inspired by studies of the asylum such as Foucault's *History of Madness* (1961; reprint, London: Routledge, 2006), Erving Goffman's sociological description of "total institutions" in *Asylums: Essays on the Social Situation of Mental Patients and Other Inmates* (New York: Anchor Books, 1961), or David J. Rothman's *The Discovery of the Asylum: Social Order and Disorder in the New Republic* (Boston: Little, Brown, 1971) (in addition to *Discipline and Punish*)—has had remarkable staying power.

24. Miron's excellent study, *Prisons, Asylums, and the Public: Institutional Visiting in the Nineteenth Century* (Toronto: University of Toronto Press, 2011), tracks the vast enterprise of prison and asylum tourism in nineteenth-century North America. As will be apparent here, my work is deeply indebted to the groundwork she has laid.

25. For the phrase "Model Prison," see Henry Mayhew and John Binny, *The Criminal Prisons of London and Scenes of Prison Life* (London: Griffin, Bohn & Company, 1862), 119, 123 (and 112–96 for a detailed description of their tour of this "Model Prison").

26. "Report of the Warden," *Journals of the Legislative Assembly of the Province of Canada*, vol. 6, Appendix N (Montreal: R. Campbell, 1847); quoted in Miron, *Prisons*, 45.

27. Samuel Gridley Howe, *An Essay on the Separate and Congregate Systems of Prison Discipline* (Boston: W. D. Ticknor, 1846), 46; cited in Miron, *Prisons*, 47.

28. These numbers are based on the estimates in Norman Johnston, "Noble Ideas Collide with Reality," in *Crucible of Good Intentions: Eastern State Penitentiary*, ed. Norman Johnston (Philadelphia: Philadelphia Museum of Art, 1994), 47, 57; quoted in Miron, *Prisons*, 142.

29. S. G. Lathrop, *Crime and Its Punishment, and Life in the Penitentiary* (Joliet, IL: the Author, 1866), 226; quoted in Miron, *Prisons*, 17.

30. John Josiah Munro, *The New York Tombs Inside and Out!* (Brooklyn, NY: the Author, 1909), 226.

31. Enoch Cobb Wines and Theodore W. Dwight, *Report on the Prisons and Reformatories of the United States and Canada* (Albany: Van Benthuysen & Sons, 1867), 218.

32. For instance, in 1846 the Massachusetts State Prison made $1,500 from admission tickets. Howe, *An Essay on the Separate and Congregate Systems*, 46; cited in Miron, *Prisons*, 47. Howe's and my calculations are based on the multiplication of the annual number of visitors by the admission price of 25 cents, which seems to have remained remarkably stable between the 1820s and 1860s, as the Wines and Dwight quote above suggests, but is likely to have gone up later in the century. Calculating historical monetary equivalences is historiographically complex, and "hundreds of thousands of dollars" is, of course, merely a rough estimate, based on the thoughtful metrics offered at http://www.measuringworth.com/uscompare (accessed May 6, 2015).

33. J. C. Myers, *Sketches on a Tour through the Northern and Eastern States, the Canadas and Nova Scotia* (Harrisonburg: J. H. Wartmann and Brothers, 1849), 116; quoted in Miron, *Prisons*, 61.

34. "BLACKWELL'S ISLAND. A Summer-day's Tour," *New York Times*, July 8, 1866, 8.

35. "A Visit to the Islands in the East River," *New York Daily Tribune*, September 13, 1849, 2.

36. Robina and Kathleen Lizars, *Humours of '37: Grave, Gay and Grim* (Toronto: W. Briggs, 1897), 351–52; quoted in Miron, *Prisons*, 85.

37. "Scenes in Prison," *Free Enquirer* 1, no. 39 (September 7, 1834): 311.

38. "A Visit to the State Prison," *New York Times*, June 16, 1859, 1; quoted in Miron, *Prisons*, 105

39. Moodie, *Life in the Clearings versus the Bush* (Toronto: McLelland and Steward, 1989), 190; quoted in Miron, *Prisons*, 64.

40. Dickens, *American Notes for General Circulation*, 2 vols. (London: Chapman and Hall, 1842), vol. 1, 199.

41. "Scenes in Prison," *The Free Enquirer (1828–1835)* 1, no. 39 (September 7, 1834): 311.

42. Mayhew and Binny, *Criminal Prisons*, 118.

43. Ellice, *The Diary of Jane Ellice*, ed. Patricia Godsell (Toronto: Oberon Press, 1975), 100; quoted in part in Miron, *Prisons*, 80.

44. Howe, *Essay on the Separate and Congregate Systems*, 47.

45. "Über die Bestimmung im § 8 des StGb, dass die Vollstreckung eines Todesurteils durch Glockengeläut anzukündigen sei," quoted in Richard J. Evans, *Rituals of Retribution: Capital Punishment in German 1600–1987* (Oxford: Oxford University Press, 1996), 305.

46. Howe, *Essay on the Separate and Congregate Systems*, 47 (paraphrasing such claims in a counter-argument).

47. "An Exploration of the Tombs," *New York Times*, March 16, 1862, 3.

48. Gershom Powers, *A Brief Account of the Construction, Management and Discipline of the New York State Prison at Auburn* (Auburn: U. F. Doubleday, 1826), 10.

49. Dodd, *Thoughts in Prison*, 62–63.

50. *Rules and Regulations and By-Laws for the Government and Discipline of the Albany County Penitentiary* (Albany: Joel Munsell, 1849), 4; quoted in Miron, *Prisons*, 35.

51. Wines and Dwight, *Report*, 218.

52. Powers, *Brief Account*, 2.

53. Benjamin Rush, "An Enquiry into the Effects of Public Punishments Upon Criminals, and Upon Society," *Essays Literary, Moral and Philosophical*, ed. Michael Meranze (Schenectady, NY: Union College Press, 1988), 82; quoted in Kristin Boudreau, *The Spectacle of Death: Populist Literary Responses to American Capital Cases* (Amherst, NY: Prometheus, 2006), 19.

54. In "Thoughts upon Female Education," a lecture delivered later that year, Rush criticized the "abortive sympathy" created by novel reading in terms that echo similar critiques of the theater during the period. Rush, *Essays Literary, Moral and Philosophical*, 48; quoted in Bourdreau, *Spectacle*, 22. I am indebted to Boudreau's discussion of "abortive sympathy" in these two texts.

55. "Annual Report of the Warden of the Reformatory Prison of Lower Canada," *Second Annual Report of the Board of Inspectors of Asylums, Prisons, &c 1861, Sessional Papers*, Session 1862, no. 19 (Quebec: Hunter, Rose, and Lemieux, 1862); quoted in Miron, *Prisons*, 44.

56. Wines, *State of Prisons*, 242 (but see his critique of prison tourism in Wines and Dwight, *Report*, 218).

57. "American Prisons," *North American Review* 103, no. 213 (October 1866): 410; quoted in Miron, *Prisons*, 152.

58. Howe, *Essay on the Separate and Congregate Systems*, 47.

59. Ibid. (italics removed).

60. Dorothea Dix, *Remarks on Prisons and Prison Discipline* (Boston: Munroe & Francis, 1845), 10.

61. Quoted in Wines and Dwight, *Report*, 218.

62. Powers, *Brief Account*, 59.

63. Joseph R. Roach, "Theatre History and the Ideology of the Aesthetic," *Theatre Journal* 41, no. 2 (1989): 155–68.

64. James R. Brice, *Secrets of the Mount-Pleasant State Prison, Revealed and Exposed* (Albany, NY: the Author, 1839), 41–42.

65. George Moore, *Journal of a Voyage across the Atlantic* (London: s.n., 1845), 63.

66. Ibid.

67. See David J. Rothman, "Perfecting the Prison," in *The Oxford History of the Prison: The Practice of Punishment in Western Society*, ed. Norval Morris and David J. Rothman (New York: Oxford, 1995), 110.

68. T. R. Woodhouse, ed., "A Trip to Upper Canada, August 1835. From the Diary of John Armour, Jr.," *Ontario History* 14, no. 3 (1953), 133; quoted in Miron, *Prisons*, 106.

69. Powers, *Brief Account*, 10.

70. For Fried, paintings express "theatricality" when subjects break the "fourth wall," looking directly at the spectators or the painter, posing for them. Paintings express "absorption" when subjects are absorbed in the scene, seemingly unaware of the presence of spectators or painter. Michael Fried, *Absorption and Theatricality: Painting and Beholder in the Age of Diderot* (Berkeley: University of California Press, 1980).

71. "The Tread Mill," *Niles's Weekly Register* 23 (November 9, 1822), 159.

72. Mayhew and Binny, *Criminal Prisons*, 304.

73. James Williams, *A Narrative of Events since the 1st of August, 1834* (London: the Central Emancipation Committee, 1839), 5.

74. Mayhew and Binny, *Criminal Prisons*, 303. A few prisons (especially in the United States) did use treadmills to mill grain or cut lumber, but even these, when supply or demand failed, were to be used merely symbolically. "Should the supply of grain, at any

time, fail, it is not necessary that the labour of the prisoners should be suspended; nor can they be aware of the circumstance; the supply of labour may, therefore be considered as unfailing." James Hardie, *The History of the Tread-Mill* (New York: S. Marks, 1824), 17–18.

75. Mayhew and Binny, *Criminal Prisons*, 307.

76. Ibid., 303.

77. Ibid., 308. Mayhew and Binny estimate that this took approximately eight and a half hours. It was one of the ironies of the crank that it was often imposed as a punishment for shamming illness, which many prisoners did in an attempt to get out of the treadmill or shot drill: that is, prisoners were punished for shamming, but it was in fact the prison's sham performances that were the reason for their shamming, and their punishment produced yet more shamming.

78. Hippisley, *Prison Labour, etc: Correspondence and Communications Addressed to His Majesty's Principal Secretary of State for the Home Department* (London: W. Nicol, 1823), 190–91.

79. Mayhew and Binny, *Criminal Prisons*, 308.

80. Ibid., 309.

81. On the expense of the treadmill, see Anon., *Thoughts on Prison Labour* (London: Rodwell and Martin, 1824), 3. David Dyer reported in 1868 that some British prisons were "approaching to self-support," but cites extremely low prisoner earnings: "the country [is] spending between two or three millions sterling on crime." Dyer, *Impressions of Prison Life in Great Britain* (Albany: J. Munsell, 1868), 22–23.

82. Mayhew and Binny, *Criminal Prisons*, 303.

83. Ibid., 492.

84. This was the reason that nineteenth-century prisons put not only felons but also vagrants on the treadmill and crank. Indeed, many argued that criminals were criminals not because they were naturally vicious, or poor, but simply because "vagrants and rogues"—more-or-less indistinguishable—did not like to work. For "vagrants and rogues," see "Tread Mill," *Niles's Weekly Register* 23 (November 9, 1822), 158. For a nonjudgmental version of the view that criminals were criminals because they did not like to work, see Mayhew and Binny, *Criminal Prisons*, 108.

85. Great Britain [Parliament. House of Commons], *Parliamentary Papers 1875*, 84 vols. (London: HMSO, 1875), vol. 51, 226, 230.

86. Chesterton, *Revelations of Prison Life*, 2 vols. (London: Hurst and Blackett, 1856), vol. 1, 224–25.

87. Hardie, *History of the Tread-Mill*, 36–37.

88. Ibid., 10.

89. On injuries and deaths, see Mayhew and Binny, *Criminal Prisons*, 288; and Ignatieff, *Just Measure*, 177.

90. See, for instance, "The Notion of Expenditure," in *Visions of Excess: Selected Writings, 1927–1939*, trans. Allan Stoekl (Minneapolis: University of Minnesota Press, 1985), 116–29.

91. Powers, *Brief Account*, 59.

92. Chesterton, *Revelations of Prison Life*, vol. 2, 93.

93. Francis Lieber, *A Popular Essay on Subjects of Penal Law* (Philadelphia: Society for Alleviating the Miseries of Public Prisons, 1838), 85. Lieber explains further: "Now every one knows how easy it is to communicate a considerable train of ideas by mere indications, if we speak to one of our profession on a subject belonging to it, because he reasons as we do, knows our chain of thoughts, and three, four points will be sufficient to construe the whole figure. So do familiar friends understand each other rapidly by a few words in their correspondence, so has the commander to write but a few words to his generals on whole vast positions; so does the nurse understand the few incoherent sounds of the infant" (85).

94. C. D. Arfwedson, *The United States and Canada in 1832, 1822, and 1834* (London: Bentley, 1834), vol. 2, 210; quoted in Miron, *Prisons*, 94.

95. Wines and Dwight, *Report*, 219.

96. Brice, *Secrets of the Mount-Pleasant State Prison*, 48–49.

97. Ellice, *Diary*, 100; quoted in part in Miron, *Prisons*, 80.

98. Davidson, *Fashionable Tour*, 143.

99. Mayhew and Binny, *Criminal Prisons*, 304–5.

100. Ibid., 311.

101. Ibid., 141–42.

102. Ibid., 141.

103. Brice, *Secrets of the Mount-Pleasant State Prison*, 42.

104. Ibid., 41–42.

105. See Mark Colvin, *Penitentiaries, Reformatories and Chain Gangs: Social Theory and the History of Punishment in Nineteenth-Century America* (Houndmills: Macmillan, 1997), 93–94.

106. Ibid., 102.

107. "The Negro Convict, More, Showered to Death," *Harper's Weekly*, December 18, 1858, 808–9.

108. Ibid. The article also illustrates the "crown": a locked metal head cage that is "rather a badge of disgrace than a method of torture" (809).

109. It is useful to separate, first, judicially mandated corporal punishment for criminal offenses from corporal punishment generated from within the prison, and then to separate the latter into specific punishments mandated by prison rules, punishments allowed at the discretion of the guards, and unauthorized violence acting as "punishment." And yet the boundaries are not always clear. For instance, it was hard to distinguish discretionary from unauthorized punishments, or to say when a guard was going too far. The lawsuits that arose (and, indeed, continue to arise) around these questions would require a separate study.

110. Foucault, *Power/Knowledge: Selected Interviews and Other Writings 1972–1977* (Brighton, Sussex: Harvester, 1980), 155.

111. These must be "banished from [prison] walls." "Flogging in Prisons," *New-York Daily Tribune*, Febuary 4, 1846, 2.

112. Packard, *Vindication of the Separate System*, 19.

113. Austin Sarat, *Gruesome Spectacles: Botched Executions and America's Death Penalty* (Stanford: Stanford University Press, 2014), 8.

114. Dickens, "To the Editor of the Times," *The Times* (London), November 14, 1849, 4.

115. *The Tread-Mill . . . A Description of the Tread-Mill* [broadside] ([London]: J. Catnach, n.d. [c. 1822])

116. Wines, *State of Prisons*, 242 (quoting Psalms 74:20).

117. Mayhew and Binney, *Criminal Prisons*, 135–36.

118. Rainey Bethea, executed in 1936, was the last person to be publicly executed in the United States. Although most states had outlawed public flogging by the 1930s, Delaware continued to flog publicly until 1952. The Texas Prison Rodeo began in 1931, the Oklahoma Prison Rodeo in 1940. The Louisiana State Penitentiary still stages regular Angola Prison Rodeos, each attended by at least 20,000 people and earning close to a half a million dollars. "The Angola Prison Rodeo: Life, Death and Raging Bulls," *The Economist*, May 8, 2014, http://www.economist.com/news/united-states/21601853-god-and-daredevilry-give-prisoners-hope-and-dignity-says-burl-cain-life-death-and-raging (accessed May 6, 2017).

119. http://simplyghostnights.co.uk/venues/buckingham-old-gaol-museum/; https://www.easternstate.org/halloween/node/3 (both accessed May 6, 2017).

120. Mark Joyella, "On Friday Night, Highest-Rated Non-Fox Cable News Show (In Demo) . . . Was MSNBC's *Lockup*," Mediaite, April 18, 2011, http://www.mediaite.com/tv/on-friday-night-highest-rated-non-fox-cable-news-show-in-demo-was-msnbcs-lockup/ (accessed May 6, 2017).

121. Unless otherwise noted, all of the following fan quotes were posted in late 2016 or 2017 on the *Lockup* Facebook page: https://www.facebook.com/msnbcLockup/ (accessed May 6, 2017).

122. Review of "Behind Bars: Rookie Year," Season One, August 25, 2016, https://www.amazon.com/Behind-Bars-Rookie-Year-Season/product-reviews/B013JPDEZO/ref=cm_cr_dp_d_btm?ie=UTF8&reviewerType=all_reviews&sortBy=recent (accessed May 6, 2017).

123. See James Parker, "Prison Porn: MSNBC's *Lockup* Documentary Series, about Life behind Bars, Is Exploitative and Debasing, and as Poignant a Show as Can Be Found on TV," *The Atlantic*, March 2010, https://www.theatlantic.com/magazine/archive/2010/03/prison-porn/307906/ (accessed May 6, 2017).

124. See, for instance, the essay by Mansfield Frazier (a formerly incarcerated journalist): "The Saddest Reality Stars of All: Prisoners," *Daily Beast*, May 19, 2013: "It's akin to caging animals and then poking them with sticks for the amusement of the audience—the only difference is, here they use cameras instead of sticks." http://www.thedailybeast.com/articles/2013/05/19/the-saddest-reality-stars-of-all-prisoners.html (accessed May 6, 2017). I cite Frazier repeatedly here because his searing critique is so persuasive, posing the biggest challenge I have found to any defense of prison reality shows.

125. Ibid. See also Adam Johnson, "After Exploiting Prisoners for Years, MSNBC Still Won't Cover the National Prison Strike," AlterNet, October 12, 2016, http://www.alternet.org/media/after-exploiting-prisoners-years-msnbc-still-wont-cover-national-prison-strike (accessed May 6, 2017). It is worth noting that at least one *Lockup* episode focused on a 5,000-person prison protest. Tom Jackman, "'Lockup,' MSNBC Reality Show, Films Six Episodes in Fairfax County Jail," *Washington Post*, December 23, 2013, https://www.washingtonpost.com/blogs/local/wp/2013/12/23/lockup-msnbc-reality-show-films-six-episodes-in-fairfax-county-jail/?utm_term=.c8049e0bb164 (accessed May 6, 2017).

126. "The question is, can people who are in custody really freely consent? What if they refused to participate—would there be retaliation from their warders? Would those who did participate be rewarded in some manner? An extra piece of chicken is a big incentive in a county jail." Frazier, "The Saddest Reality Stars."

127. Ibid. (That *Lockup* shows "the few demented souls," the most "unhinged inhabitants," makes it harder to change public views about prisoners, thus making reentry harder and recidivism more likely.)

128. On the neoliberal ideology behind the "good prisoner," see Aurora Wallace, "Better Here than There: Prison Narratives in Reality Television," in *Punishment in Popular Culture*, ed. Charles J. Ogletree Jr. and Austin Sarat (New York: NYU Press, 2015), 55–75. Wallace does not, unfortunately, offer any examples, focusing instead on a third form of ideology, best represented by *Lockup Abroad*: the presentation of foreign prisons as houses of horror, and U.S. prisons as havens of humanity.

129. Mark Abadi, "7 People Went Undercover as Inmates for 2 Months, and They Revealed Harrowing Details about an Indiana Jail," *Business Insider*, March 10, 2016, http://www.businessinsider.com/60-days-in-follows-undercover-inmates-2016–3 (accessed May 6, 2017).

130. "Formerly Incarcerated Women Hope to Raise Awareness of the Plight of Women in the Justice System," Bossip, February 1, 2017, https://bossip.com/1469883/exclusive-female-former-federal-inmates-to-launch-reality-show-docu-series-to-expose-mass-incarceration/ (accessed May 6, 2017).

131. For instance, *Lockup* producer Susan Carney: "I don't think it would surprise anyone to learn that socioeconomics and skin color can play big roles in who gets locked up and for how long. People with financial resources can usually bond out of jail more often than those without resources and they can usually hire private attorneys who, unlike public defenders, can focus more attention on their case. All the public defenders I've encountered have massive case loads and rarely have the time and access they need for individual clients, especially if their clients are behind bars. Also, sentencing laws for various non-violent crimes often seem excessive and unfairly skewed against people who are poor and who are minorities." "Lockup Producer Susan Carney Answers Your Questions," MSNBC, May 30, 2014, http://www.msnbc.com/lockup/producer-susan-carney-answers-your-questions-0 (accessed May 6, 2017).

132. http://www.prisontalk.com/forums/showthread.php?t=264326 (accessed May 6, 2017).

133. http://www.prisontalk.com/forums/archive/index.php/t-210661.html.(accessed May 6, 2017).

134. http://www.prisontalk.com/forums/showthread.php?t=264375 (accessed May 6, 2017).

135. http://www.prisontalk.com/forums/showthread.php?t=264326 (accessed May 6, 2017).

136. Frazier, "The Saddest Reality Stars."

137. Quoted in Erik Sherman, "How American Prisons Became a Bizarre Tourist Mecca," *Fortune,* August 17, 2016, http://fortune.com/2016/08/17/prison-tourism-museums/ (accessed May 6, 2017). Eisen is responding here to critics of prison museums.

138. With 693 prisoners for every 100,000 people, the United States has the highest incarceration rate in the world (other than the Seychelles), over six times that of Canada, for instance, and almost six times that of the United Kingdom. World Prison Brief, Institute for Criminal Policy Research (Birkbeck, University of London), http://www.prisonstudies.org/highest-to-lowest/prison_population_rate?field_region_taxonomy_tid=All (accessed May 6, 2017). At the same time, according to Michael P. Jacobson, the UK's "tough on crime" policies in the past decades have followed the American model, leading the prison population to double between 1995 and 2016. Michael P. Jacobson, "Tough Talk on Crime Has Led to a Crisis in Britain's Prisons," *The Guardian,* May 5, 2016, https://www.theguardian.com/commentisfree/2016/may/05/tough-talk-crime-crisis-britains-prisons-suicides-assaults (accessed May 6, 2017).

139. On the booming private prison industry in the United States, see James Surowiecki, "Trump Sets Private Prisons Free," *New Yorker,* December 5, 2016, http://www.newyorker.com/magazine/2016/12/05/trump-sets-private-prisons-free (accessed May 6, 2017). On the large number of private prisons in the UK and Australia, see Kuang Keng Kuek Ser, "Australia and the UK Have a Higher Proportion of Inmates in Private Prisons than the US," PRI's The World, September 6, 2016, https://www.pri.org/stories/2016–09–01/australia-uk-have-higher-proportion-inmates-private-prisons-us (accessed May 6, 2017).

140. According to Joe Vignati, research comparing *Scared Straight* participants to a control group has shown that *Scared Straight* programs actually *increase* the odds of offending. Joe Vignati, "'Beyond Scared Straight' is Beyond Common Sense," Juvenile Justice Information Exchange, January 11, 2011, http://jjie.org/2011/01/11/joe-vignatibeyond-scared-straight-beyond-common-sense/8684/ (accessed May 6, 2017).

CHAPTER 2

"This Is a Trial, Not a Performance!"

Staging the Time of the Law

RYAN HARTIGAN

Delgamuukw v. R: A Prologue

> Every conception of history is invariably accompanied by a certain experience of time which is implicit in it, conditions it, and thereby has to be elucidated.
>
> –Giorgio Agamben, *Infancy and History: The Destruction of Experience*

Chief Justice McEachern's stentorian rebuke to the songs, dances, and narratives of the First Nations claimants, "This is a trial, not a performance!"[1] remains one of the most memorable episodes in the crackling proceedings of *Delgamuukw v. R,* which took place in British Columbia, Canada, between 1987 and 1991. Often known as the McEachern Decision after the presiding judge, the release of McEachern's 394-page *Reasons for Judgment* made the outcome public on Friday, March 8, 1991. The action, initiated in 1984 by Gitksan and Wet'suwet'en peoples in northwest British Columbia, asserted ownership and legal jurisdiction over 133 hereditary territories in a total area of 54,000 square kilometers—larger than the province of Nova Scotia. This was a claim under what is commonly referred to in the law as native land title, or Aboriginal title and rights. The case gathered 374 days spent in court; 141 days spent taking evidence out of court; over 61 witnesses were heard in court; transcripts of testimony fill 23,503 pages of text; and 82 binders hold 9,200 pages of exhibits.

The claim arose on the basis of a refusal by the Province of British Columbia to negotiate land title under the Gitksan-Wet'suwet'en Declaration of ownership and jurisdiction, which had been accepted by the Canadian Federal government in 1977. As the Province failed to act on the Declaration, fifty-four hereditary chiefs representing seventy-six Houses took the Province to court. The chiefs, through their legal counsel, made the argument that traditional law and claims to territory remained in effect unless changed with their consent. Chief Justice McEachern rejected these claims and their underpinnings, holding that the claimants were never sovereign over these lands; that they held no Aboriginal title to the land; that use rights were weak and limited in area; and, moreover, that the extinguishment of *even* these use rights could occur by inference based on actions throughout and subsequent to the colonial period.[2]

Pivotally, Gitksan and Wet'suwet'en presented the weight of their evidence in the form of performative evidence and oral tradition, claiming these as archival practices demarcating their existence in and claims to usage and possession of the territory. Gitksan oral histories of *adaawk,* which provided sacred memories of ancestors, histories, and territory, were offered alongside Wet'suwet'en of *kungax,* spiritual songs, dances and performances.[3] Both were offered as collective traditions inherited as a key part of coming into social recognition and, therefore, positioned as forming specialized knowledge, which was rigorous insofar as it was assessed and held to account by elders and their peoples. In further evidence, the claimants submitted totem poles, house crests, and regalia.[4]

The collective trial proceedings and their later appeal to the Supreme Court of Canada in 1997 are rightly considered a landmark in Canadian legal history: indeed, according to leading Native American scholar Jace Weaver, perhaps one of the most significant cases in Indigenous jurisprudence, and certainly among the most famous.[5] The notability of the case, however, turns not only on its assessment of the claimants' Aboriginal rights/Native title to land, and the alleged legal extinguishments of said rights, but also on the articulations and rationale of McEachern's courtroom as indicated in his behavior at trial and underscored in the publication of his *Reasons for Judgment,* which, as Bruce Miller has commented, is fascinating insofar as it was attractively packaged and priced; deceptively simple in its claims to straightforward commonsense language; and priced relatively cheaply, with an apparent intent toward wide distribution. As a result, it carried the potential for circulating its account to large numbers of people—and in doing so, seeding an account which was rightfully greeted with shock and outrage by First Nations and academics, let alone Indigenous peoples globally.[6]

An investigation of the judge's reasoning and comportment is remarkably fertile material for interrogating assumptions regarding performance, legality, textuality, and embodiment. Jacqueline Shea Murphy suggests that at the *Delgamuukw* trial, the judge "rehearsed familiar attitudes about the relation between performances and legal enactments,"[7] and his attitude demonstrates a familiar hierarchy of efficacy, where documents, treaties, and contracts are deemed to have legal weight or consequence, and the courtroom is unable to deal with performance, which "may be interesting or amusing" but "doesn't actually prove anything, make anything actual, or serve as official record of having made anything actual in the past."[8]

Murphy's response takes the courtroom as a metonym for written culture and document, and is explicitly to the rebuke of the judge, opposes it to the culture of performance introduced by the claimants. This is understandable, given the forcefulness of McEachern's own statement: "This is a trial, not a performance!" This response certainly seems to speak to an unbridgeable divide between performed evidence and written records. On Murphy's conflation, this also speaks to an identification of the former with a performative culture and the latter with legal culture. In this emphasis, a courtroom is a place where facts are decided upon and rulings are made, law is created and reflected in documents, and "a performance" does not carry legal weight.

Yet this relies on a literal reading that accepts that the judge's attempt to rigidly parse these categories is self-evident. What if, instead, "This is a trial, not a performance!" is a statement issued and performed by an exasperated judge, unwilling to have the regulated forms, rituals, and understandings of history of his courtroom displaced by performative testimony that breaks these regulated forms and sets its own temporal conditions? In stating that "the judge rehearsed familiar attitudes about the relation between performances and legal enactments," is it perhaps overlooked that the linguistic slippage is revealing, namely, that the judge "rehearsed"? Can performative culture and written culture be opposed so readily? Or is this attempt to continually reoppose them an ongoing struggle in which McEachern participates, cooperates, and unwittingly complicates?

Consequently, I take the opportunity to more fully pursue the court's staging of the encounter between law and performance and, more particularly, the courtroom's disciplining of temporality and history through confronting performative testimony with its own performative enactments.

Ergo, I do not examine the significance of the *Delgamuukw* proceedings in terms of evaluating its assessment of the claim to territory itself: on this point, the claim was unsuccessful at trial level, and at appellate level, while the appeal was upheld, it was found that another trial would be necessary in order to make a finding on the land dispute. Nor, more particularly, is this chapter a detailed engagement with the law of what is known variously as Aboriginal title, Indigenous title, or Native title: this would be a gargantuan undertaking and, in any instance, Chief Justice McEachern's ruling was viewed by many as in conflict with, if not seriously contradictory of numerous Supreme Court of Canada rulings dealing with constitutional Aboriginal and treaty rights.[9]

Rather, I concentrate upon *Delgamuukw v. R* as a meeting point of performative and written culture, of Indigenous memory and Anglo-derived juridical practices, and of law and performance. It is an encounter with the tropes of legal performance as enacted by a judge whose demeanor has been the subject of much critique, and whose responses to the performed evidence were seen variously as inappropriate, biased, or analytically flawed. I do not operate in the mode of a jurist or a legal scholar. I take up the critical labors of a scholar working across Indigenous history, theater and performance studies, and the anthropology of law—albeit a scholar with a near-forgotten past as an errant near-completed student in law school—and desire to be in conversation with legal specialists who would have much more to say than I about the jurisprudence thereof. I also recognize, and even foreground, that I am not carefully parsing the categories of theatricality and performativity as I might were I to be speaking with a specialist theater and performance studies forum, and trust that any errors or slippages that may occur in this overview prove to be productive for further discussions rather than causes for irising in upon more careful definitions in order to have a disciplinary stoush.

In this, I am somewhat taking a cue from Julie Stone Peters's article "Legal Performance Good and Bad," which demonstrates the value in an overarching conversation that places "performance," "performativity," and "theatricality" into broader dialogue in the interest of a sweeping encounter with law's ambivalent relationships with each of these items. Peters notes that "theatricality" invokes the theater, and also the historical burden of Jonas Barish's memorable identification of what he calls the "antitheatrical prejudice," a discourse that associates acting, lying, artifice, hypocrisy, and, I would add, inefficacy. She identifies "Performance" as deriving critical standing from the field of "Performance Studies," extending drama and theater studies into rituals, ceremonies, sporting events, and defining performance as "twice behaved behavior": behavior that has been rehearsed or carries the implication of rehearsal and repetition.[10]

While performance is often positioned, in the epigrammatic coining of Victor Turner, as culture creating, "making, not faking" compared with the theatrical implications of fakery and falsehood,[11] where performances *are* comparatively a practice that make "something happen" in the world, I take Peters's precis as productive in demurring from a more specialist discussion here (and would certainly direct the reader to refer to the article), considering law as a slippery beast that is indeed twice-behaved behavior; that replays social conflict and conventions; that alchemically turns history into dramatic narrative; that fictionalizes thought experiments, surrogates figures from history and interpellates them into the present as cultural memory re-performed;[12] that uses the language of the specifically theatrical, where counsel are said to "act as" representatives and speak "on behalf" of the clients; where judges are placed on a raised stage, separate from the public gallery as audience, and where the process is arranged, aestheticized, and rehearsed. As this blend of categories might suggest, and as Peters goes on to productively suggest, "this double nature—law's conjoint performativity and theatricality—are both problem and power."[13]

With this in mind, consider this chapter an investigation into that "both" of problem and power, using the frame of the conjoint and a loose rubric of performance, in order to move to Chief Justice McEachern's own processes, and in which he himself does not parse the categories of performance in which he participates or denies filiation. In working expansively, I am considerably guided by the work of Dara Culhane in her magisterial account of the *Delgamuukw* case, *The Pleasure of the Crown: Anthropology, Law and First Nations*.[14] I trust that this expansive, broad consideration of embodiment, audience, and aesthetics will not be unduly hamstrung by operating in something other than a rigorously parsed set of terms.

I wish to dwell upon the ways in which McEachern's courtroom mixes categories in a broad dismissal of performance that seeks to demarcate law from any association with the word, and I examine McEachern's overt hostility, even in his literal statements, *toward* Gitksan and Wet'suwet'en performance as testimony. From the claimants' perspective, this was undertaken in a considerable effort toward supplying expert testimony, and, as Dara Culhane observes, "the Gitksan and Wet'suwet'en approached the court and its proceedings with dignity, sincerity and integrity."[15] What they were met with was a chief justice who explicitly invoked

Thomas Hobbes, specifically referring to and in fact quoting Hobbes's famous adage regarding the state of nature, as "nasty, brutish and short," in order to define the state of Gitksan-Wet'suwet'en peoples in the nineteenth century.[16]

The level of McEachern's hostility now begins to flicker into legibility. The detail of this encounter exposes the manner in which law and performance, so vigorously contrasted by Chief Justice McEachern's divide of trial and performance, are in fact far from contrasting. They are more than related or even permeable to each other. In the courtroom and its wider dispersals, they are assembled of *competing practices*, of similar material. I explore this first through the relationship between the forms of the court and its human actions and relations. I here trace the contours of the courtroom's feedback loop, of interactions between its things, its symbols, its control of time and lived circumstances, and the theatricality of its processes.

That wider background then gives way to a focus upon McEachern's construction of history, in the form of the architecture of his reasoning that undergirds his assessment of Gitksan-Wet'suwet'en civilization itself. This forms a specifically framed regulation of temporality, evaluating the claimants in terms of what McEachern considered was an appropriate level of a civilization located in modernity, which he denied was present in the Gitksan and Wet'suwet'en peoples by the time of colonization. Through this denial, the chief justice therefore supplied the terms in which he found the claim lacking—a neat feedback loop. In McEachern's doctrine, this was a teleological narrative of discovery, occupation, and settlement, and culminated in a juridical declaration regarding the certainty of the temporal point at which British Columbian (later Canadian) sovereignty came into being. This suggests that the proceedings specifically demonstrate the manner in which the constant denial of the ability of the claimants' performed evidence to obtain as convincing is a necessary denial, not only in the trial at hand, but indeed, in his opinion, the practice of law more generally: because it displays the presence of an alternative, competing history.

This is crucial, because if McEachern's court and, by extension, judicial authority were to admit that it was performing, it would, in turn, be forced to admit that it was in competition with a model of performance that lay before it and made very different claims to history. To do so would be to unpick the very basis of legal certainty, and as it was a sovereignty-based claim, for the courtroom to invite the anxiety that its own foundations of authority were also uncertain. In other words, McEachern's narrativizing of history is a temporal operation of distraction, one that undertakes an internal logic in order to affirm Derrida's provocation that "the origin of authority . . . the position of the law can't by definition rest on anything but [itself]."[17]

The vehemence of McEachern's rigid distinction in his phrase "This is a trial, not a performance!" is self-evidently an exercise in proposing a contrast—and a stark one—between the tasks and practices of the courtroom, which is strongly implied to be a decorous and efficacious activity, and performance, an unseemly and unruly one that does not belong within such a frame. Moreover, positioning performance in this manner makes it at best an unhelpful supplement and, at worst, a completely unwelcome distraction from the task at hand. In doing so, his statements resonate with Stanley Fish's memorably tendentious, if not polemic, piece "The Law Wishes to Have a Formal Existence," where Fish declares:

> The law wishes to have a formal existence. That means, first of all, that the law does not wish to be absorbed by, or declared subordinate to, some other—nonlegal—structure of concern; the law wishes, in a word, to be distinct, not something else. And second, the law wishes in its distinctness to be perspicuous; that is, it desires that the components of its autonomous existence be self-declaring and not in need of piecing out by some supplementary discourse.[18]

McEachern's efforts are certainly of a kind with Fish's provocation. The very attempt to commonsensically deny that society would deem the trial itself to be performance, in comparison with Gitksan and Wet'suwet'en practices of performative testimony—and its denunciation, with the implication of bad mannered children being admonished—implies a scrambling attempt to continually display the appearance of difference, and by displaying a public stance of disapproval, to construct, demonstrate, and reenact that appearance of difference. More simply, the effort to create this distinction, and affirm it to be so, is itself performance. The visibility of the foregrounded denial is betrayed by the background specter of a courtroom designating what is and what is not acceptable performance, in an anxious ritual of inclusion and exclusion.

This balancing act, near paradoxical in its energy, is what Philip Auslander problematizes as the law itself attributing to performance "the same ontological qualities—existence in the moment and persistence only as memory—as those who see performance resisting the law," which, he goes on to note, makes performance *available* and *useful* to the law in other, more comprehensive ways.[19] Indeed, the strong preference of the law for live performance, as demonstrated in its resistance to what Auslander refers to in shorthand as the PRVT (the prerecorded videotape trial), demonstrate what he contends is a resistance to the idea of recording what amounted to a transcript of the trial before the trial itself had occurred. As a result, the PRVT "fought an inevitably losing battle against a fundamental premise of American jurisprudence: that a trial is an ontologically live event."[20]

The Theatrical Forms of the Colonial Courtroom: A Preamble

> The trial is preeminently a theatrical form.
>
> —Susan Sontag, *Against Interpretation*

A courtroom is a materialization of impressive edifices and testaments to stability. To Indigenous peoples in particular, its forms and shapes are a transfer of the monoliths of colonial history into concrete representations. The power of these symbols and structures lies not simply in memorialization, but in interlocuting colonial *practices,* circulating and realized in their repetition in the lived circumstances of those subject to the law. Embodiment provides a medium for the percolation of documents, which are themselves by no means the source of stability they might claim to be. In this set of interactions, textuality and archival practices collaborate, corroborate, and complicate. Ann Laura Stoler provides helpful remarks regarding these slippages between textual declarations and embodied circulations, suggesting that rather than authoritative sources of singular declarations, colonial administrations produced social categories and rules of classification as the result of unsure and hesitant documentation and sensibilities, and "nor is there much that is hegemonic about how these taxonomies worked on the ground."[21]

Indeed, the very suppleness of colonial law exists much less in its stability and centralization than in its diffusion throughout the fabric of society. Documents drafted for different purposes can easily be retooled to suit new governing strategies, and laws themselves become a palimpsest of previous legal histories and rulings. The customary becomes normative: first entrenched, and then *assumed,* as the result of repetition. By this, I extend Rebecca Schneider's observation that the repeatability of an action, the endurance of a performative practice, "however fractured or partial or incomplete, has a kind of staying power."[22] Moreover, as she later goes on to discuss, texts necessarily meet bodies and engage in repetition and revision, and that an archive, far from "a place of arrest," is one constructed even in its moment by "the eye that reads and the tongue that mouths," even before the process of citation, enactment, and revelation of the false promise of preservation.[23]

Diana Taylor's influential Performance Studies text, *The Archive and the Repertoire,* positions what she calls a *repertoire*—"performances, gestures, orality, movement, dance, singing,"[24] historically undervalued and presented as disappearing—in contrast to an *archive* of written culture, defined by the fixedness and stability of writing. These practices of the repertoire, she argues, also act as transmissions of knowledge, as capable of *acts of transfer,* despite being historically presented as mutable, unsteady, disappearing, and reliable. This is an attitude that seems to percolate through Chief Justice McEachern's contrast in his statement, "This is a trial, not a performance!" Taylor simultaneously weaves in the recognition that notwithstanding historical privileging of the latter, the two frequently work "in tandem and . . . alongside other systems of transmission,"[25] but notwithstanding that recognition of interaction somewhat presents the archive as, in the words of W. B. Worthen, "the prison house and graveyard of active performance culture,"[26] since it is argued that unchanging texts, such as the dramatic text of Antigone, assure a stable signifier.[27]

Legality, the courtroom, and its products are presented as something of a metonym for written culture, somewhat ameliorated in terms of recognizing trials as a site where performed and documented behaviors are both required, and which are a nexus of the interaction of archive and repertoire. Notwithstanding and perhaps precisely in the argument of interaction, according to Worthen's reading of the theoretical apparatus, writing in the archive is seen to have an "oppressive force," where writing "remains positioned here as a means of inscribing or documenting behavior, rather than as an instrument for the production of new behavior, new performance."[28]

Written culture and performed or oral culture certainly do interact extensively within the courtroom, even and especially in legal history. Indeed, the flow between the two is not as unidirectional as might seem to be implied in the above examples. As observed by Paul Collins, it was not until the 1800s that the U.S. Supreme Court required parties to submit written briefs. Prior to this, cases were carried out in an oral manner, with oral arguments sometimes lasting for days, and "thus the concept of legal proceedings being carried out in primarily written form is a relatively new phenomenon."[29] It was longstanding tradition for advocates at the King's Bench in the United Kingdom to present their material orally to the court. For arguments to the House of Lords, as the highest tribunal in the country, actual written filings were extremely succinct, consisting of a few sentences and the basic issue presented in the appeal.

In this process, it was oral argument, performance, that authenticated the text rather than the reverse. The basis for the practice in England was that the entire judicial process had to be seen to be completely open to public scrutiny: everything the judge learned about the case had to be presented in open court, which was seen, therefore, to diminish the possibility of out-of-court influence and to demonstrate the veracity and integrity of proceedings.[30] In such a setting, the comportment of the judge was vital, as was the interplay between political rhetoric and oral argument that reinforced the interaction between the courtroom and the wider circulation of its rulings into lived experience.

Elizabeth Freeman's comments regarding the colonial state are especially productive in focusing this chapter's claim that these dispersed, performative practices of the law, insofar as they provide the basis for the quotidian, *also* form pivotal demarcations of state-governed temporality. She notes that the colonial state intervened early into temporality, directly inscribing itself into the bodies of the people through the colonial calendar. As indigenous rhythms become skewed, and time itself was reconstructed, the colony required the managing of time—particularly "productive" time—through the parsing of a meaningful life through an official timeline.[31] The forcing of temporal synchrony is, therefore, a mechanism for subduing and disciplining colonial bodies: its power lies not in overt confrontation, but in the taming of alternative cultural temporalities, secured by the repetition of social formations, and those timelines held to be compatible with an official record. This is at least as much true, if not more so, given the impact of this temporal operation upon the quotidian.

These reconstructions of time depend upon the idea of linear progress, and a chronopolitics of development: an enfolding of the temporal, swallowed and held in the belly of the body politic, excreted as social hierarchy, and crucial in securing and policing the false unity of "a self-same, national subject evolving through time."[32] In Freeman's argument, the structural alteration of the minutiae of people's lives contrasts two temporal models, the Indigenous and the colonial, where the former must surely give way to the latter. This denial that peoples exist in the same time is what Johannes Fabian calls an *allochronic* discursive claim, a deliberate attempt to twist chronos, time itself, and to locate Indigenous culture as pastness. This rhetorical move contrasts Indigenous time with the time of the law, juxtaposing as a temporal schema which precedes a culture of modernity and hence one of legal efficacy.

Allochronism, in Fabian's claim, is not at all a categorical error: it is a deliberate exercise in "choosing to misunderstand" and constructing a gulf between two claims to history. This provides the justification for colonial power, underpinned by and exercising the temporal schema of the colonizers, which is valorized as measurable, rational, and productive. As a result, it provides the linchpin for abandoning Indigenous ideas of time and history altogether.[33] It is a device that provides its own internal justification when juxtaposed with the official calendar, which provides a temporal schema valorized as measurable, rational, and productive, and abandoning Indigenous ideas of time and history as belonging to the past and, if you will, to past-ness.

The fact that this involves a deft operation in performative cloaking, obscuring the courtroom's own internal tension between its various temporalities, is most visibly displayed in the figure of the judge itself.[34] Judicial rulings dwell in a temporal ambivalence insofar as they work across time as both cloaked reconstructions of pastness and constructions occurring as statements in the present; make statements that draw from the dead and are issued by the living; are propped by pastness, and make declarations in the present, which impact upon futurity; and shift between the quotidian time of lived experience and of evidence, the moments of law being practiced by the officers of the court and the judge, and the timelessness of what might be called the difference between the temporality of the practices of law and the suspended temporality, perhaps even the intemporality of The Law itself as a system that stands outside of time,[35] and which only acquires form as it is embodied, enacted, and performed.

Michelle Castañeda suggests that legal ritual is "drenched in the aura of its theological past," and that this is most visibly revealed in the image of the judicial robe itself, which enacts the temporal drag of the medieval upon the present, and "betrays the agency of the robe acting on bodies and on time."[36] In this register, judges become both oracles of an impersonal, infallible, and absolute law even as they are deemed to be performing secular rationality in opposition to Indigenous temporal schema. They are transmuted, through the donning of the robe, into the sacred immortality of the judicial office: a temporal intermediary with the ability to speak for, as, and with the dead.

The robe, Castañeda argues, is what supplies this property of "temporal extroversion,"[37] a theatrical externalization of the legal system's continuity, and what becomes an item of faith in the temporal flow of legal pronouncement. Just as the office is handed down across time, and metonymized by the concomitant handing down of the robe, it displays itself as in a genealogy: a participant in a linear history that the display and inhabitance of the judicial robe itself subsequently authenticates and therefore assures the seamlessness of origins and a necessarily successivist history of legal rulings and temporal flow both.

This aesthetic visibility of the judge resonates with a formative statement within the law itself: that the visibility of the judge's performance is no less than a mechanism for securing the rule of law itself. In the oft-quoted 1924 judgment of *R v. Sussex Justices, Ex parte McCarthy,* Lord Hewart CJ founded a core legal principle that illuminates how law and performance move beyond the terms of reflective metaphor as practices grounded in *entwined constitutive metaphor.* The chief justice's principle foregrounds the courtroom as the privileged exemplar of observable legal enforceability. The case primarily speaks to the central principle of the courtroom needing to be freed from even the *appearance* of bias in its rulings, and the necessity of the recusal of judges should bias even be an implication. Yet in its imbrication with visibility, I would argue it also refracts a sense of spectatorship, of viewing, of the courtroom process itself necessarily being staged and even legally ascertained by the act of observation of the courtroom, both internally and externally to its physical location: "a long line of cases shows that it is not merely of some importance but is of fundamental importance that justice should not only be done, but should manifestly and undoubtedly *be seen to be done.*"[38]

My claim here resonates with Philip Auslander's contention that to consider performance in the frame of the law as only continuing in its existence in spectatorial memory, and otherwise to disappear forever, is to oversimplify the courtroom's complicated engagement with the fact that "live performance, is, in fact, essential to legal procedure."[39] Much like the earlier traditions referred to in the U.S. Supreme Court and the UK's King's Bench, Auslander poses that direct, live observation is an inherent part of the legal process; indeed, that testimony itself is a present performance, and that the ontological state of liveness is privileged within a legal context. In this sense, the workings of memory must play out in the temporal condition of presentness in order to be legally disciplined and form correct adjudication.

In this claim, I also take heed of the suggestion of Tracy C. Davis, who does not limit theatricality to the specific location of a theater, arguing that, instead, it can and does emerge elsewhere according to conditions of spectating. Moreover, she does not locate theatricality solely as a quality created by a performance, but as a choice made by a spectator to view performance in a certain way. Spectating depends upon the presence of a spectator where "a person must decide to be a spectator . . . engaged and conscious of the transaction of display and reception."[40] Theatricality, therefore, is neither a purely aesthetic effect nor a relationship drawn between theater and lived reality, but an addressing of "spectating in civil society," where the state itself becomes a theater in its institutions, key in which, she notes, is the courtroom.[41]

The courtroom's performance practice therefore summons the tools of theatricality and the attitude of spectatorship: a process of assembling, directing, aestheticizing, and managing the shape and politics of spectacle. It is one thing to suggest that the aesthetic presentation of a court bears some metaphorical relationship to the aesthetically theatrical, with demarcated stage and judicial costume, but quite another to note that its processes of selection, presentation, and privileging of embodied processes also refract a theatrical sensibility, and one that is only too keen to disguise its operations: that law and performance might perhaps be not simply reflective metaphors, but *mutually constitutive* ones. In this cooperative both/and sense, to repeat the earlier reference to the adage, we make the law and the law makes us.

Delgamuukw v. R: Time, Performance and the attitude of terra nullius

> Today, we live by legalized time. . . . There is no choice.
>
> –Anthony Aveni, *Empires of Time: Calendars, Clocks, and Cultures*

In the colonial imaginary, Indigenous bodies are always seen to be vanishing. The identity of colonial nations cannot be conceived of without Indigenous peoples, and yet at the same time, linear, successivist, teleological histories proceeding from settlement to modernity are keenly problematized by the fact that these stubborn Indigenous peoples simply will not vanish in the face of claims to buzzwords and phrases such as "progress" and "forgetting the past and moving on." John Frow comments that "Indigenous peoples inhabit modernity not as an archaic remnant but as a fold, a complication of its singular but fractured and internally disparate time."[42] In Canada, as in Australia and Aotearoa-New Zealand, advocacy for territory and sovereignty is in a curious relationship with "the atemporal locus of Law and personhood," and "the normative rhythm of a modernization process"[43] is set against any claim to historicity of an Indigenous people. As a result, clashing social and legal forces draw together a heterogenous cluster of time(s), and Indigenous self-determination is always a claim propped on the assertion of historicity; as Homi Bhabha suggests, colonial power always involves a contestation and stabilization of ambivalent and disjunctive temporalities.[44]

This spatiotemporal weave of time and space, and the colonial queasiness this evokes, bears relation with Gelder and Jacobs's comments on the postcolonial status of Australia, in their monograph *Uncanny Australia*. In brief, they sketch Freud's formulation of "the uncanny" through the use of *heimlich* and *unheimlich,* the former being glossed as "home" and the latter as unfamiliar, strange, inaccessible and unhomely. An "uncanny" experience, therefore, results in these two apparently opposed words circulating through each other: "one has the experience, in other words, of being in place and 'out of place' simultaneously."[45] The simultaneity is the crucial element, as it is not simply the unfamiliar in itself that generates the anxiety of "the uncanny," but the uneasiness of the familiar and unfamiliar inhabiting each other. This acquires a temporal dimension for postcolonial claims over self-determination and territory, as "in this moment of decolonization, what is 'ours' is also potentially, or even always already, 'theirs': the one is becoming the other, the familiar is becoming strange."[46]

Delgamuukw v. R materializes a site where Indigenous bodies not only reappear, but refuse to be quiet, activating the collision of "ours" and "theirs." The claimants, in providing performed evidence as testimony, self-consciously introduced multiple, disjunctive temporalities into the courtroom, insofar as they placed their own Indigenous historical modes into conversation with those of the colonial-derived court; petitioned for a space where Gitksan and Wet'suwet'en practices stood on a footing with Anglo-derived jurisprudence; pointed up the survivance of temporal schema that competed with the linear history of the courtroom; and activated the postcolonial uncanny, effecting and affecting British Columbia's—and by extension, Canada's—sense of itself.

As plaintiffs, the Gitksan and Wet'suwet'en peoples were bound to establish much more than their society's structuring in temporally different form alongside the Crown's settlers. The evidentiary standard expected of them was considerably higher—or, more correctly, inherently unbalanced. To utilize Johannes Fabian's theorizations in this context, establishing the existence of Aboriginal rights, haunted by the *terra nullius* doctrine, directly denies that the condition of being coeval, which means the condition of existing in the same time and temporal schema, is possible.[47] In fact, it *requires* this denial in order to obtain. A ruling on the establishment of Indigenous occupancy of the land, by definition, necessitates a temporal schema and understanding of history and civilization that can be reconciled with the law. The court is identified with time and civilization marching into the future, and the pre-civilization of the claimants, which is not even deemed sophisticated enough as a civilization to have proper legal standing, is identified as pastness and vanishment. This temporal compatibility is held to be a necessary precondition in even bringing the claim, as without establishing a temporal framework of title comprehensible to the court, a party does not have legal standing to possess rights. Yagalahl (Dora Wilson), a member of the Gitksan-Wet'suwet'en Litigation Team, was under no illusion about what was at stake: "Like I said, our culture was on trial. We were told we didn't exist. . . . Ownership and jurisdiction is not something new for us. We have practised that. It is thousands of years old. We only want recognition. . . . We are right here before your very eyes."[48]

I begin here with the court's treatment of the claimants' attempts to lodge performance practices and cultural memory as evidentiary submissions. Simply put, this type of performance makes the court, and the judge, what I might refer to, in shorthand, as legally "anxious." Rather than demonstrating the definitive ability of the court to exclude performance as evidence, these moments show juridical operations upon performance-as-evidence, and a judge parsing them as to what performance is convincing, and what is found to be unconvincing—even and especially when it is purely at the level of oral delivery. It is not so much wrong as insufficient to account for this exclusion purely in terms of overly rehearsed—pun intended—tropes of legal documentation and embodied practices being opposed to each other in performance theory.

This opposition simply does not occur even internally to the courtroom, inasmuch as verbal testimony and statements by expert witnesses do not so much augment documentation as provide a differing and interlocuting form of evidence. Therefore, any characterization of particular performative evidence as inefficacious evidence speaks not to its opposition to the world of the courtroom, but to its *relationship*. The disclosure of the courtroom as an anxious space is nothing less than the revelation of the court's own modes of performative display, the unraveling of the court's claims to definitive legitimacy, and hence its claims to absolute certainty. As a result, it is (by definition) incumbent upon juridical power to ensure that performance practices which are not participants in the court's evidentiary modelings are deemed to be lacking in usefulness.

I then proceed to a more specific example of the court's regulation of temporality via its carefully determined, perhaps even overdetermined performance process of examining the unbroken claim of Gitksan and Wet'suwet'en to the land. In this case, the court's decision regarding continuous occupation, and hence Aboriginal rights/Native title, was haunted by the history of *terra nullius* doctrine, of which more will be said later: a concept of law which declares that upon declaring a region "empty land," where no one was deemed to have settled and the territory considered uninhabited, that the colonizing power could then acquire possession by mere assertion. The court's role is to affirm this assertion by playing out the legal tests that affirm its own authority to reach the decision. Should this seem like a painful paradox to the reader: it illustrates the necessarily paradoxical case of the law on the subject.

This process requires a courtroom to visibly play out the steps of the test that originates from within its own rehearsed doctrines, much as the visible performance of process was so necessary for the UK King's Bench, where the judge's receipt of material was to be observed by and track at the same rate as its audience, both internally to the courtroom and, by extension, externally to it. In other words, it *performs*. The tests for whether the doctrine applies necessarily emerge from within the law, and involve the court's explicit regulation of temporal schema: it affirms a foundational moment. The doctrine involves a narrative of discovery, occupation, and settlement, and culminates in a juridical declaration regarding the certainty of the temporal point at which sovereignty comes into being.

This suggests that the reason for the court's anxiety regarding performance as evidence, which asserts an unbroken chain of cultural memory and history has not so much to do with the fundamental incompatibility of such an activity, but the necessity of making such moments incompatible with the court's own performative practices. For native land title to be affirmed, a party to legal proceedings must establish that their claim to land and jurisdiction is not subject to extinguishment by Crown sovereignty. Moreover, even if those claims can be sustained, the claimant must evidentially substantiate that they were already present on the land in a form of society whose history and social organization can be deemed acceptable in the court's eyes.[49] In legal essence, this means that the burden of proof lies not upon the Crown, but upon the petitioning party, to disprove that the court's existing definition of occupation—and, therefore, its own basis for power—obtains. It is an extraordinarily high requirement in terms of evidence.

Performance and Testimony: The Ancestors as Evidence

> It is very sad that some of the most powerful witnesses in the court case . . . have now died, but they saw within themselves the strength and the need to go and give their evidence in court.
>
> –Medig'm Gyamk (Neil Sterrit) in Dara Culhane, *The Pleasure of the Crown*

The main evidence submitted by Gitksan and Wet'suwet'en in support of their claims to ownership, organization, borders, and laws took the form of the performance of *adaawk* and *kungax* as a form of expert testimony. This was done to illustrate their having lived in an organized society, with boundaries, laws, and of having occupied and owned their territories. It was a deliberate and highly considered attempt to bring their oral histories and temporal conditions into direct conversation with those of the court. Lawyers for the Gitksan and Wet'suwet'en argued that they were supplying a mechanism for the Court to try to gain a sense of understanding "across both a profound cultural divide, and from a distance of 200 years and more."[50] As, by definition, the clear authorities on such knowledge were elders, chiefs, and members of Gitksan and Wet'suwet'en communities, they were key expert witnesses.

This is not without precedent in legal terms, and a carefully considered attempt to mesh their performative evidence with the acceptable performance forms of the court. There is a long-standing tradition in Anglo-derived law, originating in the sixteenth century, whereby expert testimony stands on a footing with evidentiary submissions of documents and eyewitness testimonies. Specialized knowledge is seen as a core aspect of supplementing knowledge beyond that which a legal expert or a reasonable person might be expected to possess.[51] Expert witness testimony is evaluated on the basis of the convincing nature of the explanation, the demonstration of specialized knowledge, and the judge's perception of the demeanor of the expert, particularly under cross-examination. The primary test as to whether an expert is necessary at trial is whether their expertise falls within the experience and knowledge of the judge or jury. Despite the frequent assumption that performance is necessarily supplanted by documentation in archive and legal culture, expert witnesses are, in effect, a walking fusion of archive and repertoire, of written knowledge and of performance of that knowledge.[52]

As a foreshadowing of the problems which the claimants would face from Chief Justice McEachern, it is worth commenting that judges are most receptive to expert testimony that claims the status of dispassionate conclusions rather than revealing ambiguity or controversial interpretations. As a result, in this claim, the expert witnesses testifying on behalf of the Gitksan and Wet'suwet'en are held to account against the supposedly value neutral "historical record," which, as Eric Reiter contends, means that "the constitution of this record—who establishes it, and what it contains and does not contain—is invisible in the decisions, and the record itself becomes a fact."[53] The irony in terms of the ranking of knowledge is that the claims of historians or legal experts may well synthesize the anthropological evidence that the courts seek to distinguish from the historical record. Once expert testimony is admitted, at that point the court treats it "as unmediated 'fact,'"[54] at which point quotations from the expert become presented without footnotes, detaching any controversy in favor of the courtroom performing "an artificial unanimity."[55]

Given that the expert witness's identity and nearly all documents used to prepare the testimony will become discoverable upon their testimony, experienced counsel advise an expert witness not to take notes on documents because all the notes will be available to the other party, and instead to convincingly testify. Adopting this basic model, the claimants submitted that they were necessarily the experts in their own history. The Gitksan oral histories of *adaawk,* and Wet'suwet'en territorial songs of *kungax,* were offered as collective traditions inherited as a key part of coming into social recognition, and therefore as specialized knowledge. In further evidence, the claimants submitted totem poles, house crests, and regalia.[56]

The Crown originally sought to exclude this testimony, but *not* on the basis that it was performed testimony. Rather, their objection was that the testimony was inadmissible under the rules of evidence, specifically the prohibition on hearsay. The hearsay rule principally claims that a witness's statement must be available for cross-examination in court, and be based upon what the witnesses themselves see and hear rather than their repeating what they have been told by a third party. The presence of the witness is not simply necessary to authenticate evidence: in a sense, it is part of the evidence. This demonstrates, once more, the promiscuous traffic between archive and repertoire, and between written and performative culture.

In the case of the Crown's petition for exclusion, they claimed that oral histories necessarily constituted hearsay. The contention was that the performance relied upon ancestral knowledge, and since these figures were deceased, they were not available for cross-examination. Gitksan and Wet'suwet'en chiefs, elders, lawyers, and witnesses strove to assist the chief justice by making *adaawk* and *kungax* legible to him, drawing analogy between distinctions in evidence and hearsay, opinion and knowledge, and lay people and experts.[57] *Adaawk* were explained as Gitksan oral histories comprising a collection of sacred memories and reminisces about ancestors, histories, and territories, documenting continuous ownership and occupation of land and usage of resources. *Kungax* were positioned as Wet'suwet'en songs about territories and their relationships. The rights to perform these forms were noted as privileges and responsibilities of particular individuals and House groups. The guardianship and practice of these performance forms, their content, the conventions of oratory and style, and the songs and dances that accompanied the narratives, were all noted as taking many years to learn. As a result, chiefs and elders were necessarily custodians of this knowledge, overseeing their rigor and consistency, and correcting errors in content and form.[58]

In anticipation of any skepticism expressed toward their performed evidence, Gitksan and Wet'suwet'en supported their testimony with expert witnesses drawn from cartography, paleobotany, geomorphology, forest ecology, fishery biology, ethnoarchaeology, linguistics, historical geography, anthropology, and history.[59] In many instances, witnesses were members of Gitksan and Wet'suwet'en Houses who were considered to be both experts in their own culture and also formally academically or professionally qualified.

Were performance in *Delgamuukw v. R* prima facie incompatible with the courtroom, as was earlier contended by Jacqueline Shea Murphy, this is where the claim would have stalled. But it did not. The juridical determination in an early procedural stage of the trial was that the submissions were indeed ruled admissible.[60] McEachern held that he was satisfied that the *adaawk* and *kungax* had gone through a "sifting process" which had lent them an "enhanced trustworthiness" in his eyes. However, he added, "Historical facts sought to be adduced must be truly historical and not anecdotal," admitting the performance evidence and testimony, but also stating that he would assess its persuasiveness and rigor as the trial proceeded. Chief Justice McEachern supplied two principal criteria whereby he might determine the weight of performance evidence. First, he said that he would distinguish between what "a deceased elder said he or his elders did, and what they believed," and allow on the former to obtain as evidence. Second, he identified the plaintiff's culturally specific definition and identification of the distinction between folklore ("antimahlaswx" in Gitksan) and what could be considered laws, traditions, or histories, and would only allow the latter three to stand.[61]

Moreover, and once more particularly salient to the question of the meeting point of written and performative culture, he referred explicitly to precedents set in cases where oral tradition had been assessed as evidence. He stated that from the case of *Kruger v. R,* he would extract the direction that evaluation should be based on "facts pertinent to that Band and that land, and not on any global basis." Especially crucial was his second reliance upon the law of *R v. Simon,* where the former chief justice of the Supreme Court of Canada had found that to require written evidence where oral tradition was the only source of evidence available was to "impose an impossible burden of proof."[62]

As the trial proceeded, Chief Justice McEachern became increasingly agitated about his attempted distinction between "historical facts" and "beliefs." He was particularly irritable at having to witness the perfomative testimony in its entirety, and especial exception to witnesses singing in court. It was at this point that he directly rebuked elders, in the quote that began this chapter, "This is a trial, not a performance." He added, acidly, that the point of the music was lost on him as he had "a tin ear."[63] The performed evidence was not faulted because it was performative, but because it was specifically excluded by the court based upon being unacceptable performance—lacking insofar as it did not meet McEachern's desire to separate fact and belief, lacking insofar as it was deemed to be insufficiently dispassionate in form, and excessive in its volume, its length, and its ornate emotive qualities. In this setting, McEachern set himself as a performative arbiter, disputing that what was placed before him was acceptable, and found it to be embedded in affect rather than legal effect.

In his ruling, the judge dismissed the efficacy of the performances as evidence, writing, "I am not able to accept *adaawk, kungax* and oral traditions as reliable bases."[64] By accepting that performative evidence could be lodged, but denying it weight, McEachern acted in precisely the way he had claimed he would not, based on *R v. Simon:* setting an impossibly high bar for the plaintiffs given that their testimony was essentially the only proof that they had.[65] The attitude of the court was that this material lost the ability to narrate facts objectively, a tone that had already been struck in aggressive cross-examining of the claimants' witness Heather Harris—a non-Indigenous woman who had married into a Gitksan family and been adopted into a House and clan, and also held a degree in anthropology. While testifying about genealogy and matrilineal kinship systems, she was halted in cross-examination by the lawyer Marvyn Koenigsberg, acting on behalf of the Crown, who suggested that she had lost her capacity for scholarly analysis and "gone native,"[66] a colonialist slur used to discredit her and imply that she had somehow crossed over from European to Indigenous culture, and consequently lost her veracity as an expert witness.

The court's process of excluding these types of performance as incompatible with the acceptable forms of the court also mark up an exclusion of temporal schema and historical modes deemed to be incompatible with its own methodology. The resistance of the court to the performed testimony and oral tradition of the claimants, according to Eric Reiter, was not an issue of this evidence not being written down and lacking claims to textual stability. Rather, it was an issue of temporality and narrative. Gitksan and Wet'suwet'en performances were overtly narrativized, amalgamating history, geography, spirituality, community norms, and performative modes. Its spiraling approach to history and narrative defy linear narrative and linear, progressivist history, and its fusion of subjects is performed passionately and without a difficulty in shifting narrative voice. Chief Justice McEachern stated, at one point, "I have great difficulty, as did many witnesses, separating histories and declarations of aboriginal interests and stories."[67]

To introduce an overtly theatrical framing, and paraphrase Shakespeare's *Hamlet,* "McEachern and the court doth protest too much, methinks." The sheer venom of the judge's statements, the declarations of strict parsing, are an attempt to make a cogent division between history and narrative, where "the former is scientific and so immediately useful to a court of law, while the latter is suspect because of its lack of verifiability."[68] The performance of the judge's declarations becomes an authoritative declaration compared with the performance that confronted him, which extended to his assessment of the performance *qua* performance. McEachern's tone is reminiscent of a grumpy and unimpressed *New York Times* theater critic, supplementing his misgivings about the performance's efficacy as evidence by faulting the performance on his own assessment of its merit, which he declared was poorly organized, rehearsed, and performed: "I am far from satisfied that there is any consistency among the Gitksan and Wet'suwet'en Houses about these matters. The early witnesses suggested that the adaawk are well formulated. . . . I am not persuaded that this is so."[69]

Colonialism and the Whimsy of Evaluating "Civilization"

> The estimation of the rights of aboriginal tribes is always inherently difficult. Some tribes are so low in the scale of social organization that their usages and conceptions of rights and duties are not to be reconciled with the institutions or the legal ideas of civilized society. Such a gulf cannot be bridged.
>
> –Privy Council, *Re Southern Rhodesia*

The basis of the Gitksan and Wet'suwet'en claim was that they were the descendants of peoples who had lived in that same territory, in an unbroken genealogy without contesting claim. Neither the Gitksan or Wet'suwet'en ever entered into treaties with Britain or Canada. There was no war by which the land was acquired in conquest. There were no sales of land or rights to either individual settlers, or to the British or Canadian governments. The response of the Province of British Columbia and the Government of Canada was that since British Columbia's incorporation into Canada in 1871, all successive governments had taken the position that no Aboriginal rights as recognized by "civilized law" existed prior to Britain declaring sovereignty over the territory. Furthermore, the Province asserted that *even if* those rights had existed, they were necessarily extinguished by the simple act of the Province of British Columbia asserting sovereignty over these lands.[70]

As Eric Reiter notes, law is necessarily a self-authenticating practice. It includes and excludes evidence, defines and assesses significance, controls the narrative version of the past that stands for and represents past events and their impact upon the present. Reiter goes on to suggest that in this register, the power of the word is exercised and internally justified by the law in terms of the construction of and authorizations of historical narratives, and the uses to which it is put. As a result, judging as process involves the act of constructing a narrative that tethers evidence with a throughline. The judgment itself, conferred in judicial pronouncement, performs these narratives "an aura of factual finality that masks their narrative origins,"[71] which involves a feedback loop of pieces of fact to tethering narrative and back again in order to transmute them into overarching fact.

Should this appear to contain elements of paradox, the reader is forgiven for being dizzied by the creative process that is taking place, but should make no mistake: the courtroom's participation in the means of theatricality, as earlier noted in this chapter, extends to the construction of the dramatic narrative and its events, which are then ascertained by the visible means of the court and its declaration that these are the facts that obtain. The claim to dispassionately observing evidence is a foregrounded and visible presentation, but the deployment of history by judges becomes "a powerful force for the construction and preservation of orthodoxy,"[72] which is underpinned and presented as continuity in law by both the mechanics of precedent-based reasoning and the images of continuity made visible by items such as the judicial robe extending connections across time. It confers "a particular view of the past, of the legal order, and the relationship between the two."[73]

McEachern's judgment is haunted by *terra nullius* doctrine, and particularly the existence of cases such as *Re Southern Rhodesia,* which historically form one of the most explicit examples of the performance of colonizing power in the courtroom. The doctrine's invocation involves the portrayal of Indigenous peoples as primitive, warlike, uncertain in their claim to any specific territory and precarious in their lifestyles. A memorandum of the Privy Council issued in 1722 consolidated imperial attitudes and law by establishing rules for founding British sovereignty in two possible situations. The first option, often referred to as the doctrine of discovery, of occupation or of settlement was an application to be applied where the land discovered was deemed to be vacant and uninhabited by human beings. The second option was the application of conquest, where Indigenous populations were encountered and conquered, and British sovereignty was deemed to come into being.[74]

The reader is likely to ask at this point whether the concept of *terra nullius* was ever truly in play, particularly with the ongoing presence of Indigenous peoples occupying and using the land in different areas that were "discovered" by colonial explorers, albeit in ways that remained starkly different to British usage. The answer is that regions where Indigenous peoples were already in occupation were "simply legally *deemed to be uninhabited*"[75] if the people involved were deemed to be "insufficiently evolved" as a civilization. In British Columbia, the doctrine of *terra nullius* and acquisition of sovereignty by assertion legitimized the colonial government's occupation, and indeed, its failure to enter into treaties with First Nations—as they did not legally "exist," they need not be regarded as negotiating parties. Ergo, as Dara Culhane observes, "when Aboriginal people say today that they have had to go to court to prove they exist, they are speaking not just poetically, but also *literally*."[76]

The determination of a civilization being insufficiently evolved, and therefore precarious in its claims to existence, is also a temporal problem. It is contrasted with the stabilization of this society and certainty of recognizable claims to land upon the Crown's declaration of sovereignty and introduction of the Anglo-derived rule of law. It is an inherently linear model in which one can still find survivances of Thomas Hobbes's seventeenth-century political philosophy in which he famously characterized the "state of nature" of "primitive life" as one of where life is "nasty, brutish, and short." John Locke would later extend this by asserting that Aboriginal peoples lived in a pre-political state, had no perception of systems of property or government, and therefore the promise of higher productivity by Europeans justified their acquisition of land, governed by the natural law of their relative degree of development.[77]

A particularly flagrant example of this kind of reasoning is that of Lord Sumner's 1919 decision in *Re Southern Rhodesia*. Lord Sumner's primary determination is clear: "Some tribes are so low in the scale of social organization that their usages and conceptions of rights and duties are not to be reconciled with the institutions or legal ideas of civilized society."[78] It requires testimony regarding the ways in which a society managed resources, maintained social order, occupied a specific territory, and tracked their connection to land. In all cases, Lord Sumner declared that these had to be assessed according to what, in the court's opinion, constitutes "an organized society." If a claimant cannot establish that they were sufficiently "organized," nor that they had unbroken occupation and usage of specific areas of land, then they cannot sustain their claim to occupy it. Additionally, the particular application of permanent occupation and land usage, rather than anything resembling intermittent or nomadic practices, smuggles Locke's principles into the law's application: land which was not "used," in the judge's opinion, meant that it was not occupied.

In *Delgamuukw v. R,* the claimants sought to make their understanding of time comprehensible to the court by adopting the legal term "time immemorial." As Yagalahl's earlier remark indicates, Gitksan and Wet'suwet'en did not in fact see their models of temporality as intrinsically problematic for the court. They argued that at the time of European arrival, their peoples had thousands of years of occupation and were already supporting themselves through hunting, fishing, and natural resources. Their society was matrilineally figured, and highly organized into clans and houses led by chiefs, with institutional processes and protocols equating to law. Their appropriation of the term "time immemorial" was an effort to translate these elements to the court, indicating both that they had been there since the beginning of time, and that the ancestors were and are still with them.[79]

Should foregrounding the case of *Re Southern Rhodesia* seem an unfairly harsh line of reasoning with which to characterize Chief Justice McEachern's ruling, his words speak for themselves. Swayed by the evidence from the Crown that Gitksan and Wet'suwet'en were nomadic peoples, and further unconvinced that they were more than minimally socially evolved, he pronounced that "I have no doubt that life in the territory was extremely difficult, and many of the badges of civilization, as we of European culture understand that term, were indeed absent,"[80] evidence of his process of assessing Gitksan and Wet'suwet'en society on the basis of their conformity to European practice and temporal conditions.

This harks back to Johannes Fabian's claim, as made earlier in this chapter, that a key tool of colonial power is the act of deliberately shifting the temporal conditions of two civilizations into allochronism, a condition where the two parties were said to be incompatible as they existed in different temporal schemas. Elizabeth Freeman refers to this fusion of temporality and political power as *chronopolitics,* a politics of time, which here falls into relief as an analytic. Gitksan and Wet'suwet'en oral traditions and performative evidence, in summoning alternative temporal conditions and historical claims challenging the smooth narrative constructions of the court, forge cracks and disunities that reveal and place doubt in the modality of time that haunts its colonial conception of history. Moreover, they trouble the courtroom's own performative display of these as inherently self-authenticating, and perhaps even begin to dismantle the successionist chronopolitics that underpin both its assessment of civilization, and also the precedent-based reasoning that is at the heart of its legal adjudications.[81]

In this setting, oral traditions are a temporally troubling precolonial relic that refuse to disappear in the face of civilizing influence, embarrassingly refusing to disappear. By referring to the word "embarrass," I use it in two registers. The first is the original use of "embarrass" as a noun, meaning an obstacle. The verb derived from it, in this context, suggests an encumbrance, an impeding, a perplexing or a throwing into doubt and difficulty. This means that the performative testimony offered by the claimants, and rejected so vividly in his statement "This is a trial, not a performance!" refuses the norms of its viewing public, and particularly the courtroom and the judge at its head. In contrast to the claims of measured, dispassionate narratives of history, the claimants offer impassioned singing, dancing, and orature, placing an affective dimension at the heart of their claim rather than detaching it as an evidentiary precondition. As a result, the kinetic histories of these performance forms "embarrass" any foreclosure of colonial linear temporal history and its claims to "progress" and "civilization," vividly bodying forth not only an alternative temporal schema, but one that is hypervisible and *refuses to disappear.*[82]

Chief Justice McEachern unequivocally refused the usage of "time immemorial" by the claimants, finding that the ancestors of the plaintiff were not continuously occupied and used, and that in any case their civilization had practices "which some persons of different cultural background classified as barbaric,"[83] echoing nineteenth century depictions of civilization's evolution. He invoked Thomas Hobbes explicitly, stating that the lives of Gitksan and Wet'suwet'en were "nasty, brutish and short,"[84] dismissing that Native social institutions and organizations were more than instinctive at best, instead concluding that "they more likely acted as they did because of survival instincts which varied from village to village."[85] It is not clear from *Reasons for Judgment* what McEachern meant by "instincts," but it is worth noting that it carries the connotations of unpremeditated and unmediated actions purely governed by non-intellectual processes and therefore not constructive of a model of civilization.

As a final flourish, and perhaps an unintentionally hilarious illustration of the attempt to stabilize temporal claims that lay at the heart of his judgment, Chief Justice McEachern rejected the claimants' use of "time immemorial" as particularly incompatible with the historical assessments of the court. In a piece of "common sense" moralizing about what was allegedly accepted wisdom, he went on to state that "'Time immemorial,' as everyone knows, is a legal expression referring to the year 1189 (the beginning of the reign of Richard II), as specified in the Statute of

Westminster, 1275."[86] As Bruce G. Miller points out, such examples of appealing to "common sense" smuggle in "a sort of epistemology," appealing to preexisting notions of social and cultural norms, and necessarily excluding those that are deemed to be incompatible with those preexisting notions. The appeal to common sense employed in the *Delgamuukw* decision, and even more so in McEachern's publication of *Reasons for Judgment,* are "a form of misrepresentation," which is particularly problematic in placing Western documents and modes of argumentation on a footing with Indigenous oral and performative traditions and their very different structurings and narratives of history.[87]

The exposure of the central philosophical machinery of *terra nullius* doctrine reveals its elaborate performative construction. Its processes of decision making place a patina of certainty upon what is inherently a discretionary decision by the judge as an embodied agent. Despite the courtroom being embedded within the historical forms of life that it structures, at the same time it purports to occupy a detached realm of decision making. The certainty of the law relies upon this double movement. While upholding structure, the law distances itself from the space of quotidian life within social structure. The definitive pronouncement that a society does not fulfill the requirements for being sufficiently advanced and "organized" is one in which the law answers the questions it has posed by itself, within the framework of the sovereignty that it has already asserted and then tests in order to reassert.

Concluding Remarks

> It is queer the use of the word native always means people who belong somewhere else, because they had once belonged somewhere else. That shows that the white race does not really think they belong anywhere because they think of everybody else as a native.
>
> –Gertrude Stein in Jane Malcolm, *Two Lives: Gertrude and Alice*

As I noted toward the beginning of this chapter, the adage says, "We make the law and the law makes us." The interaction between the carefully staged proceedings of the courtroom, how this legal world is represented in judicial robe and adversarial rejoinder, and how the symbols of the legal world both refract and rejoin the wider dispersals of legality beyond its walls are a potent illustration of how objects and images constrain, enable, and theatricalize behavior. McEachern's courtroom does not reject performance because it *is* performance, but rejects it as incompatible with the performative modes of the courtroom itself. It is an anxious temporal exclusion, narrativizing what is and is not temporally able to stand on an equal footing with McEachern's legal reasoning, and making historical parsings on that basis.

There are a series of questions, it seems to me, that raise themselves: what does this mean, in practice? By revealing the performative constructions and modes of the courtroom, by revealing its exclusions and inclusions and processes of selection, what might be revealed? In the specific case at hand, *Delgamuukw v. R,* are there implications that could be taken up by seeing the manner in which temporal modes are rendered irreconcilable, and Indigenous histories are worked upon to make them unequal in footing with McEachern's narrativizing of history? What might we do in recognizing that the lives of Indigenous peoples become particularly vulnerable to misrepresentation, oversimplification, and deliberate mystification in the chronopolitical processes of the law?

That the law might become increasingly self-aware of the centrality of these processes, and develop new modes of encountering their problematics, is verging on a truism. The courtroom itself is made of performance, constructed as a theater, staging justice. The law's paradoxical claim to timeless objectivity alongside foundational laws is undone from within itself by the time of the proceedings, the time of the witnesses' recollections, and the histories that we must ethically account for. Certainly, the implications for theater and performance studies are considerable: recognizing the promiscuous traffic between written culture and performative culture, the feedback loop of temporal and performative processes that are *made-to-be-compatible,* and the ways in which the archive is continuously remade considerably illustrate and add weight to Rebecca Schneider's contention that "the advantage gained by the promise of preservation in a house divided between writing on the one hand and repertoires of (given to disappear) embodied knowledge on the other is only the advantage of the social secret it props and the privilege of the patriarchic it protects: that the distinction is bogus."[88]

The Supreme Court of Canada offers some illumination on these points, in some brief remarks as to their holding when they heard the *Delgamuukw v. R* appeal. Chief Justice Lamer enjoined with the argument of this chapter in pointing up the history of biases against oral tradition, although as Eric Reiter points out, "Translating this appreciation into practice is another matter."[89] If an increased awareness of hearing performative evidence is undertaken, this is only a start, since there is little material change if these are still seen as a resource "to be mined for whatever 'facts' can survive scrutiny against the 'historical record.'"[90]

Chief Justice Lamer indeed made additional claims, contending that there had to be a high degree of openness not simply to hearing oral tradition, but to its epistemology:

> This appeal requires us to apply not only the first principle in *Van der Peet* but the second principle as well, and adapt the rules of evidence so that the aboriginal perspective on their practices, customs and traditions and on their relationship with the land, are given due weight by the courts. In practical terms, this requires the courts to come to terms with the oral histories of aboriginal societies, which, for many aboriginal nations, are the only record of their past.[91]

While such an attempt to "come to terms" requires a considerable shift in traditions of evidence law in order to recognize Indigenous oral tradition and performative testimony as holding a unique status, it also requires a temporal operation, where there is deemed to be a relationship, with an assessment of power differential, between Indigenous and non-Indigenous evidence about the past:

> Notwithstanding the challenges created by the use of oral histories as proof of historical facts, the laws of evidence must be adapted in order that this type of evidence can be accommodated and *placed on an equal footing* with the types of historical evidence that courts are familiar with, which largely consists of historical documents.[92]

Nonetheless, while the Supreme Court placed this challenge in front of the law, it only partially acquitted it, and displayed the ongoing internal struggles of the law. Immediately prior to these two statements about a pluralist approach, and openness to oral tradition, the Court somewhat reaffirms and reasserts the authority of dominant narratives and indicates that Indigenous evidence must be made to fit within it:

> In other words, although the doctrine of aboriginal rights is a common law doctrine, aboriginal rights are truly *sui generis*, and demand a unique approach to the treatment of evidence which accords due weight to the perspective of aboriginal peoples. However, that accommodation must be done in a manner which does not strain "the Canadian and constitutional structure."[93]

The challenges of this kind of reconciliation of epistemology have been taken up since, although tracing them in depth is beyond the boundaries of this chapter. The 2007 judgment of Justice Vickers of the British Columbia Supreme Court in *Tsilhqot'in Nation* foreground a more refined and granular assessment of historical evidence and history, emphasizing that in encountering oral tradition, "Courts must undergo their own process of decolonization," that judges must not simply rest at "positivistic or scientific" notions of claims to "objective truth," and that the law has to "set aside some closely held beliefs."[94] Although the case resulted in the land claim being ruled out, on procedural grounds, as to an award of the entirety of the lands claimed, the court recommended that the parties proceeded to negotiation, further adding that the evidence submitted had made out a claim to large parts of the territory in question, providing an affirmative basis from which to advance negotiations. These negotiations were nonetheless unsuccessful. The case continued to be appealed, until in the 2014 Supreme Court of Canada decision ruled that their evidence obtained and the Tsilhqot'in did indeed have a claim to the 680 square miles they had historically occupied.

Within the Commonwealth more widely, and since Canadian, Australian, and Aotearoa-New Zealand rulings and legislation on Indigenous law inform and percolate through each other, I add a final coda from the Ngāi Tūhoe people, a Māori iwi (loosely, "tribe") of Aotearoa-New Zealand, whose performative traditions were successful in bodying forth alternative forms of cosmology and history; this is the subject of my current research. Under Te Urewera Act 2014, the region ceases to be vested in the Crown, ceases to be Crown land, and ceases to be a national park. Moreover, the former Te Urewera National Park is created as a "legal entity" with "all the rights, powers, duties, and liabilities of a legal person."[95] It is a revolutionary encounter between the law and Indigenous cultural memory, with far-reaching implications for the standing of land itself, and suggests that when the law is placed into dialogue with Indigenous knowledge, decolonizing its constructions of history and narrative, and, most of all, comes into awareness of its performative interactions with oral tradition, it might prove to be less an item of discipline for rendering performative and temporal modes incompatible, and instead contains the seed of possibility for an interlocuting, collaborative, and optimistic relationship between past, present, and futurity.

NOTES

1. Dara Culhane, *The Pleasure of the Crown: Anthropology, Law, and First Nations* (Burnaby, BC: Talon Books, 1998), 123.
2. Bruce G. Miller, "Introduction," *BC Studies* 95, no. 3 (Autumn 1992): 3–4.
3. Jacqueline Shea Murphy, *The People Have Never Stopped Dancing* (Minneapolis: University of Minnesota Press, 2007), 217.
4. Culhane, *The Pleasure of the Crown*, 119–20.

5. Personal conversation with Jace Weaver at conference "In the Balance: Indigeneity, Performance, Globalization" London, October 24, 2013.

6. Miller, "Introduction," 5.

7. Murphy, *The People Have Never Stopped Dancing*, 218.

8. Ibid.

9. Mary Hurley, "Aboriginal Title: The Supreme Court of Canada Decision in Delgamuukw V. Bc" (January 1998, revised February 2000), http://www.lop.parl.gc.ca/content/lop/ResearchPublications/bp459-e.htm.

10. Julie Stone Peters, "Legal Performance Good and Bad," *Law, Culture and the Humanities* 4, no. 2 (2008): 182–85. On antitheatrical prejudice, see the memorable work of Jonas Barish, *The Antitheatrical Prejudice* (Berkeley: University of California Press, 1981).

11. Lorne Dwight Conquergood, "Of Caravans and Carnivals: Performance Studies in Motion," in *Cultural Struggles: Performance, Ethnography and Praxis*, ed. E. Patrick Johnson (Ann Arbor: University of Michigan Press, 2013), 27.

12. See Joseph Roach, *Cities of the Dead: Circum-Atlantic Performance* (New York: Columbia University Press, 1996), most particularly defined at 2–3.

13. Peters, "Legal Performance," 185.

14. Culhane, *The Pleasure of the Crown*, 119–20.

15. "Adding Insult to Injury: Her Majesty's Royal Anthropologist," *BC Studies* 95, no. 3 (Autumn 1992).

16. Miller, "Introduction," 5.

17. Jacques Derrida, "Force of Law: The 'Mystical Foundation of Authority,'" in *Deconstruction and the Possibility of Justice* ed. Drucilla Cornell, Michel Rosenfeld, and David Gray Carlson (New York: Routledge, 1992), 14.

18. Stanley Fish, "The Law Wishes to Have a Formal Existence," *The Fate of Law*, ed. Austin Sarat and Thomas Kearns, Amherst Series in Law, Jurisprudence, and Social Thought (Ann Arbor: University of Michigan Press, 1991), 159.

19. Philip Auslander, "Legally Live: Law, Performance, Memory," in *Liveness: Performance in a Mediatized Culture* (New York: Routledge, 1999), Ebook.

20. Ibid.

21. Ann Laura Stoler, *Along the Archival Grain: Epistemic Anxieties and Colonial Common Sense* (Princeton, NJ: Princeton University Press, 2009), 1.

22. Rebecca Schneider, *Performing Remains: Art and War in Times of Theatrical Reenactment* (New York: Routledge, 2011), 37.

23. Ibid., 106

24. Diana Taylor, *The Archive and the Repertoire: Performing Cultural Memory in the Americas* (Durham, NC: Duke University Press, 2003), 15.

25. Ibid., 21.

26. William B. Worthen, "Antigone's Bones," *TDR/The Drama Review* 52, no. 3 (2008): 11.

27. Taylor, *The Archive and the Repertoire*, 19.

28. Worthen, "Antigone's Bones," 12n3.

29. Paul Collins, personal email, March 4, 2015.

30. David C. Frederick, "Supreme Court Advocacy in the Early Nineteenth Century," *Journal of Supreme Court History* 30, no. 1 (2005): 2.

31. Elizabeth Freeman, "Time Binds, or Erotohistoriography," *Social Text* 23, no. 3 (2005): 57–58.

32. Prasenjit Duara, *Rescuing History from the Nation* (Chicago: University of Chicago Press, 1995), 3.

33. Johannes Fabian, *Time and the Other: How Anthropology Makes Its Object* (New York: Columbia University Press, 1983), 32.

34. I am exceedingly and enduringly grateful to my colleague Michelle Castañeda for having theorized upon the body of the judge, the costume of the judicial robe, and their dual relationship with temporality. I will be explicitly referring to the ideas expressed in her unpublished conference paper "Asylum, Credibility, and the Totemic Performance of Judicial Authority," which she delivered at the PSi (Performance Studies International) 19 Conference held at Stanford University in June 2013.

35. Scott J. Shapiro, *Legality* (Cambridge, MA: Belknap Press of Harvard University Press, 2011), 7–8.

36. Castañeda, "Asylum, Credibility," 1.

37. Ibid., 5.

38. *R v. Sussex Justices, Ex parte McCarthy* [1924] 1 KB 256, 624 (emphasis added).

39. Auslander, "Legally Live."

40. Tracy C. Davis, "Theatricality and Civil Society," in *Theatricality*, ed. Thomas Postlewait and Tracy C. Davis (Cambridge: Cambridge University Press, 2003), 128–29.

41. Ibid., 151.

42. John Frow, "A Politics of Stolen Time," in *Timespace: Geographies of Temporality*, ed. Jon Thrift and Nigel May (New York: Routledge 2001), 73.

43. Ibid.

44. Homi K. Bhabha, *The Location of Culture* (New York: Routledge, 2004), 203.

45. Ken Gelder and Jane M. Jacobs, *Uncanny Australia: Sacredness and Identity in a Postcolonial Nation* (Melbourne: Melbourne University Press, 1994) 23.

46. Ibid.

47. Fabian, *Time and the Other*, 30–33.

48. Yagalahl (Dora Wilson), "It Will Always Be the Truth," in *Aboriginal Title in British Columbia: Delgamuukw v. The Queen*, ed. Frank Cassidy (Lantzville: Oolichan Books and Institute for Research on Public Policy 1992), 119–205.

49. Culhane, *The Pleasure of the Crown*, 37, 113.

50. Ibid.

51. Ibid.

52. Bryan A. Garner, ed., *Black's Law Dictionary*, 10th ed. (St. Paul: Thomson West, 2014), c.v. "Evidence," "Expert," "Witness."

53. Eric H. Reiter, "Fact, Narrative, and the Judicial Uses of History: Delgamuukw and Beyond," *Indigenous Law Journal* 8 (2010): 68–69.

54. Ibid., 69.

55. Ibid.

56. Culhane, *The Pleasure of the Crown*, 119–20.

57. Ibid., 120.

58. Ibid.

59. Ibid., 124.

60. Reiter, "Fact, Narrative, and the Judicial Uses of History," 69.

61. Culhane, *The Pleasure of the Crown*, 122.

62. Ibid.

63. Ibid., 123.

64. Murphy, *The People Have Never Stopped Dancing*, 217.

65. Reiter, "Fact, Narrative, and the Judicial Uses of History," 69.

66. Culhane, *The Pleasure of the Crown*, 125.

67. Reiter, "Fact, Narrative, and the Judicial Uses of History," 69–70.

68. Ibid., 70

69. Culhane, *The Pleasure of the Crown*, 258.

70. Culhane, *The Pleasure of the Crown*, 27.

71. Reiter, "Fact, Narrative, and the Judicial Uses of History," 57.

72. Ibid.

73. Ibid.

74. Culhane, *The Pleasure of the Crown*, 47.

75. Ibid., 48.

76. Ibid.

77. See John Locke, *John Locke: Two Treatises on Government. A Critical Edition with an Introduction and Apparatus Criticus* (Cambridge: Cambridge University Press, 1964).

78. *Re Southern Rhodesia* (1918), [1919] A.C. 211 at 233 (P.C.)

79. Culhane, *The Pleasure of the Crown*. See at 37, 112, 124, 130–31.

80. Allan McEachern, *Reasons for Judgment: Delgamuukw v. BC* (Smithers, BC: Supreme Court of British Columbia, 1991) 31.

81. For more on this topic, see Ryan Hartigan, "Embarrassing Time, Performing Disunity: Rugby, the Haka, and Aotearoa-New Zealand in the United Kingdom," *Performance Research* 16, no. 2 (2011).

82. Ibid., 39.

83. McEachern, *Reasons for Judgment*, 34.

84. Ibid., 13.

85. Ibid., 213.

86. Ibid., 82.

87. Bruce G. Miller, "Common Sense and Plain Language," *BC Studies* 95 (1992): 55–56.

88. Schneider, *Performing Remains*, 106.

89. Reiter, "Fact, Narrative, and the Judicial Uses of History," 70.

90. Ibid.

91. Quoted in ibid., 73.

92. Quoted in ibid., 74 (emphasis added).

93. Quoted in ibid.

94. Quoted in ibid., 76.

95. Jacinta Ruru, "Tūhoe-Crown Settlement—Te Urewera Act 2014," *Māori Law Review* (October 2014).

CHAPTER 3

Reenactability

ANN PELLEGRINI AND KAREN SHIMAKAWA

Introduction

In recent years "reenactment" has become one of the most vital—or should we say "re-vitalizing"—areas of performance practice. From the live re-performances of Marina Abramovíc's and others' iconic performances at the Guggenheim Museum ("Seven Easy Pieces," 2005) and MoMA ("The Artist is Present," 2010) to André Lepecki's re-productions of Allan Kaprow's "18 Happenings in 6 Parts" (Munich and New York, 2006/2011), to the longer-standing (and often derided) practices of weekend history buffs painstakingly recreating Renaissance England or key battles of the American Civil War: both "professional" and "amateur" artists are challenging the idea that a performance once performed is over. They relive both the historical past and past performances.

This preoccupation with reenactment, moreover, often finds expression in the performance of specifically *legal* (or para-legal/political) events: from mainstream theater works like Moisés Kaufman's *Gross Indecency: The Three Trials of Oscar Wilde* (1997) or the off-Broadway documentary theater work *Her Opponent* (2017), a gender-inverted reenactment of excerpts from the Clinton-Trump presidential debates; to performance art (*Combatant Status Review Tribunals, pp. 002954–003064: A Public Reading* at MoMA, New York, 2011 and 2012); to public forum events such as *All The President's Men,* a Public Theater (New York)/National Theatre (London) collaborative restaging of the Trump cabinet appointees' nomination hearings; to countless "mock" historical (re-)trials (including the trial of Socrates, *Brown v. Board of Education,* and that perennial favorite, Shakespeare's *Hamlet*) performed by high school students, celebrities, and the occasional Supreme Court justice.[1]

We could also add to this accounting the cultural phenomenon of "Judge TV" reality television shows that feature many retired judges playing the part of a "real" judge in an as-if court of "law." As Sarah Kozinn argues in her recent study of the genre, for the parties who "litigate" their disputes on these shows, and for much of the viewing audience, Judge TV offers a reparative fantasy of how the law *should* work on behalf of people "like them."[2] Kozinn argues that the pleasure (and labor) of these staged (quasi)legal proceedings offers us ways of scrutinizing closely the inner workings (procedural and psychic) of the law in ways that the "actual" enactment (i.e., congressional hearings, small claims court proceedings, etc.) apparently cannot.

Performance theorists, too, have turned their attention to reenactment (most notably Rebecca Schneider's important 2011 book *Performing Remains*) to reconsider how live performance remains and returns. Such reconsiderations of the time(s) of performance, by both artists and scholars, are offered as criticism of (or corrective to) an earlier and nearly canonized view that what distinguishes performance from other arts is that it disappears irretrievably.[3] The boom in recent theatrical reenactment has prompted performance scholars to make their own return and once again examine performance's distinctive quality of "liveness" as ever-retreating, burdensome, mediated, or otherwise.

Despite this relatively recent turn to "reenactment," however, the fact of reenactment or, perhaps more accurately, the multiple ways reenactments make facts happen are not new at all, neither as practice nor as theoretical preoccupation. Think, for example, of the key role played by reenactment or (our preferred term, "reenactability") in J. L. Austin's *How to Do Things with Words,* a published collection of lectures on linguistic philosophy delivered at Harvard in 1955,[4] that became a founding text in performance studies, as well as in queer theory via Judith Butler's reworking of speech act theory in the context of citational practices of sex and gender.[5]

The force of performativity, of the *doing* that an utterance (or other citational practice) can do, depends in large part on its insertion into a temporal schema that looks to the past and/as the future simultaneously. A legal term for this temporal paradox is "precedent," which indicates the dependence of a judicial ruling in the present, governing social relations in the future, on a preexisting finding in the past. Nevertheless, while legal and performance scholars frequently observe the ways in which law and "theatricality" collude or collide, the specifically *reenacted* character of law has not been as deeply examined. In this essay we investigate how the quality of *reenactability* both authorizes and imperils the law. We turn to some surprising recent theatrical-legal reenactments by law professionals and theatrical amateurs (the Asian American Bar Association of New York) as a way of understanding some of the ways law generates its binding authority, and how theatrical reenactment might itself disrupt the reiterative force of law's implicit reliance on reenactability.

Oyez, Oyez, Oyez: Parasitic Repetition in Legal Speech

Our turn toward theatrical precedent may even constitute our ironic refusal of the wall Austin seeks to build between "felicitous" performative utterances in everyday life and the infelicity of theatrical speech: "a performative utterance will . . . be *in a peculiar way* hollow or void," he cautions,

> if said by an actor on the stage, or if introduced in a poem, or spoken in soliloquy. This applies in a similar manner to any and every utterance—a sea-change in special circumstances. Language in such circumstances is in special ways—intelligibly—used not seriously, but in ways parasitic upon its normal use—ways which fall under the *etiolations* of language.[6]

For Austin, what deactivates a performative utterance onstage is the hollow echo-chamber effect: the "special circumstance" of theatricality—that is, of language that openly avows and explicitly stages its quality as enacted and reenactable—saps its power. Austin's programmatic and, arguably, anxious disqualification of theatrical performances has already been the subject of much criticism in performance studies (Auslander, Schechner) and elsewhere (Derrida, Felman, and Sedgwick). For the purposes of this essay, we are interested in the way Austin makes that distinction—his characterization of theatrical language as a form of *parasitism* that etiolates the force of language—in relation to law's temporality.

Indeed, Austin's dismissal of language sapped of its performativity on stage is perhaps his attempt to diffuse the long-recognized power of theatricality. Accusations of parasitism have long dogged theater and performance. Plato's ultimate banishment of mimesis from the ideal Republic, on the grounds that mimesis degrades the real, is perhaps a founding example of the anti-theatrical prejudice that has shaped western philosophy, theology, and law. The danger—and allure—of the simulation is that it may overpower and even replace the real, by seducing audiences to identify with the false. Performance may be a shadow of reality, a sham, Plato seems to imply, but it does something to and in the real. This *something* may be, in Alan Read's terms, the "placebo of performance."[7] We will come back to this possibility below.

In response to Austin's characterization of the dystrophic effects of theatricality, Jacques Derrida returns (differently) to Plato's recognition of the power of imitation, posing the question (in "Signature Event Context"), "is this risk [of falling into the trap of the degraded, non-serious etiolation] rather its internal and positive condition of possibility?"[8] It is *only* in relation to the theatrical parasite, perhaps, that the "host" utterance has meaning and force. Michel Serres's extended meditation on the role of the parasite builds on Derrida and allows us to deepen this inquiry into the parasite-host dynamic inherent in (legal) speech acts.[9] Serres characterizes parasitism as foundational to culture: "The parasite is the essence of relation," he writes. "It is necessary for the relation and ineluctable by the overturning of the force that tries to exclude it." Notably, Serres identifies the parasite-host dynamic as ubiquitous and mutual social (linguistic) practice: "We parasite each other to speak, to eat, to organize injustice and legal extortion; for these projects everyone is good. . . . If parasitism in general supposes that the host is a milieu or that the productions of the host constitute the environment, the niche necessary to the survival of the one placed there or who moves around there, we are all parasites of our own language(s)." In Serres's formulation, then, theatrical utterances do not simply define "normal" discourse by contrasting/lesser example. Rather, the logic of theatrical parasitism structures language itself and, like Plato's mimeticism or Butler's iterability, troubles the Austinian hierarchy of the felicitous citation versus its hollowed-out, reenacted cousin.

Law, too, relies on the ongoing (if intermittent) disavowal of the theatrical nature of its utterances. Robert Cover famously wrote that while "we do not talk our prisoners into jail," the uttering of a judge's sentence is freighted with state power sufficient to performatively coerce that action usually without the aid of physical force.[10] But, as Oscar Chase has argued, it is precisely in the spectacular adherence to ritual performance conventions and norms that legal proceedings derive their power of social control.[11] In other words, the elaborate staging and choreography of legal proceedings—their theatricality—are anything but hollow. Is it possible that the lawyer's deployment of legal speech (i.e., reenactment) partakes in a parasite-host dynamic that, rather than etiolating its force, in effect constitutes the system of law?

The proleptic character of law extends beyond the ritual forms of speech and gesture that characterize legal proceedings; the logic of *stare decisis* that forms a philosophical bedrock for much of our contemporary legal milieu favors, when it does not demand, reiteration. Judicial opinions are most often credible and enforceable to the extent that they are accepted as (ostensibly) reiterating previously established statutory norms and precedents; even when overruling a prior ruling, the adjudicator is deemed to be aligning their decision with a preexisting, overriding principle. While the invocation of precedent might not rise to the level of "reenactment" in the strict sense, the extravagant citational conventions governing legal writing often come close, and the oral delivery of an opinion replete with quotations from governing authorities can take the form of a series of reenacted excerpts collaged into a "new" iteration of the rule. Indeed, the charge of judicial "activism" might be understood as an accusation of a "hollow" performance of legal reenactment—an instance where the more recent utterance does not track or sync up with prior iterations closely enough, thereby exposing not only the parasitic nature of legal decision making but its vulnerability. For all the citation-heavy attempts to stabilize law and the norms it upholds, such repetitions also open a scar of difference and mutability.

What of the ostentation of a *theatrical* reenactment of legal proceedings, then? Might the "hollow" utterance of the lawyer-actor not only "etiolate" the utterance's (legal) performative effect (by virtue of the "special circumstances" of theatrical performance), but draw focus to the special, theatrical circumstances of legal performativity itself?

Hurts So Good: Re-enacting Legal Injury

Members of the Asian American Bar Association of New York (AABANY) launched their theatrical careers in 2006, when Judge Denny Chin (U.S. Court of Appeals, 2d Cir.) recruited them to participate in a reenactment of the 1951 trial of Ethel Rosenberg at an annual meeting of the National Asian Pacific American Bar Association. Chin (who presided over such high profile cases as the U.N. Oil for Food scandal and the trial of Bernie Madoff) along with his wife, Kathy Hirata Chin (a partner in the downtown corporate law firm Cadwalader, Wickersham, & Taft), and other members of AABANY, have scripted and produced trial reenactments on a nearly annual basis since then. Drawing from court transcripts, briefs, personal correspondence, and news accounts surrounding some of the better known legal cases in Asian American history, Chin and other members create plays that combine voiceover narration with dramatic restaging of arguments at trial. These one-hour documentary dramas[12] are most often played before attorneys (offering CLE credit) and student groups, and at cultural and community events.[13]

Such dramatic forays by legal practitioners/aficionados are not unique to AABANY; as noted above, the "public mock trial" has long been a popular form of edutainment. For example, the Landmark Center, a cultural/arts center in Minneapolis–St. Paul, formerly the home of the Federal Courts Building, annually produces reenactments of trials that took place there with a cast of local lawyers and judges to sold-out audiences.[14] The annual "Scopes Trial Play & Festival," sponsored by Bryan College and the City of Dayton, includes a reenactment of that trial in situ performed by local actors and students and regularly attracts over 2,000 people to "play" the gallery.[15] This return to the historical case is an outlier in re-performances of the famous "monkey trial." The 1925 Scopes trial has remained alive in U.S. popular memory in large part through the 1955 fictionalized treatment in the play *Inherit the Wind* and subsequent 1960 film starring Spencer Tracy. The play remains a staple of high school theatrical productions. One of Serres's points is that parasites press their hosts to adapt to them: in an extraordinary example of performative parasitism, scenes and verbatim language from *Inherit the Wind* have been quoted in legal opinions. As Tad Guterman observes, such references suggest no difference between (legal) case and play-script.[16] Who is borrowing authority from whom here? Finally, and in a more recent example of crossover between legal case and theatrical reenactment, MarriageTrial.com used professional actors to re-perform daily transcripts of the 2010 California Proposition 8 marriage equality trial (*Perry v. Schwarzenegger*) as a form of daily blogging on the proceedings.[17] In this last instance, the team behind the re-performance intentionally sought to compensate for the fact that live TV coverage of the trial had been blocked by the courts. Rationales for all these undertakings range from education (including practice-based research), to hobbyist/tourist pastime, to charity-event entertainment, to public service.

Interestingly, the cases AABANY selects for reenactment are typically not stories of Asian Americans prevailing under the law, but rather instances of Asian American racist subjection: the U.S. Supreme Court case of Minoru Yasui (in which the justices ruled that wartime incarceration on the basis of ethnicity is constitutional); the case of Takao Ozawa (barred from citizenship at a time when U.S. naturalization laws admitted only "free white persons" and blacks); or their self-described "greatest hit," the infamous Vincent Chin murder trial, in which two unemployed white Detroit auto workers reportedly mistook Chin for one of those "little [Japanese] motherfuckers" who "stole [their] jobs" and subsequently beat him to death with a baseball bat in plain view of several eye witnesses. In the state criminal trial (on which Judge Chin based his script), the defendants' charges were pleaded down to manslaughter, they served no jail time (receiving three years' probation instead), and were fined $3,000 plus court costs. These cases, especially *Yasui* (along with its companion case *United States v. Hirabayashi*) and the Chin murder trial, are typically viewed as low points in the legal history of Asian America; the cases remain good law, and illustrate the ways U.S. law has figured Asian Americans as excludable from full citizenship rights.

Yet these Asian American lawyers- and judges-turned-thespians stage these reenactments, playing not only the parts of the subjugated Asian Americans, but their adversaries, judges, and juries—precisely the mouthpieces of those laws and rulings that sought to exclude, devalue, and erase Asian Americanness in law and/or in fact. What is to be gained by such inhabitations of an abject legal history? What might these "parasitic" theatrical performances tell us about the nature of legal (mis)recognition and the force of reenacted law?

In *Infinitely Demanding*, Simon Critchley (synthesizing the work of Levinas, Lacan, Badiou, and Løgstrup) has argued that to be a conscious subject is, in part, to be uncomfortable—or rather, it is to manage the discomfort engendered by our necessarily imperfect, incomplete knowledge of the world (including the other), and our less-than-full mastery over our environment or even ourselves. Building on Critchley, we suggest that this ontological discomfort has bodily, affective, and psychic dimensions and is linked to the discomfort that garners legal protections. How does the law manage the discomfort that is the by-product or trace of subject formation? What kinds of harms, and whose, is the law prepared to recognize and redress? Is law equipped to address, let alone, alleviate ontological discomfort? In Critchley's view, the task of *managing* discomfort is an ethical one: the ethical subject is produced by an active, self-reflexive engagement with ontological discomfort. For this essay, we are considering the parasitic nature of *performance* as providing ways to manage that discomfort—not necessarily to allay it, but to allow audiences to abide with "fictionalized" difference (and the discomfort it provokes) for some limited duration.

The reenactments that AABANY presents are not elaborate theatrical affairs: they most frequently take place in hotel ballrooms or law school classrooms, with conference tables and lecterns serving as the USSC Justices' bench and witness stand.[18] The performers, given their limited rehearsal availability, read their parts rather than memorize them; with the exception of judges' robes, period/character costumes are eschewed; because nearly all performers are amateurs[19] and Asian American, acting is minimal, and casting is race- and gender-blind. AABANY's reenactments do not strive for historical or emotional verisimilitude; the performers go through the motions more or less awkwardly, and dramatic tension is minimal. In other words, these performances are as "hollow" (and therefore safely "infelicitous" in Austin's terms) as one could imagine. Still, the circling back of *reenacted* performance raises the stakes of the discomfort management. On the one hand, the "distance" (of intervening time) and the non-realist, alienated elements of the performance serve as spectacular reminders that that abject past is *not* the performers' present. Indeed, as spectacle goes, the performances are not very spectacular; in truth, they can be kind of boring. But the relative emotional containment or earnestness of the performance style may help shore up a defensive fantasy or wish that these cases and the racism they upheld belong to a different era. On the other hand, these historical assaults on Asian American political subjecthood have contributed substantially to the lived possibilities in the present for Asian Americans (including the performers themselves). As a result, the chosen subject matter (the history of racial subordination of Asians in American law), the use of archival material, and the proximity of political identities potentially collapse time, flooding the space of the present (including the literal space of the re-performance) with the "bad" feelings of the past. In this respect, we could even say that the past bores into the defenses of the present. This affective layering and overflow bring into sharp relief the tension between "good" and "bad" theatricalities in legal performance,[20] and the work that performative parasitism can do.[21]

That the past returns to affect, and affectively saturate and re-code, the present introduces another parasitism into the scene of our investigation: namely, the parasitism of psychoanalysis on theater. Consider, in this connection, the affective work the AABANY reenactments seem to do for and on both participants and audiences. When asked, the AABANY players (usually represented by Judge Chin or Kathy Chin) say they value the exercise for its pedagogical value—they not only perform these scripts, they also encourage other groups to use them for similarly educational purposes. But with equal frequency the participants speak of the *pleasure* they derive from doing these performances.

Frank Wu, former dean of the Hastings School of Law and honorary member of this acting troupe, writes in the foreword to a special issue of the *AABANY Law Review* that includes five of their scripts: "We are attracted to trials, because we love stories. We create meaning out of what might seem absurd, because it *sustains* us,"[22] and Judge Chin often speaks of the "fun" he has doing these reenactments, writing (in the same special issue's "Introduction"):

> We have enjoyed these projects immensely, and they have been satisfying on several levels. First, it has been instructive to go back and re-visit—or, in some instances, visit for the first time—these important cases in Asian-American legal history. Second, these cases raise issues that still reverberate today; there are still lessons to learn. Third, from a litigator's point of view, it has been fun to see how a case was tried, for example, in the Territory of Hawaii in the 1930s or in federal court in San Francisco in the 1940s, and many of the litigation techniques and strategies would be effective today. Fourth, we have enjoyed the opportunity to be creative and to "perform" before live audiences (who receive CLE credit). Finally, we believe we are helping introduce a whole new generation of Asian-Americans and others to these important cases.[23]

How is it that reembodying these roles can be construed as "enjoyable," especially to attorneys who are well aware of the legal ramifications of these rulings? Although this might speak to the drudgery of legal work, if that were all it were—*pleasure-seeking*—there are plenty of "happier" texts one might choose to re-perform. In the case of Japanese American internment, for example, one need only turn to the 1984 *coram nobis* re-trial of Fred Korematsu, in which District Court Judge Marilyn Patel not only reversed his conviction on a technicality, but also apologized on behalf of a racist nation at war.[24] The players opt instead for the earlier case that affirms the contingency of Asian American political inclusion. Why? What happens if we go, as it were, "beyond the pleasure principle"?

The compulsion to act out unpleasurable phenomena was first explored by Freud in his 1914 essay "Remembering, Repeating, and Working Through" and further elaborated in his 1919 study *Beyond the Pleasure Principle*. "Remembering, Repeating, and Working Through" is one of Freud's few papers on technique. In it, he explores the role of repetition, what he also calls "acting out," and its relation to memory. Remembering, Freud writes, is "reproduction in the psychical field."[25] As a translation of event into representation, memory implies the transformation and symbolization of mental processes into language as well as their insertion into time.[26] All too commonly, however, a patient does not know anything of what she has forgotten and repressed; instead, she or he acts it out. That is, the patient "reproduces it not as a memory, but as an action; he *repeats* it, without, of course, knowing that he is repeating it."[27] Freud is writing about patients and, especially, what happens between couch and chair during a treatment; but his observations about the compulsion to repeat instead of symbolize have ample application outside the consulting room as well.

Freud offers several examples to illustrate repetition phenomena, all of which show how the patient actively recreates and re-lives attitudes, relationships, and incidents from the past—playing them out with and on the analyst—not as past events but as "a present-day force."[28] The "patient repeats instead of remembering."[29] This is one of the most repeated claims of Freudian psychoanalysis. A key goal of the treatment is to transform repetition into remembering, into representation, but how? The analyst enlists the patient's compulsion to repeat, giving it room to move and assert itself within the contained and staged space of the consulting room. This is a literal space; it is also a metaphoric one—the "definite field" of transference[30]—within which repetition can acquire new and representable meanings. The play of transference provides a transit point between repeating and remembering, acting out and symbolization. It helps the patient transform and "place" a past event into the past—as memory.

From another vantage point, though, we could equally say that the process of remembering transforms and re-places the patient. In saying this we follow a line of flight made possible by Dominique Scarfone in his richly suggestive return to the role of repetition in psychoanalytic theory and practice. Scarfone reminds us that the "mutative value" of remembering, which analytic work makes possible, does not derive from the "mere filling in of blanks."[31] This is because such a conception of the work of remembering—as a matter of recall—posits a subject "external to the [remembered material] itself."[32] As in: Before I did not recall this, now I do. But in either instance, there I am. In contrast to this picture of a solidified subject who fills in the blank, Scarfone offers that "remembering in the specifically Freudian sense suggests that the subject is, so to speak, the remembered itself. By recomposing itself the soul also transforms itself."[33] More prosaically put, Scarfone's point, extrapolated from Freud's account of the relationship between repeating and remembering, is that the thing "remembered" does not exist *not* because it is not yet represented or representable. Rather, for the subject to "remember" it, a transformation in herself is necessary. That is, the subject that remembers is not the same subject that did not. Repetition under the specific conditions of the analytic relationship and the "playground" (Freud's term) of transference re-members her.[34]

This possibility rhymes with the transformative work performed by AABANY. Their performances of reenactment take something that was not "remembered"—in the sense that it was not "reproduced" in the *socio*-psychic field of representation and historical time—and turns it into memory. In this regard, theatrical reenactment functions analogously to transference, as a route of transit between repeating and remembering. Where we see AABANY's performances of reenactment crucially differing, however, is in the way they work with and in time. They help to transform un- or under-metabolized events into cultural memory, but they also never let the audience or the performers forget that the racism of the past is not over: racism persists. But it can also be confronted in different ways. Confronting and redressing racism and the inequalities it supports require the transformation of the compulsion to repeat into the injunction to remember. The burden of remembering is not equal. In the U.S., racialized subjects are required to do this kind of memory work—holding onto the persistence of racism—because white subjects don't have to, may actively refuse to do so, and may even throw up obstacles to people of color on the road to remembering.[35]

Memory work is thus labor, and labor disproportionately undertaken by racialized subjects. But within the deliberate theater of reenactment such labor can take on fresh sensations. There is a potential yield of pleasure in this: the result of containing and metabolizing the painful affects and effects of "bad" law, of giving them into meaning and being given anew, re-membered. There may be lightness in this, an enjoyment, even, that carries beyond the make-do theatrical spaces inhabited by AABANY and into the "actual" realm of life and law.

In Richard Posner's view, levity is precisely what must be guarded against in trial reenactments: "Reenactments of real trials are the most promising form of the public mock trial," he writes, "though they too often miscarry. The participants, notably including the judges, find it almost impossible to refrain from joking and to avoid anachronisms."[36] So troubling does he find the penchant for laughter in these settings, he indicates (ominously) the "Average Number of Jokes by Judges (5.88)" in such proceedings.[37] "If low comedy is what the mock-trial market wants," he laments, "so be it. My own view . . . is that the only possible value of a mock trial is educational."[38] Setting aside Judge Posner's curious segregation of pedagogy from punchlines,[39] we wonder at his emphasis on avoiding anachronism. It seems to us an impossible charge or fantasy.

Now, most commentators on reenactment, in documentary film, history-tourism, or high art, recognize the inherent pleasure of reenacting —regardless of the seriousness of the historical referent. Or perhaps it is *in precise relation to* that seriousness: likening reenactment to fantasy, documentary film theorist Bill Nichols argues that "reenactments . . . foil the desire to preserve the past in the amber of an omniscient wholeness, the comprehensive view we like to think we have that accounts for what has come to pass."[40] Contra Judge Posner, then, anachronism is an unavoidable feature of re-performance. By summoning and re-playing the past, re-performance puts time out of joint (a potentially discomforting unbinding) so as to create fresh insertion points for meaning in this time (binding). The hyphen that links "re" and "performance" cannot close or fill in the gap between past and present. It can, however, mark the wavering between pleasure/discomfort, binding/unbinding, same/different.[41] However much a given re-performance might aspire to an exacting duplication (and not all re-performances do), sincerity always misses its mark. And yet, the miscarriages that Judge Posner warns against—humor where it does not belong, the contamination of a "pure" past with the present—are built into reenactment as such. And, as Nichols notes, this queer sort of failure may itself become a sincere form of pleasure. Perhaps even a kind of camp sincerity.

Re-enactment and Para-legal Reparation

In her essay on "Paranoid Reading and Reparative Reading," Eve Sedgwick points to the ubiquity of what she calls (following Paul Ricoeur) "a hermeneutics of suspicion," by which she means a form of analysis that identifies and calls out instances of exclusion, subordination, and injury—a form of analysis that she says has come to be "widely understood as a mandatory injunction rather than a possibility among other possibilities."[42] This mode of critique, according to Sedgwick, is fundamentally paranoid: a "strong theory" of negative affect that places its faith in "exposure." She is calling to our attention a naïve belief that, if only one is made aware of the injurious nature of a particular behavior, its value as an object of desire and source of pleasure will immediately dissipate and that person will no longer act or feel in the same way. Accordingly, once we recognize the virulent racism and faulty logic of these cases, it follows that we can (and must) have no choice but to decry the verdicts (and the individuals responsible for promulgating them) as hated, abjected (or abjecting) historical artifacts that are best forgotten and, at the very least, must be neatly packaged as stern warnings/object lessons. Such is the reading amongst some early feminist critics of camp: it is misogynist parody and should therefore be condemned. Insert scare quotes or trigger warning here.

But camp traffics in the off-kilter quotation. "Camp," as Susan Sontag famously wrote "sees everything in quotation marks. It's not a lamp, but a 'lamp'; not a woman, but a 'woman.' To perceive Camp in objects and persons is to understand Being-as-Playing-a-Role. It is the farthest extension, in sensibility, of the metaphor of life as theater."[43] Moreover, many feminists have queerly mined camp for the lamp-light it shines on the fabrication of gender as nature. Butler's account of gender performativity may be the most famous example here, but it is noteworthy that she credits Esther Newton's ethnography of female impersonators, *Mother Camp*,[44] for showing Butler—at a time when Butler says she needed such lessons in creative falsity to feel less false herself—the way *any* gender is assumed and put on again, and again.[45] This insight crucially informs Butler's conception of gender as an imitative practice whose performance fabricates its own origins and passes them off as law. Although it is most strongly associated with (white) gay male cultural practices, as an aesthetic and affective style and as a proto-ethic, camp can also disrupt racial (racist) conventions and stereotypes.[46]

Given that camp seems to produce such pleasure and *communitas* amongst subordinated minority subjects, in contrast to Posner, we will have our cake and eat it, too; seriousness and levity are not opposed values or experiences. Reenactment activates not just cognitive processes—intellectual engagement, history lessons—it also sets in motion affective overflows, pleasurable and discomforting. Conceptual artist Pope.L writes similarly about the *communitas* of reenactment. Likening it to karaoke, he offers, "Drinking alcohol, loud carousing, singing off-key late into the darkness collaborate in a ritual obliteration, the goal being: community-cohesion via public obliteration. Can you reenact something until it's rendered completely invisible? Until its true color finally shows through? A transparent color suffused in dust, cobwebs, and melancholy?"[47] For Pope.L, the collectivity that (camp) reenactment can make of minoritized subjects sees and un-sees past events in the inviting, melancholy darkness of the karaoke booth.

Sedgwick writes, "The desire of a reparative impulse . . . is additive and accretive. Its fear, a realistic one, is that the culture surrounding it is inadequate or inimical to its nurture; it wants to assemble and confer plentitude on an object that will then have resources to offer to an inchoate self."[48] Now to be clear: lawyers and judges dramatizing historical trials are not equivalent to gay camp and its accretions! The kind of nurturing that Sedgwick contemplates as an effect of parody or camp performance is very different from the kind of (educational, non-parodic, if also not-fully-realist) performances we are looking at here. Still, might it be possible to draw lessons from camp and the conferral of plentitude it offers? Paradoxically, this plenitude derives in part from camp's refusal to refuse negativity, whether a negativity of bad feelings or bad history or, as in the case of AABANY's reenactments, bad law. This refusal to refuse—or, to put it differently, the investment in conscripting what would otherwise be discarded as refuse and waste—is the fierce and life-sustaining signature of what José Muñoz calls disidentification.[49] It is a willingness to play with, rework, and claim toxic materials.

Whereas the value of camp for Sedgwick seems to derive from a kind of affectionate, horizontal, nurturing and affective-bond-building reparation, the reparative effect we are tracking here is in the act of re-embodying histories of exclusion or abjection. Sedgwick may have even laid too much stress on the nurturing side of camp, leaving out of view the ways it has functioned as a bitchy weapon of choice to be wielded amongst gay men, as they read each other down. Moreover, in addition to its intra-group role, camp has historically served to put up a performative shield to deflect the insults, degrading stereotypes, and worse of a homophobic dominant culture. As Newton affirms in *Mother Camp,* "Camp humor is a system of laughing at one's incongruous position instead of crying."[50] Camp does not will away pain or injury; it works with it and transforms it. To repeat: this is not the same thing as relegating it to the past as over and done. Something similar may be at work in the way AABANY replays past traumas. For Asian Americans, the category of "citizen" has always been overdetermined: racialized (as Neil Gotanda has argued) as perpetually foreign, the stakes of citizenship are not just about legal status, but also about legible, full personhood itself. So to inhabit these abject histories is, potentially, a way for Asian Americans to insert themselves imaginatively into this history of the citizen-subject. Elsewhere, one of us has written about a similar phenomenon in terms of "critical mimesis"—the way Asian Americans (and others) might find some value in the inhabitation of abject embodiments, when those embodiments are, finally, the only routes to social legibility.[51] That project worked more along the lines of a camp aesthetic—"playing" performatively with abject stereotypes so as to de-authorize them. But the AABANY reenactments are something else:

a "straight" rendition of hateful histories that do not attempt to defuse through humor. Nonetheless, there remains something compelling in the pleasure that performance *as performance* can produce.

"What we can best learn from such practices," Sedgwick points out, "are, perhaps, the many ways selves and communities succeed in extracting sustenance from the objects of a culture—even of a culture whose avowed desire has often been not to sustain them."[52] Our argument with regard to AABANY is that their performances body forth the discomfort that proximal difference engenders and in so doing—in fact, in their alienated, amateur rendition of that difference—enact, paradoxically, a reparative, parasitic reenactment practice that allows us to grapple with, and see in new ways, the violent performativity of law through the device of theatricalization—an intimate, somatic engagement through which we might sit with that difference and the discomfort of abjection and find (ambivalent) pleasure in doing so.

The philosopher Avishai Margalit writes, "Nostalgia, like sentimentality, is the fuel of kitsch."[53] It purifies the past of all shit, preserving a pristine picture of ourselves and, vicariously, our ancestors. Camp, by contrast, repurposes the sharp pangs, bitchy force, and even the shitty stench of history that will not or cannot clean itself up for easy at-home consumption. This reference to "home" is deliberate, given that the word "home" (*nostos,* literally "returning home") is buried in nostalgia. AABANY's reenactments are certainly not nostalgic: Who would yearn for the violent exclusions or overt and legitimated racism manifested in the legal cases they perform? But they potentially underscore the value of reinhabiting a painful past. This return to a decidedly unpurified past (indeed, to a time when the "Asian American subject" was marked as unpure) might be a way of pushing back against model minority status in the present and the contemporary demands of assimilation. It may even be that reenactment of a shitty past—a time when a subject was treated like shit, the debased paradigm of abjected materiality—de-pathologizes memory by de-idealizing it. Memory thus becomes differently available for tasks in the present, becomes, even, a way to re-member different possible futures.

Once More, with (Another) Feeling

To take up questions of reenactment and reenactability is necessarily to engage the ethics and politics of memory and history. The language of reparation crosses the threshold between law and psychoanalysis. One of the many issues raised by AABANY's performance is the splitting between reparation in a psychologized sense and reparation in the sense of redistributive justice, that is, the making up in material ways for *past* harms or the reallocating of resources *in the present* to redress the ongoing effects of past social arrangements. In the current moment, there seems scant likelihood of gaining traction for any kind of materialist reparation, whether nationally or internationally, that would involve "paying up." Instead, the best that can be offered is public rituals—for example, truth commissions—that aim to "reconcile" victims and perpetrators and in so doing consign the past of injury to a clearly defined and overcome past.[54] Are the reenactments performed by the AABANY one such public or, better, counter-public, ritual of reparation? At a cultural moment when the U.S. president justifies his own hateful, bullying speech as a counter to so-called bullies of "political correctness," those who continue to talk of past injuries, including those who point out enduring connections between injuries and injustices in the past and contemporary social problems and injustice, risk being diagnosed as hysterics of history. These "anachronists" are unable or unwilling to "move on," "heal," "forgive," and/or to become proper secular subjects of history, who "get" the right relations between past, present, future.

The Christianizing dimension of the demand to forgive bad histories, bad laws, the bad agents who authored them and/or the bystanders who "merely" benefitted from them requires further attention; it points to the way a particular religion suffuses the culture of U.S. public feelings. The demand to forgive is the flip-side of another: to love your neighbor as yourself. When applied to sharing space, including democratic social space, with others this commandment presents the genteel face of liberal multiculturalism whereby members of minoritized groups are welcomed ("loved") on the condition that they appear like or like enough to the majority that they do not disturb the fantasy of the same. But this fantasy is just that: a fantasy that wishes away all the many ways our neighbors annoy us, discomfort us, and, most assuredly, are not ourselves. How do we make room for "strangers" and for the strangeness of those we do not yet know and may never understand, let alone love, if and when we do come to know them? How do we make room for discomfort in public life without either turning to the law to "heal" it or turning away from the material conditions that continue to produce some people's discomfort as the operative condition of the majority's ongoing happiness?

"Bad law" belongs to the past, to a history of badness we have passed out of. But this bracketing of past and present is always threatened by the return of the repressed, to use the language of Freud. In more Kleinian language we could say that the splitting off of badness (past as "bad object") produces a false and, indeed, dangerously precarious sense of the goodness of the present—or, at least, a goodness that could be recaptured for the present if only those troublesome others would leave or keep silent. In this sense, "Make America Great Again" might be a form of reenactment, too—in this instance, a reenactment of a fantastically constructed non-existent but highly invested "past." If so, this is a powerful reminder that the work of reenactment—what it does in the world, how it makes worlds—has no set politics nor guaranteed effects.

Nor will it suffice simply to distinguish between reenactment as acting out (bad reenactment, bad) and reenactment as working through, the term that Freud used to refer to traumatic events that are processed and reworked. How do "we" know when things are worked through in the quote-unquote "right" direction? The positive valence usually accorded "working through" (good job!) fails to acknowledge that an ethical or political compass (and thus a particular subject positionality) underwrites such judgments. What if we approached AABANY's reenactments as insisting on the value of staying with discomfort as a route to re-membering subjectivities?

Theater emerges here as a potential laboratory for trying out new forms of social being and becoming. That this is so also points to the parasitism of psychoanalysis on theater. Psychoanalysis, as theory and practice, has got theater deep in its bones. Put another way: if "dreams are the royal road to . . . the unconscious,"[55] that road passes through the theater district. Freud's and psychoanalysis's indebtedness to theater goes far beyond the plays that he cites—and he does so frequently. In *Interpretation of Dreams,* Freud enlists both *Oedipus Rex* and *Hamlet* to support his claims about the shared mental material that underlie "typical dreams." Over the course of his discussion, the plays start to function as waking dreams. Might the dreams that are performance awaken us? And, if so, to what? These are among the questions that are acted out and transformed by AABANY.

If theater sometimes appears as symptom of illness, it also functions, or can function, as vehicle of transformation. This is psychoanalysis as homeopathy: admit just the "right" amount of repetition on the way to remembering; give transference just the "right" amount of free rein to play out the past. It does not always go as planned, for worse and for better.

The theater of analysis is scripted and improvised at once, and ego is not master (director) of its own show. Perhaps AABANY's performances of bad law play in the difference between Freud's negative appraisal of reenactment as acting out in the place of remembering and his appreciation of reenactment as a form of creatively reanimating the past in and *for* the present day, a creative re-purposing that happens in the "live" meeting between patient and analyst, perfomer and audience-become-witness.[56] Reenactment, for Freud, and for many subsequent psychoanalytic thinkers and practitioners, always occupied this uneasy, ambivalent space between blockage and transformation.

There are potential links here to recent controversies over "trigger warnings" and the demand voiced by some individuals and groups to be immunized in advance from being offended. Arguably, trigger warnings—with their reductionist conception of traumatic returns and their demand to avoid such risks at all costs—may effect a freezing or preserving of the traumatic past. Trigger warnings conceive reenactment only in the negative sense articulated by Freud, with the subject of reminiscence trapped in the theater of memory. But reenactment in the second sense, as creative reliving, pursues another risk: that of *transforming* the past into usable material for the present and future. Such a transformation risks contamination, and invites the stink of the past into the present. Because it never went away. AABANY is not great theater; but their performances of reenactment reactivate and potentially recode historical memory, producing pleasure or its possibilities in the place of abjection. History parasites us. AABANY says: yes.

NOTES

The authors would like to thank Martha Umphrey and Austin Sarat for inviting us to contribute to this collection and for their thoughtful and generative feedback; Hon. Denny Chin and Kathy Hirata Chin for sharing their insights and archival material; and Avgi Saketopoulou for her keen editorial eye.

1. Richard A. Posner, "Mock Trials and Real Justices and Judges," *Cardozo Law Review* 34 (2012–2013): 2111. Posner analyzed forty-three "Public Mock Trials" presided over by Supreme Court justices as well as state and federal judges, yielding statistical insights including "Mock Trials per year of Judicial Service" (Ruth Bader Ginsburg leads the USSC pack, with an average of 0.70 mock trials per year), percentage of jury trials (40%), and defendants' win/loss percentages (43.48%/39.13%), etc. One of Justice Ginsburg's most recent turns onstage was in a retrial of Shylock in Venice in 2016.

2. Sarah Kozinn, *Justice Performed: Courtroom TV Shows and the Theaters of Popular Law* (New York: Bloomsbury Methuen, 2015). The judges are reenacting roles they played in "real" courts of law. Together with the plaintiffs, men and women who have been recruited from suits they filed at small claims court, these real fake judges may well

dispense more justice than the plaintiffs and defendants expect to receive (and others do actually receive) in real courts of law.

3. For an influential and much-debated argument for disappearance as the ontology of performance, see Peggy Phelan, *Unmarked: The Politics of Performance* (New York: Routledge, 1993).

4. J. L. Austin, *How to Do Things with Words* (Cambridge, MA: Harvard University Press, 1962).

5. Judith Butler, *Bodies That Matter: On the Discursive Limits of Sex* (New York: Routledge, 1993), and *Excitable Speech: A Politics of the Performative* (New York: Routledge, 1997).

6. Austin, *How to Do Things with Words,* 22 (emphasis in original).

7. Alan Read, "The Placebo of Performance: Psychoanalysis in Its Place," in *Psychoanalysis and Performance,* ed. Patrick Campbell and Adrian Kear (London: Routledge, 2001), 147–65.

8. Jacques Derrida, "Signature Event Context," in *Limited Inc.,* trans. Samuel Weber and Jeffrey Mehlman (Evanston, IL: Northwestern University Press, 1988), 1–21, 17.

9. Michel Serres, *The Parasite,* trans. Lawrence R. Schehr (Minneapolis: University of Minnesota Press, 2007); published as *Le Parasite* in 1980 by Grasset et Pasquelle.

10. Robert Cover, "Violence and the Word," *Yale Law Journal* 95 (1985–1986): 1601, 1608; see also Butler, *Excitable Speech.*

11. Oscar Chase, *Law, Culture, and Ritual: Disputing Systems in Cross-Cultural Context* (New York: New York University Press, 2005).

12. See Carol Martin, *Theatre of the Real* (London: Palgrave Macmillan, 2012).

13. AABANY's repertoire also includes "22 Lewd Chinese Women (*Chy Lung v. Freeman*)," New York Historical Society, October 18, 2014; and "Iva: The Myth of Tokyo Rose—Allegiance on Trial," The Asia Society (New York), May 16, 2014.

14. www.landmarkcenter.org/programs/trials.htm (accessed April 10, 2015).

15. www.scopesfestival.com (accessed April 10, 2015).

16. Tad Guterman, "Field Tripping: The Power of *Inherit the Wind,*" *Theatre Journal* 60 (2008): 563–83; for the legal cases that cite *Inherit the Wind,* see 581n91.

17. www.marriagetrial.com (accessed April 4, 2015).

18. In at least one instance, however, the reenactment was staged in a courtroom simulacrum. The Vincent Chin trial reenactment performed at Hastings College in January 2013 was staged in the law school's Moot Court classroom, and performers were placed in the appropriate locations for judge, witnesses, defense, and prosecution.

19. In the 2013 Hastings reenactment, playwright Philip Gotanda joined the cast as one of the witnesses.

20. Julie Stone Peters, "Legal Performance Good and Bad," *Law, Culture and the Humanities* 4 (2008): 179–200. Peters argues that "the oscillation between theatricality and antitheatricality is not just a minor subplot of legal history or supplement to law, but at its heart: defining it and shaping its self-conception" (198–99).

21. There are important links to be drawn here as well to the question of catharsis and, in a more psychoanalytic vein, the problematics of "working through." We do not know in advance where expelling, letting go, working through "negative" affects will take audience or performer, for that matter. For one recent discussion of this uncertainty, see Eric Severson et al., "Trauma, Tragedy and Theater: A Conversation with Simon Critchley," in *In The Wake of Trauma,* ed. Eric Severson, David Goodman, and Brian Becker (Pittsburgh: Duquesne University Press, 2016), 9–34.

22. Frank Wu, "Foreword," *AABANY Law Review* (2012): 15 (emphasis added).

23. Judge Chin, "Introduction," *AABANY Law Review* (2012): ii.

24. That case, *Korematsu v. U.S.*, 548 F.Supp 1406 (N.D.Cal. 1984), proved instrumental in the grassroots political movement for Japanese American reparations, as discussed below.

25. Sigmund Freud, "Remembering, Repeating, and Working Through" (1914), in *The Standard Edition of the Complete Psychological Works of Sigmund Freud*, vol. 12, ed. James Strachey (London: Hogarth Press, 1958), 153.

26. See Dominique Scarfone, "Repetition: Between Presence and Meaning," *Canadian Journal of Psychoanalysis* 19, no. 1 (2011): 70–86, esp. 72–74.

27. Freud, "Remembering," 150.

28. Ibid., 151.

29. Ibid.

30. Ibid., 154.

31. Scarfone, "Repetition," 73.

32. Ibid.

33. Ibid., 74.

34. Freud, "Remembering," 154.

35. In this context, consider accusations that people of color are playing the "race card" when they call out issues of racist discrimination or assertions that affirmative action, which is aimed to address a history of racist subordination, is a form of "special rights" or "reverse racism."

36. Posner, "Mock Trials and Real Justices and Judges," 2132.

37. Ibid., "Table 3: Summary Statistics," 2123.

38. Ibid., 2148.

39. We know from Freud onward that the joke is often one of the ways that otherwise inadmissible or repressed material breaks through to consciousness and communicability (wanted and unwanted). See Freud, *Jokes and Their Relation to the Unconscious*, in *The Standard Edition of the Complete Psychological Words of Sigmund Freud*, vol. 7 (London: Hogarth Press, 1960).

40. Bill Nichols, "Documentary Reenactment and the Fantasmatic Subject," *Critical Inquiry* 35, no. 1 (Autumn 2008): 72–89, 80.

41. Scarfone, "Repetition," 74.

42. Eve Kosofsky Sedgwick, "Paranoid Reading and Reparative Reading, or, You're So Paranoid, You Probably Think This Essay Is About You," in *Touching Feeling: Affect, Pedagogy, Performativity* (Durham, NC: Duke University Press, 2003), 125.

43. Susan Sontag, "Notes on 'Camp,'" in *Against Interpretation and Other Essays* (New York: Anchor Books, 1990 [1966]), 280.

44. Esther Newton, *Mother Camp: Female Impersonators in America*, with a new preface (Chicago: University of Chicago Press, 1979).

45. Judith Butler, "Imitation and Gender Insubordination," in *The Lesbian and Gay Studies Reader*, ed. Henry Abelove, Michèle Aina Barale, and David M. Halperin (New York: Routledge, 1992), 312.

46. For camp as a proto-ethic, see Ann Pellegrini, "After Sontag: Future Notes on Camp," in *A Companion to Lesbian, Gay, Bisexual, Transgender, and Queer Studies*, ed. George E. Haggerty and Molly McGarry (Oxford: Blackwell, 2007), 166–91. For work on camp and racial performance, see especially José Esteban Muñoz, *Disdentifications* (Minneapolis: University of Minnesota Press, 1999); Nyong'o Tavia, "Racial Kitsch and Black Performance," *Yale Journal of Criticism* 15, no. 2 (Fall 2002): 371–91; and E. Patrick Johnson, *Camp Revival: Queering Gender in the Black Church* (forthcoming).

47. William Pope.L, "Canary in the Coal Mine," *Art Journal* 70, no. 3 (Fall 2011): 55–58, 55.

48. Sedgwick, "Paranoid Reading and Reparative Reading," 149.

49. José Esteban Muñoz, *Disidentifications: Queers of Color and the Performance of Politics* (Minneapolis: University of Minnesota Press, 1999).

50. Newton, *Mother Camp,* 109.

51. Karen Shimakawa, *National Abjection: The Asian American Body Onstage* (Durham, NC: Duke University Press, 2003).

52. Sedgwick, "Paranoid Reading and Reparative Reading," 150–51.

53. Avishai Margalit, "Nostalgia," *Psychoanalytic Dialogues* 21, no. 3 (2011): 271–80.

54. Robert Meister, "Human Rights and the Politics of Victimhood," *Ethics and International Affairs 16,* no. 2 (2002): 91–108.

55. Sigmund Freud, *The Interpretation of Dreams* (1900–1901), in *The Standard Edition of the Complete Psychological Works of Sigmund Freud,* vol. 5, ed. James Strachey (London: Hogarth, 1953), 608.

56. It may be significant in this connection that AABANY is mostly performing for its own, that is, Asian American audience members, so that their performance's transformation of memory and of affects associated with it blurs the lines between who is the patient, who the analyst-interpreter.

CHAPTER 4

Statements before and after Arrests

Performing at Law's Edge in Apartheid South Africa

CATHERINE M. COLE

The field of "law and literature" is by now well established, having formed a professional society, launched a journal, gestated an ample bibliography, convened regular conferences, and even become, in the words of one critic, "quaint."[1] "Law and performance," by way of contrast, has been a far more nascent, embryonic, and fractured conversation, moving in fits and starts over time, migrating from legal studies to literary studies to medieval and Renaissance studies to theater studies, rhetoric, history, and performance studies. It has not, as of yet, congealed into a coherent conversation much less a well-defined "field," despite the fact that some of its key interventions extend back at least fifty years—and much longer if we care to consider the ancients.[2]

"Despite the persistence of the trope likening law to theater, despite the vast body of critical writing on 'law and literature,' the rise of 'Performance Studies' and the more general proliferation of the term 'performance' in critical studies," wrote Julie Stone Peters in 2005, "there has been no sustained theoretical articulation of the nature of legal performance or the meaning of legal theatricality in the critical literature."[3] Two years later Dennis Kezar echoed these sentiments when he said that theater remains a "perennial blind spot" in the larger law and literature movement, even though theater and law in the early modern period were not just relevant to each other but were actually defined by an institutional co-presence.[4] Henning Grunwald expressed a similar opinion in 2012: "Despite—or perhaps partly because of—manifest structural similarities between theater and courtroom, between stage and tribunal, scholars of politics, law and culture have been slow to take seriously the performativity of law."[5] Perhaps only now, with the publication of this edited collection *Law and Performance,* is the question of the relationship of law and performance coming clearly into view.

Two superb literature reviews on "law and literature" and "law and performance" written by Julie Stone Peters and published in 2005 and 2008 respectively provide excellent introductions to each field, rich in citations and pithy in their identification of key problematics, with insights that remain relevant today.[6] Interestingly, mirrors emerge as a key metaphor in both essays. Of law and literature, Peters writes:

> In effect, through this double desire for the other and for the other's projection of the self, each discipline [law and literature] came to desire in itself what the other discipline had put there. In the disciplinary hall of mirrors, they met in the shared space of mutual projection, in work that acted out both sets of anxieties while repressing some of the most important insights of each discipline.[7]

Mirrors also figure in Peters's characterization of the relationship between law and performance, but here the cross-disciplinary conversation is not figured as a co-equal gazing down a hallway of reflections. Rather, Peters sees theater as "law's twisted mirror, its funhouse double: ever-present, substantiating, mocking, reinforcing, undermining."[8] Theater is the object that seems to simultaneously fascinate and disorient, reflect and distort, entice and repel those who think about the law. The twisted mirror may incite vertigo, or perhaps simply exhaust with novelty. For this and other reasons, the pace of the conversation has been slow. Perhaps the most inhibiting obstacle has been a set of pernicious polarities. On the one hand is the proclivity to extoll the "good" (which can be, for instance, theater's "truth," a naïve embrace of its utopian potential for transformation, or similarly, an uncritical faith in a legal liberal humanist rights discourse). On the other hand, we also see haughty (and hasty) disavowals of the "bad" (such as theater's artifice and insincerity, or law's normativity). We would do well to curb kneejerk reactions and pejorative dismissals, as these have demonstrably inhibited a scholarly conversation that has long been identified as compelling, necessary, and important.

Perhaps it is time to move beyond the "mirror stage" in the law and performance conversation, with its distortions, projections, misrecognitions, narcissisms, and innate two-dimensionality. The common mode of analysis has been analogy: metaphoric and comparative work on law and theater. This remains a valid line of inquiry, with many important explorations yet still to be done on topics such as law's space, acoustics, costume, gesture, comportment, presence, affect, voice, interactivity, spectatorship, ritual, and liveness in relation to theater. The vocabulary and theories of performativity and theatricality that arose in the 1990s and 2000s have pushed the law and performance discourse inaugurated by Milner Ball and others in the 1960s and 1970s into a far more complex theoretical register.[9] So where are we now? What avenues are most likely to advance the law and performance conversation in substantive ways?

I want to advocate for a deeper understanding of the performativity of the law, the way in which one becomes a subject before the law through performative acts, and how the law itself performs especially as it intersects with theater's simultaneous ontic and mimetic dimensions. I agree with Martha Merrill Umphrey that the full implications of Judith Butler's scholarship on performativity and the law have yet to be seriously understood, much less explored, especially in more empirically grounded ways. Among the questions that Butler's work prompts Umphrey to ask are: How do trials "do" law? How are trials "law-making (and not just law-applying or law interpreting) events *because of their performativity?*"[10] Joshua Takano Chambers-Letson's recent book *A Race So Different: Performance and Law in Asian America* provides a sophisticated navigation of the "slippery ground between performativity and performance," a nuanced appreciation of how law is situational and realized through legal habitus and aesthetic performances.[11] I appreciate his distinction between quotidian and aesthetic arenas, as well as the insistence that these are not binary oppositions. There is great value in examining the aesthetic representations of the law in relationship to "everyday" legal habitus.[12] What I propose is a course correction that balances our disproportionate focus on trials (and related legal "events" such as truth commissions and hearings) as the primary venues for exploring the relationship between law and performance.[13] We need to think more expansively about legal habitus, the performativity of law in arenas and spaces outside of the trial. If we think about law as a set of contingent enunciations performed in many locations, including, in Martha Merrill Umphrey's words, "the street corner, the interrogation room, the district attorney's office, a lynching scene and, of course, the trial," what new lines of scholarly research does this open up?[14]

My focus here is on the arrest as a situational space where the law asserts itself overtly, hailing subjects—seizing, capturing, charging, and detaining them. Louis Althusser long ago showed us that subjects are "always already" interpellated by the law. The scene of the arrest or a hailing by a police officer are merely instances that make explicit what is otherwise implicit: the law's pervasive reach as well as law's dependence upon subjects to affirm its legitimacy. That said, arrests are highly performative iterations of the law; three-dimensional, durational, visceral, and kinetic. Arrests fundamentally change the status of the person apprehended. Things are "done" with words in the course of the arrest, to use J. L. Austin's theorization of the performative.[15] In the moment of arrest, one sees the paradigmatic trope of interpellation, as theorized by Althusser:

> I shall then suggest that ideology "acts" or "functions" in such a way that it "recruits" subjects among the individuals (it recruits them all), or "transforms" the individuals into subjects (it transforms them all) by that very precise operation which I have called interpellation or hailing, and which can be imagined along the lines of the most commonplace everyday police (or other) hailing: "Hey, you there!" [Note: Hailing as an everyday practice subject to a precise ritual takes a quite "special" form in the policeman's practice of "hailing" which concerns the hailing of "suspects."
>
> Assuming that the theoretical scene I have imagined takes place in the street, the hailed individual will turn round. By this mere one-hundred-and-eighty-degree physical conversion, he becomes a subject. Why?[16]

Sometimes the arrest is witnessed by others; other times it is seen only by the officer(s) effecting the arrest and the accused. Today many arrests include witnesses who wield cell phone cameras, and these documents become additional witnesses with capacity to circulate across space and time, providing the basis for other narratives and truth claims. They provide both a proliferation of perspectives and potentially a narrowing of the range of permissible lies. Yet many arrests are unseen by witnesses, and rarely are they understood from a position that provides intimate insight into the intersubjective encounter of the arrest, the interiorized experience of an interpellation, *how* one becomes a very particular subject before the law, how it feels to be arrested. In particular, I am interested in the subjective experience of a *racialized* subject standing before the law. What is the psychic life of power for those who are arrested—or living with the perpetual threat of imminent arrest—within the domain of a racist regime?

Scholars such as Mladen Dolar and Judith Butler, among others, have taken up the concept of interpellation after Althusser.[17] Dolar's critique of Althusser asks us to consider the role of subjectivity, and specifically he questions whether there is a "kernel of interiority" that is outside of subjection, an inner register of the subject that is beyond interpellation.[18]

Dolar asks provocatively, "Could one say that love is what we find beyond interpellation?"[19] Judith Butler responds to this question by asserting that, in fact, the scene of subjection involves a passionate attachment to the law, a "strange scene of love," as the subject comes to embrace the very conditions of subjection. She says, "That the subject turns round toward the law suggests that the subject lives in passionate expectation of the law. Such love is not beyond interpellation; rather it forms the passionate circle in which the subject becomes ensnared by its own state."[20] Mary Bunch's more recent intervention introduces the concept of "unbecoming"—not only what it means to behave in ways that are, for instance, "unbecoming of a woman," but also theoretically to consider "unbecoming" as a space of resistance to the law because, as she argues, "one is also always already something other than the subject one is expected to be."[21] Bunch puts forth for queer theory the concept of an "unbecoming subject," one that inherently exposes subjectivity as a double performative—both law and the subject each granting the other the conditions of its possibility and threatening the withdrawal of those conditions.[22]

This chapter explores the possibilities of an *unbecoming* subject, one who refuses subjection, particularly racialized subjection. Is it possible to refuse or disrupt the dual performativity of the subject and the law? In order to think through such a question, we must consider how the law as a technology of race is performatively realized in scenes of subjection. As Alexander G. Weheliye has argued, both Giorgio Agamben's work on "bare life" and Michel Foucault's theories of biopolitics, despite their enormously important and field-transforming implications, have been notably subdued on questions of race:

> Bare life and biopolitics discourse not only misconstrues how profoundly race and racism shape the modern idea of the human, it also overlooks or perfunctorily writes off theorizations of race, subjection, and humanity found in black and ethnic studies, allowing bare life and biopolitics to imagine an indivisible biological substance anterior to racialization. The idea of racializing assemblages, in contrast, construes race not as a biological and cultural classification but as a set of sociopolitical processes that discipline humanity into full humans, not quite humans, and non-humans.[23]

This echoes Judith Butler's meditations on the concept of "bare life." Within general claims that bare life underwrites the actual political arrangements in which we live, Butler argues, there is not yet clarity about *how* one becomes reduced to such a condition, nor *how* certain lives are singled out, treated differentially on the basis of ethnicity and race.[24] In answer to these questions, the moment of arrest and its legal interpellations, its ontic reality and mimetic representation in performance, can give us a privileged and provocative vantage point to consider arrests as "scenes of subjection," to use a phrase from Saidiya Hartman. What do arrests as scenes of subjection stage? And what can be learned from (re)staging them theatrically?[25] And what happens to theatrical events that themselves hail both artists and audiences to a scene that is illegal, where spectators themselves may be arrested?

"I Fuck, Therefore I Am"

The racialized legal habitus of the arrest has recently been brought spectacularly into public awareness in the United States through the "Hands Up, Don't Shoot" and "Black Lives Matter" campaigns in the wake of the fatalities at the hands of police during the course of conducting arrests in Ferguson, Staten Island, Oakland, and Summerville, South Carolina—to name but a few in a long, disgraceful list. However, the arrest that commands my attention for this essay did not happen on August 9, 2014 (Michael Brown), or on July 17, 2014 (Eric Garner), or on January 1, 2009 (Oscar Grant), or in North Charleston on April 7, 2015 (Walter L. Scott). Rather, it happened in South Africa under apartheid. This fictionalized arrest appeared in a play written by Athol Fugard in 1972, *Statements after an Arrest under the Immorality Act.* Fugard's inspiration for the play was an actual arrest the playwright recorded in his notebook in 1966:

> Immorality Act case at De Aar [a town in Northern Cape]. Coloured Anglican missionary and a forty-year-old white woman, a librarian. The police caught them in bed, pulled back the sheets and took photographs.
>
> Darkness. Suddenly a blinking flash of light like a photographer's flash; a split second later a woman screams. Then stage lights up to reveal an office desk, chair and—to one side—a filing cabinet. Standing at the desk, examining a police file, Sergeant . . . He takes out a set of photographs—"They'll get four months' suspended."
>
> De Aar. Heat. Dust.
>
> "Three statements after an arrest under the Immorality Act"—Woman Man Sergeant.[26]

This shard of a dramatic idea from 1966 eventually became a one-act play that opened at the Space Theatre in Cape Town on March 27, 1972, starring Fugard himself as "Man" or "Errol" and Yvonne Bryceland as "Woman" or "Frieda."

Statements after an Arrest under the Immorality Act is one of the so-called "Statement Plays," first performed in Cape Town in 1972 and then published together in 1974 as a trilogy along with two other scripts, *Sizwe Bansi Is Dead* and *The Island,* with the latter two collaboratively co-authored by Athol Fugard, John Kani, and Winston Ntshona.[27] What ties the three plays together is the law, for it serves as the fulcrum of each drama: Passbooks—the identity card system so crucial as an apartheid legal apparatus—are at the center *Sizwe Bansi Is Dead;* the ubiquitous incarceration of black lives in such notorious prisons as Robben Island is the focus of *The Island;* and the Immorality Act, the apartheid law banning interracial sex, is the legal construct that drives the action of *Statements after an Arrest under the Immorality Act.* What access can this play, as an aesthetic performance of the law, provide to the interior, subjective experience of racialization at the moment of arrest? And how should we think about the performativity of the apartheid legal prohibitions (nakedness on stage, mixed-race audiences without separate amenities, etc.) that had to be defied in order for this play to be staged in Cape Town in 1972?

Sizwe Bansi Is Dead and *The Island* are still widely performed in repertoire today, two of the most famous South African "struggle" plays. *Statements after an Arrest,* by way of contrast, is a relatively little known play. It is seen as one of Fugard's "most ambitions and difficult works," according to Albert Wertheim.[28] Highly stylized and experimental, the play when first presented in 1972 was an aberration both in terms of Fugard's other dramatic works, as well as the aesthetics of South African theater generally. Perhaps it was because of its radical formal experimentation that South African critics didn't know how to receive the play in 1972.[29] When the show traveled abroad in 1974, London audiences may have had context to understand and appreciate the play's fractured, Brechtian style; however, they did not have an understanding of key context crucial to propelling the play's action: specifically the Immorality Act and Group Areas Act. The play eluded Fugard himself, and in frustration after the 1972 opening, he described the script in his journal as being "at many levels, possibly unavoidably because of the circumstances, the most uncompleted, even careless, work I have yet done on a stage."[30] The version of the play performed in Cape Town in 1972 was quite different from the one performed in London in 1974 and subsequently published, as evidenced by multiple script versions held at Indiana University's Lilly Library. I would have to agree with Fugard's self-reflection that the earlier version performed in Cape Town in 1972 comprised "notes for a play" rather than a well-crafted script. However, by the time the show got through the rehearsal process in London two years later, the underlying structure of the piece emerged with great clarity, as had the play's center of gravity and enunciation of theme. While *Statements after an Arrest* has been seen as a minor work in Fugard's *oeuvre,* I would argue that it is far more sophisticated dramaturgically and thematically than has been previously understood.

Furthermore, *Statements after an Arrest under the Immorality Act* provides a provocative vantage point to consider questions of subjectivity and the racialized psychic life of power. It is also an opportunity to reflect upon the law's intrusion into intimate acts. The play depicts the clandestine relationship of a couple in a small town in the Karoo in the Eastern Cape: a forty-two-year-old unmarried white librarian named Frieda Joubert and a thirty-six-year-old married "coloured" (i.e., mixed-race) man, a school principal, named Errol Philander.[31] They have an affair, one that involves Errol sneaking into the all-white neighborhood under cover of darkness to make love with Frieda on the floor of the library where she works. Together the couple creates a temporary sanctuary, a cherished yet fragile oasis where love and affection across racial lines could flourish.

The play is neatly divided into two parts: before and after an arrest, with each half radically diverging in style. The first part unfolds naturalistically, consistent with Athol Fugard's other works: realistic, quotidian dialogue between lovers conducted in the intimacy of a domestic space. However, halfway through the play, the action is radically interrupted, fractured in form at the very moment when a policeman intrudes. Just before he enters, the lovers have impulsively come together in an embrace:

> [*Against this image of the two lovers, a plain-clothes policeman,* Detective Sergeant J. du Preez, *walks on. He carries a police dossier and notebook. His statement is dictated to the audience.*]
>
> POLICEMAN: Frieda Joubert. Ten, Conradie Street. European. Errol Philander. Bontrug Location. Coloured.
>
> Charge: Immorality Act.[32]

The first thing the sergeant does is hail the lovers by name, address, and race, along with their alleged crime (and, of course, in apartheid South Africa, to hail by home address is to hail by race since the Group Areas Act proscribed where each race could live). The policeman seems to enter the same scene, the same space and time that the lovers had occupied earlier in the play, but he speaks from another time and place, narrating his experience in retrospect as he recites from his police report. He is the first character in the play to break the "fourth wall," to directly address the audience, thereby interpellating spectators into the action, implicitly suggesting their complicity with the action. Have they, like he, been lurking in the shadows, surveilling the lover's clandestine relationship? Or perhaps the audience members, like Frieda's neighbor Mrs. Buys, have been spying on the couple, even summoning the police? Following the police raid of the "private" sanctuary created on the floor of the public library, the three characters—the Sergeant, Errol, and Frieda—all provide statements. Each of these is stylistically distinct, providing a window into how the scene of the arrest performs authority and subjection in ways that expose the uneven racialization of the law.

In his notebooks, Fugard describes *Statements after an Arrest* as being fundamentally about the loneliness and isolation of the lovers—a lonely white librarian living in the arid karoo and a downtrodden coloured teacher struggling to make ends meet and find human fulfillment within a world tightly circumscribed by poverty, lack of water, lack of books, and lack of respect. The play stages, as Fugard sees it, an "encounter between two totally different worlds—both experienced as a 'loneliness'—and the slow, painful building of a 'no-mans' land where they are briefly together."[33] Errol and Frieda's illicit relationship is provoked by desperation about their respective lives. Fugard writes:

> Two people frightened of dying.
>
> One fate inside the room, another outside.
>
> The mistake of moving from being allies, to being lovers.
>
> What is the first incident or remark that provokes Philander to his final bitter sense of self? . . . What moved Philander from the center of his life—where he was living with a hollow sense of self—to its perimeter—because that is how, as a lover, he finally faces Frieda, his back turned on all he really is, and why it cannot work (the relationship), why it progresses into a self-destructive sterility.
>
> Frieda's sexual provocation (not by virtue of anything done deliberately, simply by being what she is) as the relationship develops. The initial affirmation of 'self' in an affair. Love = one of our useless defences against Death.
>
> Two things happen to Philander. He wakes up in the middle of his life, and he falls in love with Frieda.
>
> Frieda = charity, then excitement and admiration, then love.
>
> Fear?[34]

If what propels Frieda and Errol together is a desperate realization that their lives are running out, what drives them apart is the law, the way it structures where each can live, where each can work, what access each has to resources, and who they can sleep with. Their after-hours library "no-man's land," as Fugard calls it, is not actually a "no-man's land" but rather one fully under apartheid sovereignty. But once the law formally intrudes, once the police burst in, their fragile, temporary sanctuary is utterly destroyed.

Frieda and Errol's affair violates South Africa's Immorality Act. This law—first created in 1927 and further amended in 1950, 1957, 1969, 1985, and 1988—prohibited "illicit carnal intercourse between Europeans and natives and other acts in relation thereto."[35] The Act's amendment of 1950 clarified its terms: "'Illicit carnal intercourse' means carnal intercourse other than between husband and wife,"[36] Section 20A of that amendment introduced that the "men at a party" clause, thereby conflating in one law a prohibition on heterosexual interracial with homosexual sex regardless of race, which should lead us to reflect on what it means to think of the legacy of the apartheid state's regulation of both queer and hetero sexuality. The proliferation of amendments to the Immorality Act over many decades was symptomatic of the apartheid state's attempt to control one of the basic human acts: skin on skin, the connection of Self and Other. Jeanne Colleran asserts that of all the many mechanisms of apartheid—including substandard Bantu "education, detentions, imprisonment, unwarranted searches, poverty, unemployment, housing and pass laws"—it was the prohibition against skin contact that went to the "very core of the heart of South African racism."[37] The juridical obsession with interracial sex reflected, in Colleran's words, "a fear of skin contact so immense that it became pathology." While anti-apartheid theater in the 1970s and 1980s bravely took on a whole range of apartheid's many pathologies and obsessions, Athol Fugard's *Statements after an Arrest under the Immorality Act* is unique in its bold focus on interracial sex. In Fugard's notebooks, he writes, "Sex provide[s] the most primitive experience of 'self'—the double aspect/mystery of discovery and loss, both the self and 'the other.'"[38] In his rehearsal notes for the 1974 London production of this play, he says, "Sex is one of the most primitive acts of self-assertion of 'being' in relation to 'another.' 'I fuck, therefore I am.'"[39] So if one cannot fuck—and fuck the partner of one's own desire—does one cease to be? And if one ceases to be, is one still a subject?

Statements before Arrest

The play begins with two lovers in near total darkness on a blanket, naked, on the floor in the stacks of a library. In a languid, tender scene of post-coital intimacy, the lovers converse. Soon the man will have to make a furtive, dangerous, and what he describes as "shameful" trek back home to the township where his family resides. The script's character list identifies the two by gender and race: "A White Woman" and "A Coloured Man." In parentheses each is given greater personalization with a name: "Frieda Joubert" and "Errol Philander."[40] Yet within the script, the dialogue lists them only as "MAN" and "WOMAN," symbolic figures that some have read as alluding to a pre-lapsarian Adam and Eve.[41] The opening stage directions read: "A *man* and a *woman* on a blanket on the floor. Both of them are naked. He is caressing her. Dim light."[42]

At the top of the show, the woman is the first to speak—a monologue about her hair drying in the sun, a somatic narrative describing how the texture of her hair changes as the water evaporates and the smell of shampoo intensifies. She describes a small breeze lifting a floating strand (the first clue about her racial identity). This is a phenomenological narrative outside of time, intensely sensual, spoken from a body in a space of safety and repose. And yet, these are two naked people of different races lying on a blanket in apartheid South Africa. There is nothing safe about that, even behind closed doors in privacy, and certainly not on a theatrical stage. Given the extraordinary legal constraints on South African theater in the 1960s and 1970s, it is remarkable that the playwright imagined the police and censors would allow two people of *any* race to be naked for the duration of this show, much less a mixed-race couple. The apartheid state stranglehold around theater tightened significantly after 1965 when, as Martin Orkin writes, the Group Areas act prohibited "racially mixed casts or audiences" from all public entertainments unless a permit was secured. Orkin has also written about how "theater practitioners were further inhibited by the rapid succession of wide-ranging laws intensifying the process of censorship in the country."[43] Between 1974 and 1981, the censors considered 15,333 plays, and of these 9,819 were "declared undesirable."[44] Beyond the censors, producers, playwrights and actors had to contend with police harassment, surveillance, interruptions of performances, and demands that all theaters have separate amenities for different races. In addition, artists were subject to harassment and personal intimidation with house raids, arrests, and confiscation of personal identity documents. Fugard's *Notebooks* provided evidence of recurrent police raids on the rehearsals and performances by his company, multiple arrests and even imprisonment of actors, and intense censorship and withholding of permits. Notably, the two actors who performed the lovers in the original production were both white: Athol Fugard and Yvonne Bryceland. There is no evidence the police interfered with the first production of *Statements after an Arrest,* though the show seems only to have had a very short run in Cape Town. Yet still, the performance broke the law: its audiences were interracial (but more on that later).

From the beginning of the play, the couple's conversation is intimate, familiar, and affectionate. She pronounces "I love you" in the first few moments of the play. Their repartee moves easily between everyday details and larger philosophical questions as they talk expansively about the origins of the universe, books they've read, daily èncounters on the street, reminiscences about the early days of their relationship and playful imaginative digressions. Despite this calm and ease, threaded throughout the dialogue are recurring tensions. They are afraid of something, of an unidentified "them" outside of their oasis; they are afraid of being seen, of being exposed. There is a wedge in their relationship, and his marriage and family are only part of that wedge. Neither feels fully understood:

> WOMAN: You don't understand.
> MAN: Understand what? There is seeing, and being seen. Which one are you frightened of? Me or you?
> WOMAN: It's not as simple as that!
> MAN: Yes, it is![45]

The first half of the play narrates scenes of world making: discussion of an imaginary house, an imaginary day of spending the money in one's pocket, and expansive meditation on the creation of the world. But these idyllic moments are countered by disturbing stories of dismemberment, especially through animal motifs: She tells a story about two snakes that were caught in a neighbor's backyard while mating and were then killed. "Their . . . pieces kept moving . . . for a long time afterwards."[46] Errol remembers a story about his father bringing him a jackal's foot. "The animal had escaped that way . . . chewed off the foot caught in the trap. . . . I didn't know anything yet about being so frightened of something else, that you would do that to yourself. [*Pause*] That's what we're doing . . . chewing away, chewing away."[47] Disturbing images of dismemberments in the animal world are echoed by other disruptions in the natural world: the town where they live is experiencing a drought, one that threatens the livestock and the people, whose water is being rationed. In discussing the water scarcity, the conflict between Errol and Frieda, which had been, until then, subterranean and diffuse, finally ignites into a direct confrontation:

MAN: The location dam is empty. Little mud left for the goats. They're going to start bringing in for us on Monday. Got to be ready with our buckets at twelve. Two for each house.

WOMAN: Then why won't you let me send you some of mine? The borehole is still very strong. Please! It would be so easy.

MAN: Thanks, but I'll go along with Bontrug.

WOMAN: Don't thank me for something you won't take.

MAN: For the thought, then.

WOMAN: To hell with the thought! I'm not trying to be kind. It's only water, and you need it.

MAN: We all do.

WOMAN: Exactly! So your family must suffer because of your pride?

MAN [*Disbelief*]: Pride?

WOMAN: It sounds like it.

MAN: Pride doesn't use back doors!

WOMAN: Sssh, please!

MAN: Or wait until it's dark. You don't walk the way I do between the location and town with pride.[48]

Errol and Frieda are separated by differences in who does and does not have access to water or the right to enter front versus back doors, or which member of the couple must do the work of transgressing the treacherous territory of segregated living spaces between her address in a white neighborhood and his in the coloured township. Once the submerged conflict arising from their unequal subject positions under apartheid law finally erupts, Errol bursts into one of the longest speeches in the play, a torrent of words, about pride and guilt, and shame and the difference between them, about solidarity with other people in the township who are suffering, who are so internally wrung out they are like "rags." Frieda finally confesses she doesn't understand anything, and Errol retorts, "Then you can't. Don't even try."[49]

In the play's first half, dreams, reading, and learning emerge as an *oasis of possibility* for both characters. Errol recalls counseling a young boy playing in the sand to use his imagination to make a house not by replicating the constraints of his own small township home, but rather being more expansive: "If you're going to dream, give yourself five rooms, man."[50] Errol narrates how getting access to the library and books has opened his world and placed him in a larger universe, despite the severe constraints of the coloured township where he lives. Reading at night in his home, the words on the page remade him as a subject:

> They weren't just words, it wasn't just that I understood that somebody had said . . . I'm expressing myself badly. It's hard to describe. It was almost like having a . . . No! . . . it was a 'comprehension'—*ja,* of life and time . . . and there in the middle of it . . . at that precise moment . . . in Bontrug, was me. Being me, just being me there in that little room was . . . [*choosing his words carefully*] . . . the most exciting thing that had ever happened to me. I wanted that moment to last forever! It was so intense it almost hurt. I couldn't sit still."[51]

Even as spoken words elude Errol in his attempt to express his inner transformation, it is clear that the discovery of the library has given him access to a new self, a change in subjectivity as radical as the impact of his budding love and relationship with Frieda. Through books, to which she has given him access (he is not part of the public given access to this "public" library), he gains a new sense of autonomy, personhood, self-possession—a subjectivity full of excitement, a sense of optimistic possibility. "I read, therefore I am." He lives also for Frieda, for the world of love to which she has opened him. But their relation is always fraught, undercut by her sense of entitlement to *her* water, her role as the one who initiates their sexual relationship, unlocks the door to *her* space. To access everything in this new world—the books and Frieda—he must turn his back on his own family and their life in the township.

Both Frieda and Errol profess love at different moments in the play. Clearly for both of them, the affair is a sanctuary to the deprivations each faces in their respective environments—whether material, emotional, or intellectual. Yet even love cannot shield them from the social distortions of race. Overt acknowledgment of race happens only once in the first half of the play, just before the policeman burst in and arrests them. Errol has just informed Frieda that he won't leave his wife, and she responds:

> WOMAN: Go home. Take your conscience and your guilt and go back to Bontrug and look after your family. I've also got problems. I can't add your adultery to them. If you haven't got the courage to say No . . . to anybody . . . to me or her . . . I'll do it for you. Go home.
>
> MAN [*viciously*]: It would be better if I waited until it's dark . . . remember! [*Pause*] My adultery? And yours? *Ja.* Yours! If that's true of me because of you and my wife, then just as much for you because of me and your white skin. Maybe you are married to that the way I am to Bontrug.[52]

He insists that their respective fidelities to race (his to the coloured township where the Group Areas act prescribes that he live, hers to her white skin) are paramount over any fidelities based on choice or affection.[53]

Depending upon how designers interpret the script's lighting directions, the stage may be lit so darkly in the first scene, before the arrest, that the racial difference between the characters would be visually imperceptible to the audience for the first half of the play. Without a visual cue, the inequality in their social status emerges only gradually, elliptically through dialogue, or sonically through voice and accent. Race is not mentioned explicitly until well into the first scene. *Statements after an Arrest*'s bifurcated structure is also a sensorially divided one: the first half is about sound, the second half about seeing and being seen. The intrusion of the law, which happens in the middle of the play, brings exposure, light, and a sequence of six still photographic images—suggesting evidence to be used later in court. These frozen stop-action, two-dimensional images stand in contrast with the actors' continuous, embodied, three-dimensional live action before the audience.

After the Arrest

The police invasion incites a profound and thorough break in the play's style, character, tone, rhythm, and psychological representation. It is a violent disruption, though performed without violence. The Sergeant speaks initially in truncated partial sentences describing those he's arresting: "Been living here for six years." "Born here." As the representative and face of the law, he also ventriloquizes other voices: he recites a statement given by a neighbor, Mrs. Buys, who had been suspicious about the comings and goings of Errol to the back door of Frieda's library. He gives a cold and affectless speech that culminates in a description of the moment of the raid: "I saw Joubert and Philander lying side by side on a blanket on the floor. She was naked and he appeared to be wearing a vest. Sergeant Smitt started to take photographs."[54] Following this are the first of six surrealistic sequences with flashing lights and the wielding of torches (flashlights). The blinding exposures, meant to evoke camera flashes, pin the accused couple against the wall, startle them in their nakedness as they scurry about for blankets and clothing items to shield their vulnerability. Fugard had been inspired to write the play based upon newspaper stories about police raids on mixed-race couples' intimacy, and the role of photography in those raids. In his notebooks he wrote, "The

Immorality Act—at one level this country's one and unique contribution to the world of pornography. A guilt-ridden inversion of the celebration of the erect penis and moist vagina. . . . The camera flashes short-circuit the experience. . . . The point of view changes."[55] Fugard sees these staged photographic stills as

> the central image in their story—those six terrible photographs of Joubert and Philander scrambling around in the dark; twenty seconds of Hell which start with them together and end with them irrevocably apart; the twenty seconds that it takes to pass from an experience of life to an intimation of death. Those photographs were, and remain for me, the essence of the experience I wanted to explore. As I said repeatedly to Y. in Cape Town, an then again here [in London], the experience we ask an audience to share with us must be an exploration of the subtext to those photographs, and six scenes must in a sense be "Captions."[56]

Through the intrusion of the police and their flashes of light, Errol and Frieda are torn asunder; they become isolated individuals. The law becomes at times a voice, a light, a flash that intrudes on the subject and fixes both Frieda and Errol in preconceived assumptions, interpellations with which they must engage, dispute, concede, or contest. But there is no place to hide. The self is thoroughly interpellated by a state that forbids their sexuality and intimacy across racial lines. The intrusion of the camera creates a cinematic and Brechtian element in this play, freezing the action and precipitating a different point of identification for the audience.

There is no place to hide. Errol and Frieda scramble around. The torches (or flash lights) are "relentless, but we never see anything of the men behind them."[57] The stage directions report: "These 'flash-sequences' are nightmare excursions into the split second of exposure and must be approached as 'sub-text' rather than 'reality.'"[58] At first the man tries to speak, but his words fracture with desperation:

> MAN [*terrified. Covering his genitals with his trousers he talks desperately to the torch shining on him.]:* Look . . . look—before you make up your mind let me tell you something . . . I'm . . . I'm Principal . . . I . . . I won't do it again . . . I'm frightened. *Ja,* I'm frightened.[59]

He asserts the legitimacy of his job and social role (school principal), assures he won't "do it" again (commit adultery across racial lines), and then he simply confesses his present fright. As he continues to try to get his pants on without exposing himself, the whole operation becomes a "nightmare." The woman then comes forward, trying to shield the man with a blanket. The torches follow her as she speaks. Her response is rambling and almost incoherent, talking about biscuits and having tea. Her speech is fractured but not panicked. She does not feel compelled to assert her credentials or promise not to "do it" again. Instead her monologue becomes almost like a therapy session. She speaks of unhappiness, of being hurt, of feeling "sorry" for him. This is an accused who doesn't feel the need to defend herself but rather wants to rationalize her behavior, to explain it. Her monologue soon begins to disclose far too much, becoming almost an erotic narrative: "We were whispering. Whispering makes you sweat. He loosened his tie and said. . . ."[60] The stage directions say that the man realizes this disclosure must stop, that he must "correct, this vein of intimate confession." The stakes of such admissions are entirely different for him, as a coloured man; Frieda is clueless about that inequality. He tries to distract her from her overdisclosure, and his tactic is to play act the role of the deferential black supplicant pleading with a white woman for water. His performance desperately escalates and intensifies, eventually becoming what the stage directions describe as "a grotesque parody of the servile, cringing 'Coloured,'" a bowing and scraping servitude haunted by minstrel "darkey" stereotypes.[61] His sentences become staccato fragments: "Dam's empty. Little mud left. For the goats." He calls her "Miss Frieda" and gradually degenerates into begging. However, Frieda is completely unable to recognize or acknowledge Errol's role-playing. She doesn't recognize *what* this performance is, much less *why* he is doing it. She rejects his shift in character, seems irritated by it, and when he doesn't obey her order to stop, she becomes hysterical.

Here, the play's action is once again interrupted by a camera flash sequence, an interlude that inaugurates yet another attempt to tell what happened, another iteration of "statements" after the arrest. This one is told contrapuntally, with the two lovers speaking, overlapping, conveying more about the intersubjective discoveries of their unfolding relationship, how they shared the excitement of books and learning, found companionship through intellectual communion. They confess to a shared excitement about shared *learning* rather than shared sex. Their mutual confession pauses at one moment, abruptly, waiting for a response—from the sergeant? from the audience? The spectators are interpellated into *Statements after an Arrest* as Frieda and Errol seem to acknowledge the audience directly for the first time. There is an awkward pause. In this caesura, the playwright conveys that the intensity of the lovers' fear of their interrogators is equal, if not greater, to the intensity of their desire for each other. Implicitly the play performs a question: What is the audience's role in this scene? Are they witnesses? Spies? Conspirators?

We next learn about the intimate moments when Frieda and Errol's sexual relationship first began—a relationship that she had to initiate, given the enormous stakes for Errol if he had read her amorous signals incorrectly. To her credit, Frieda is very clear on her role initiating the love affair, and without this confession, Errol's fate at the hands of the law would surely have become much worse. The action is once again cut through with camera flashes, this time trapping the woman. She seems to be unaware of the flashlights, unashamed of her nakedness, and she rather launches into a private and self-absorbed reverie: "Ugly feet. The soles have got hard patches. My legs are bandy. Good calf muscles . . . probably got them riding to school on my bicycle up a very steep hill each day. Skin around my knees is just starting to get slack. I enjoy making the muscles in my thighs move. Hair is very mousy."[62] Like the opening monologue of the play about her drying hair in the sun, Frieda's speech conveys an embodied experience, intimately narrating what it means to be inside her body, a gendered body—one that is accustomed to being viewed. But her experience of surveillance is wholly unlike that of the coloured man. She is being appraised for beauty, not guilt; conformity to an ideal, not a negative stereotype. She may be concerned about her hair, or "ashamed" of her hands, and her skin may look "very old." But nevertheless, she says, "I think there is a whole lot of me in my hands somehow," a line in stark contrast with how Errol comes to perceive his own hands later in this scene.[63] Her internalization of the interpellative process is revealed in dialogue: she becomes both the interrogator asking questions and the one answering them. She asks herself about her own complicity, her guilt, and the possibility of coercion or shame. Her answers to her own questions are clipped, monosyllabic, until finally she begins to narrate the scene of seduction. For her, there is no fear in this statement of confession. She is a subject not in *subjection* but in *possession* of her body, her story, her self, and she is able to confess defiantly, even proudly: "So . . . so then . . . yes. . . . So then then we made love."[64]

Errol's trajectory through the fractured interpellative process of the arrest rides a course that is entirely different from Frieda's. Near the end of the play the policeman once again speaks, reciting a statement and showing "Exhibit A" and "Exhibit B," which are presumably the photographs that are being captured and staged before our very eyes with all the camera flashes. He tells us that at the actual moment of arrest, Frieda spoke but a few choice words: "I am not ashamed of myself," which she said she would repeat to anyone. She then apologized to Philander. But "Philander said nothing."[65] She is defiant, in possession of herself, fully present in her body, even as she has internalized the questions of her interrogator.

Errol, however, becomes increasingly desperate. He first asserts his good character, then performs the role of the bowing and scraping subservient. He gets one brief period in the interrogation where he can speak about how much it meant for him to go the library "and use the encyclopedias, and read."[66] What is so remarkable about the final segment of Fugard's play is that Errol becomes a person before the law by becoming *not* a person at all. This is a drama of *unbecoming*. His dissolution throughout the scene is not even seen by his lover, so caught up is she in her own narcissistic reverie. Her final speech narrates what it means to lose him, how she must move autonomously now. "I must be my hands again, my eyes, my ears . . . all of me but now, without you. All of me that found you must now lose you."[67] The outcome of the arrest for her is that she must shed herself of him, wash his sweat from her body, his memory from her mind. By way of contrast, the outcome of the arrest for Errol is dismemberment, annihilation. Whereas the arrest prompts her to take possession of herself and rid herself of the Other, for him the arrest is a process of ridding himself of his very being:

> Now I must understand it.
> If they take away your eyes you can't see.
> If they take away your tongue you can't taste.
> If they take away your hands you can't feel.
> If they take away your nose you can't smell.
> If they take away your ears you can't hear.
> I can see.
> I can taste.
> I can feel.
> I can smell.
> I can hear.
> [*Pause.*]
> I can't love.[68]

This poetic sequence repeats again, rehearses what it would mean if "they" take away your legs, arms, and head. He can still walk, work, and think, but he cannot love. His journey would seem to contradict Dolar's hypothesis that perhaps the interior register of love is beyond interpellation.[69] Next are the appetites: eating, drinking, and sleeping. Stripped of these, what is he? Here he shifts from saying he *can't* love to an assertion that he *won't* love. The speech compresses, narrows, and condenses. Broken, wounded language conveys his undoing as he is reduced to bare life, and even less than the bare life theorized by Agamben: he becomes a subject without a body, soul, or name:

An arm without a hand.
A leg without a foot.
A head without a body.
A man without name.[70]

Who is this force—"they"—that takes limbs and body parts and locks one away? The adversary is unnamed. Gradually "they" becomes "God," a force of interpellation even greater than the law:

So, I tell God I don't smoke and I don't drink and I know the price of bread. But he says it makes no difference and that he wants back what is left. And then I start to give him the other parts. I give him my feet and my legs, I give him my head and body, I give him my arms, until at last there is nothing left, just my hands and they are empty. But he takes them back too. And then there is only the emptiness left. But he doesn't want that. Because it's me. It's all that is left of me.
They arrest it all the same.[71]

Errol's statements after the arrest divest him of everything. The law makes him less than human, less than animal, less than a sentient being. Even when reduced to a dismembered, disembodied emptiness, he still does not possess his own "emptiness" for "they" arrest his emptiness all the same.[72]

Errol's monologue presciently prefigures Judith Butler's speculations about the possibility of agency for the slave through desubjectivization. Butler concludes her meditation on interpellation in *The Psychic Life of Power* by saying:

In a Nietzchean vein, such a slave morality may be predicated upon the sober calculation that it is better to "be" enslaved in such a way than not to "be" at all. But the terms that constrain the option to being versus no being "call for" another kind of response. Under what conditions does a law monopolize the

> terms of existence in so thorough a way? Or is this a theological fantasy of the law? Is there a possibility of being elsewhere or otherwise, without denying our complicity in the law that we oppose? Such possibility would require a different kind of turn, one that, enabled by the law, turns away from the law, resisting its lure of identity, an agency that outruns and counters the conditions of its emergence. Such a turn demands a willingness *not* to be—a critical desubjectivation—in order to expose the law as less powerful than it seems. What forms might linguistic survival take in this desubjectivized domain? How would one know one's existence?[73]

Errol's unbecoming performs the strategic calculation that it is better not to "be" at all than to "be" a coloured man arrested under the Immorality Act in apartheid South Africa.

Unseen and Unbecoming

Statements after an Arrest under the Immorality Act dramatizes the vastly different impact that the law's racialized interpellation has on each character. And yet it does not show us *how* that inequality is created, beyond the Sergeant's initial hailing of each suspect by race at the very moment of the arrest. Just as we never see the men behind the cameras and flashlights, we never see law enforcement in this play actually arresting anyone or conducting an interrogation. Nor do we see how apartheid's racialized law impacts these two suspects, one white, the other coloured. The psychic life of power for the oppressor, the Sergeant, also remains unseen. The playwright withholds this information. Why? The play raises the question of what is unseen. By withholding mimetic representation, the play may provide its most potent representation of all.

Elizabeth Maddock Dillon, in her book *New World Drama: The Performative Commons in the Atlantic World, 1649–1849*, asserts that "the signifying economy of the theater operates in two registers: one that is *ontic* (thingly, material, resolutely present) and one that is *mimetic* (referential, immaterial, gesturing toward a scene located elsewhere").[74] Here she is amplifying on the pathbreaking work of theorist Bert O. States, who famously wrote, "There is a sense in which signs [in the theater] . . . achieve their vitality . . . not simply by signifying the world but by being of it."[75] The simultaneity of the mimetic and ontic is a defining quality of the theater, one that distinguishes it from, say, novels. Novels have received a far greater attention in recent scholarship on questions of human rights, law, and the literary. I am thinking here in particular of the work of Joseph Slaughter and Elizabeth S. Anker, both of whom focus on human rights issues in relation to the novel.[76] How does the genre of theater compare with the novel in relationship to law and human rights? As a genre, theater (as opposed to "drama," meaning only the script) "has the body" (*habeus corpus*). What does this body do? What does it reveal? What does it withhold? How does it function in both ontic and mimetic ways simultaneously, and what are the consequences of this fundamental instability between these two dimensions? How and what does theater's ontic + mimetic perform?

Fugard's *Statements after an Arrest* not only signifies a violation of the law through the couple's mix-race affair; the performance of the play actually *was* a defiance of the law. Theater's potency in apartheid South Africa was equaled by its vulnerability—a vulnerability that surely would have been felt as much by the audience at the opening of *Statements after an Arrest* as by the actors and producers. The Space, the Cape Town theater where *Statements* premiered in 1972, was a new fringe theater staging plays to mixed-race audiences in defiance of myriad prohibitions, pervasive censorship, and relentless police surveillance, raids, and harassment. In fact, *Statements* was the Space Theatre's first production. The Space can be seen as a "white" institution inasmuch as white liberals funded it and dominated its artistic leadership. However, the founders deliberately decided to admit all races, and in this—its assembly of persons normally segregated, its fostering of forbidden intimacies across colour lines—the theater functioned as potent ontic instantiation of the transgressions mimetically represented by the characters Frieda and Errol in *Statements after an Arrest*. From its inception, the Space violated the law. According to the Separate Amenities Act of 1955 and also Proclamation R26 of 1965, both racially mixed audiences and racially mixed casts were prohibited in public entertainments without a permit.[77] In the unlikely event that a permit for mixed-race audiences was issued, then a theater had to have separate amenities for each race: separate entrances, seats, and restrooms. Furthermore, apartheid law stipulated that event spaces used by one race could not then be used by another. The first performance of *Statements after an Arrest* was cast with all-white actors, with the playwright himself playing the role of the coloured man, Errol Philander. So on the casting front, the producers were legally in the clear. However, the audience was racially mixed, and this was a calculated gamble. As founder of the Space, Brian Astbury recalls:

> Then during the run [of *Statements*] our final problem arose. Those that—in this country—shouldn't have been allowed entrance came to buy tickets.

> And we had, at the beginning, determined that if we were going to have to turn people away we were going to have to be forced to do so by the full and visible weight of the law. So from the start, everybody was allowed in. And we waited for the law to stop us.[78]

From its premier, *Statements after an Arrest* provoked the possibility that its title would become predictive—that the audience itself might end up giving statements after *their own* arrests for being in the theater that night. In the meantime, the theater waited—for the law in the form of the police or Special Branch to show up, for citations to be issued, for actual arrests of actors and spectators to be effected. Theater was a space for not just imagining but for doing what the law disallowed. Like the library after hours for Frieda and Errol, the Space Theatre was for many an oasis of possibility for imagining that which the law forbid; but it was nevertheless entirely subject to the law, which could intrude, overrule, and unmake things at any moment.

When policemen as characters burst into a dimly lit scene of love in *Statements after an Arrest* wielding cameras and blinding flashlights, law enforcement announced itself mimetically as light, exposure, a blinding glare. The police violently intrude on an intimate, domestic space, and in doing so they completely disrupt the artificial no-man's-land that Errol and Frieda have created. The police expose this affair as being fully subject to apartheid law. At the same time this mimetic reality within the play was paralleled, even more potently, by the ontic reality of the Space Theatre itself. Just as Errol and Frieda's were fully aware that their clandestine affair was never "outside" the law, South Africa theater audiences knew very well they risked arrest by attending this show, and this may well have added drama and anxiety to the moment of the police raid within the script. Was this a mimetic or ontic raid? There was likely to be confusion.

From the very beginning of the play, Frieda and Errol are spooked and anxious, despite their surface calm and equanimity. They are worried about exposure, about discovery, about who might be lighting a match that suddenly flares in the darkness. The two have created a bubble where a coloured man and a white woman can lie naked on a blanket in a tender embrace of love, but they know this private space is a play world that can be destroyed in an instant. Not unlike the imaginary house made of sand that Errol reports on early in the play when he describes a child at play, his relationship with Frieda is an imaginary house of sand. Yet, still, Errol's affair—like the coaching he gives the child—is expansive. ("If you're going to dream, give yourself five rooms, man," he had told the playing child.)[79] In Frieda, he has given himself the equivalent of "five rooms." Errol knows that fantasies and works of imagination are performative: they create *spaces of possibility*, potentialities for new dispensations, experiences of how things could be otherwise. So too did the Space Theatre. Like Errol and Frieda, Cape Town's Space Theatre attempted to create a protected space that was a "no-man's land" at law's edge in apartheid South Africa—a space where many races could assemble together, be intimate with one another, bare their souls, sit together in a mixed-race audience sharing hope that such fraternity could be unmolested by the police. The Space was a place where one could hold—at least for an hour or two—the fantasy of being a subject not in complete subjection to apartheid law. To attend or not to attend the theater—that was a choice, an action of legal significance that the audience had to make. In light of the ontological reality of naked players and a mixed-race audience in their own act of infidelity to the state, the play and its production were together and separately acts of immorality. The simultaneity of the mimetic and ontic realms in theater means that, in the case of this play, immorality *acted:* the live performance of the play *did something* with words, and bodies, and time, and space, and light and darkness.

South African Minister of Justice Dullah once described apartheid as a dual state whereby whites enjoyed parliamentary democracy and blacks lived under dictatorship. This line of reasoning has been taken up at length by scholar Jens Meierhenrich.[80] The country's "schizophrenic institutional structure," in Meierhenrich's words, created conditions whereby contrasting legal norms for whites and nonwhites had to be repeatedly instantiated, enacted, made performatively manifest. Especially in the wake of the Sharpeville massacre in 1960, the law became at once unstable and increasingly rigid, enforced in capricious ways through repeated declarations of states of emergency. One saw the suspension of normal legal procedures through states of exception, the authorization of ever-escalating periods of detention without trial, the proliferation of bannings and a whole host of other legal intrusions into daily life. The condition of the law in this period of apartheid South Africa was inherently unstable and dualistic. It was this very instability that created the potential for performative moments of intervention and defiance.

In terms of dramatic action, the law as depicted in *Statements* appears to treat Errol and Frieda equally. Other than hailing them by their race, the arresting officer doesn't single out either Frieda or Errol, or treat them in different ways—at least that we *see.* We don't see the actual arrest; it is only narrated. We don't see the actual interrogation, but only snippets of it, particularly as the interrogator's voice is internalized by Frieda. In earlier early versions of the play—including the version performed in Cape Town in 1972—Fugard gave the police a far more prominent role. The play previously had not just one but two policemen, both introduced from the very beginning of the play rather than only entering halfway through. In this early version of the play, the police were as central as characters as Errol and Frieda became in the final version. What Fugard shows us in the revised script is rather how the two accused have internalized the stakes of this arrest in such radically different ways. Clarity about this focus emerged during the London rehearsals in 1974—when actor Ben Kingsley played Errol and Yvonne Bryceland, Fugard's longtime South African collaborator, played Frieda. Here Fugard discovered the play's final form. We see in revisions a telescoping of focus so that Frieda and Errol are clearly the center of the play—their relationship, subjectivity, intersubjectivity, and thwarted love.[81] Errol's narrative of his desubjectivization after his arrest becomes the play's true center of gravity. The choice to minimize representation of law enforcement intensified, implicitly, a questioning of the audience. Do the spectators become, in effect, aligned with the unseen wielders of the flashlights and cameras, the intruders on an act of intimacy, the interrogators, the judges to whom the two accused address their statements?

Fugard's notebooks reveal that he was most interested in the couple: their relationship, their interior lives, their loneliness, their thwarted attempt to connect with an Other, and the way a racist set of laws shape their individual characters and fracture their relationship. He dramatizes the police as an inciting incident, which is not to say that Fugard failed to grasp the perversion and gross immorality of the Immorality Act itself. If Fugard had been interested in focusing more on the police, *Statements* would most likely have been banned. As Martin Orkin reminds us, apartheid legislation forbade "any real discussion or representation of police and prison conditions in South Africa."[82] This is likely why one never sees the guards or prison wardens Fugard's play *The Island*.

Instead, Fugard casts a light on Frieda and Errol. What does this light reveal? We see that Frieda stands before the law as a full person. She is defiant, confessional, introspective, free to disclose. For Errol, the arrest instigates a rapid devolution into panic, stereotype, and disintegration of self that reduces him to bare life, and even less—a subject with no body, no limbs, no soul, whose only possession is his own of emptiness, and even that—that emptiness—can be incarcerated. Errol and Frieda begin the play with the appearance of Edenic purity and equality. Once caught in their act of love, there is a dual state of play. For her the way forward is that "all of me that found you must now lose you"; for him the way forward has nothing to do with dependence, or confession, or guilt, or even shame. For him, there is no place from which to speak, no role in which to be. His only possible strategy is a dissolution of his very being. He is reduced to pure will.

This is a devastating conclusion to a play that begins with such tender intimacy, a love story that began with nakedness, honest intimacy in a darkened room, a tender embrace. The intrusion of the policeman, his dictation, as well as the photographs, camera flashes, and flashlights wielded by unseen forces representing the law, violently annihilate a precarious bond. In the dual state, fragile moments of tenderness and equanimity across racial lines could exist, but law's intrusion (magnified in the play's bifurcated structure and style) violently tears the two apart. Performatively, the law strips Frieda of entanglement with the racial Other. She becomes again a solo being. Performatively, the law strips Errol of his very being. In all of this, the audience is ambiguously cast as witness, spy, accomplice interrogator, or fellow potential arrestees.

Two key ideas animated Fugard's revisions of this manuscript after the play opened in 1972. First he said, "I want *their* [the couple's] story to contain the policeman's statement, rather than have the *policeman's* statement contain their story."[83] He also was exploring having the couple's fear and apology and explanation to the audience be "equal, if not greater, to their relationship to each other."[84] Fugard stages a reframing of the performative elements of interpellation during arrest. Rather than the law hailing the subject, the subjects (Frieda and Errol) hail the law through the "statement" of the play itself. Fugard wants *their* story to contain the policeman's statement, rather than vice versa. This is a radical reframing—certainly in the context of apartheid South Africa where the law so routinely, pervasively, and insidiously subjected people's lives to its force. Fugard also wanted the play to reframe the complicity and intersubjectivity of the lover's relationship with each other. Their intimacy and infidelity becomes, in the course of the play, matched by the bond between audience and the two lovers, a bond both of intimacy and infidelity, as well as legal vulnerability. For the audience, this vulnerability is more real than anything represented on stage. They were hailed by the performance at the Space, and by attending, they broke the law.

Conclusion: Laws of Probability

While the three "Statement" plays (*Sizwe Bansi Is Dead, The Island,* and *Statements after an Arrest under the Immorality Act*) are not generally performed as a trilogy, their publication together in one book suggests a trilogy. These plays *are* statements—uttered performances at law's edge between the human and the inhumane, aesthetic representations of moments of legal interpellation that give insight into legal habitus, the interiority of the psychic life of power, and the capacity of dreams, relationships, and imagination to carve out finite worlds of respite where agency is envisioned, and if not felicitously performed, at least *rehearsed*. Given that all three scripts were composed and premiered in a climate of intense censorship where the theater was routinely subjected to editorial interference, bannings, surveillance by spies, raids by the Special Branch, and arrests of playwrights and actors, the "Statement" trilogy provides a provocative point of entry for thinking about the way in which one becomes—and *unbecomes*—a subject before the law, and how the law and race were tightly imbricated in apartheid South Africa.

The most searing image of this play is the final monologue by Errol, after his arrest. Through extraordinary and poetically distilled language, we witness an implosion of self. He tells of the disintegration his body, the loss of limbs, the erasure of his entire material realty, his corporeal being. Yet all the while, Errol nevertheless asserts his will. Even when his limbs and all his body parts have been seized, when he is nothing but emptiness, and even then when that emptiness is arrested, he still says:

> Now I'm here.
> There is nothing here.
> They can't interfere with God any more.[85]

In these final moments, Errol's speech echoes, unwittingly, ideas of theorists who have wrestled with the paradoxes of interpellation. Does the divine provide a space outside interpellation? Does love or desire offer a sanctuary outside interpellation? In Errol's narrative we see several "turns," harkening back to Althusser's interpellation scene, the policeman's hail: Errol turns away from Frieda his lover, and we know that in turning *to* her previously, he had implicitly turned away from the rest of his life: his wife, family, and his community in the coloured township. Caught between these worlds at the moment of his arrest, Errol turns yet again, this time away from Frieda, away from his family, and away from the law. His refuge is to become an *unbecoming* subject, a consciousness without flesh, a will without materiality. He says, "Now I'm here" and, at the same time, "There is nothing here." Errol's self-negation dramatizes a subject refusing interpellation within a racist state, an unbecoming, an attempt to become not a subject at all.

Sara Ahmed in *Willful Subjects* argues, "To queer the will is to show how the will has already been given a queer potential. . . . Willfulness might be a conversion point: How a potential is converted into a threat."[86] She also asserts, "Perhaps self-certainty is not how the will becomes what is given to a subject, but how a subject can become itself: 'I have a will' understood not only as a sign of existence, 'I will *therefore* I am' but as an impulse to existence: 'I will *then* I am.'"[87] Errol is a willful subject whose unbecoming performs rather "I am *not*—and yet still, *I will*." His disintegration can hardly be seen as liberation—this is a reduction of self, a distillation to a pure essence of will, devoid of body. However, we may nevertheless read in his final monologue an insistence on another way of being, one that preserves something of the epiphanies he experienced through his affair, through reading books, through using his imagination, through creating a no-man's land sanctuary in a darkened room on a library floor with a lover of his own choice, even if that choice destroys his life. Might Errol eventually, after the action of this play concludes, become something else altogether? He asserts, if not *agency*, then at least a *willfulness*, first through a becoming tied to sexuality, intimacy, and self-discovery, and then, when his becoming is arrested, literally stopped mid-stream by the invasion of apartheid law, his unbecoming does contain the seeds of something else, something not yet seen, known or understood, where "they" can no longer interfere. Errol's will at the end of *Statements* is all he has; it's all he is. Pushed, conscripted, reduced, annihilated, in a corner that is a space of non-being, his will lives on, makes a claim to agency beyond all sovereign forces. His will persists as a dematerialized essence that continues to exert a performative force after all else is gone.

Willfulness also drove the theater artists who ran the Space Theatre on Long Street in Cape Town, the venue that staged as its first production *Statements after an Arrest under the Immorality Act* in March 1972. The theater's ontic reality provided a mimetic space not only to represent the world of apartheid South Africa otherwise, but to hail and interpellate its apartheid-era audience into an aspired nonracist future. The theater operated in defiance of apartheid laws about segregation and separate amenities; it danced around prohibitions about freedom of assembly across racial lines; it willfully asserted freedom of expression.

In a one-man show entitled *No Space on Long Street* retrospectively celebrating in 1997 the twenty-fifth anniversary of the founding of the Space, actor, comedian, and Space founding veteran Pieter-Dirk Uys recalled the opening of the Space Theatre in 1972 (Uys served as one of the theater's core innovators and artists during its ten-year existence):

> The Space / Die Ruimte opened round the 27th march 1972 with a new play by Athol Fugard: *Statements after an arrest under the Immorality Act.*
> The Space's colours were nailed to the mast.
> The impossible was probable.
> It was the beginning of freedom of expression in the theatre. . . .
> The Space became the conscience of a generation.[88]

There was much about the Space that was improbable: its fiscal viability, its production timelines, its lack of technical support, stable staffing, finalized scripts, adequate electricity, proper plumbing, or a living wage for its artists. Disruptions by security police and the censors were so pervasive and capricious the law almost became a kind of co-producing agent, inserting unpredictable provocations around which the theater producers and artists constantly improvised. As Uys recalls in *No Space on Long Street:*

> We did a season of my plays: *Selle Ou Storie*—they banned the script but you could see the play; *Karnaval*—they banned the play but you could read the script; and *God's Forgotten* the play that should have been banned but wasn't. The pressures of three productions, no money, censorship and fear, exhaustion and the silly feeling of not being loved.[89]

Of course, the apartheid state had full power and capacity to shut down the theater entirely at any time. But the censors and Security Police did not wish to make The Space into a political martyr. Their strategy seems to have been rather to tire the artists out, to undermine them slowly with a kind of "slow censorship," a bureaucratic bloodletting as a durational endurance act. As one censor says in Uys's 1997 retrospective play: "We will just ban you for 'obscenity' and 'blasphemy" and bankrupt you! We know how to do our job."[90] Slow oppression undermined the theater through exhaustion rather than outright extermination. John Vorster, the South African prime minister, tells Elsabe, a censor who routinely surveils the Space Theatre and is a key character in Uys's *No Space on Long Street:* "You see, Elsabe, we in power are also artists in what we do."[91]

Despite all that was improbable about the Space, the artists went forth making theater and breaking apartheid laws for ten years. The state, too, played its part—banning, raiding, spying, infiltrating, arresting, and undermining revenue streams. Raids were the most overt insertions of the law, and, just like the raid on Errol and Frieda in *Statements,* raids on the Space Theatre were usually prompted by a nosy neighbor. Elsabe in Uys's play *No Space on Long Street* recalls:

> It was during the performance of Tennessee Williams's *Glass Menagerie.* One of my favourite plays. A wonderful production by Bill Tanner. I could've killed them! With Yvonne Bryceland at her most moving moment, suddenly like the Gestapo, these barbarians storm in. And why? Because some fool phoned them that there are blacks in the theatre and it is against the law![92]

The police burst into the Space Theatre's production of *Glass Menagerie,* just as the police burst in on Errol and Frieda in *Statements:* "The lights went on, and the magic was gone," Elsabe recalls.[93] Yet her own subject position was complicated: the character Elsabe in *No Space on Long Street* was actually a "prominent member" of the Censor board. It was her duty to attend the Space Theatre on a regular basis. What the state may not have realized, she confesses, is that they had put a "chocoholic in charge of a chocolate factory."[94] She loved and supported much of what the Space was doing. Theater is a volatile, capricious, and unpredictable zone: in performing some roles we may un-become them. The chief censor of the Space becomes one of its biggest fans. Her objection to the police interrupting the production of *Glass Menagerie* was at core a jurisdictional question—who has the authority to make such decisions, the police or the censors? Whose opinion about what infractions are tolerable and which are intolerable will prevail? The law has many agents with many different opinions.

The Space's willful defiance and improbable tenacity provided an incubation space for at least some people in South Africa to perform, to enact, to rehearse, and to "make belief" through the "make believe." Like Errol and Frieda, the Space artists created a temporary sanctuary, a cherished yet fragile oasis where love and affection across racial lines could flourish. Such a space, however vulnerable, was nevertheless potent. In this space alternate realities came to appear not just *possible* but *probable.* Uys recalled in 1997:

> Twenty-five years ago. Before sanctions, before the Mandela t-shirts, before it was fashionable and right to be anti-apartheid, there was a dream that came true. It was called The Space Theatre and it started its journey in a sprawling warehouse off Long Street, between Bloem and Buiten. It was the place where the alphabet of South African Theatre was reinvented. It was poor and yet gave great riches to the community. It was one of the beginnings of freedom of expression. It was the end of apartheid in the arts.[95]

Theater is a form that requires for its very existence freedom of assembly, freedom of expression, and the presence of the body. As such, theaters like the Space that pitch up at law's edge—that must defy the law in order to exist—have capacity to incubate potential futures, contingent realities that not only make visible the law's reach, but rehearse and reveal the law's limits. As such, theater has capacity to perform something else—something not yet seen, known, or understood.

NOTES

My sincere thanks to the superb staff at Indiana University's Lilly Library, who facilitated access to Athol Fugard's archives. I am grateful also to Stanford doctoral student Kellen Hoxworth, who conducted research on my behalf at the National English Literary Museum in Grahamstown, South Africa. The University of California, Berkeley, provided generous funding through a Humanities Research Fellowship. Previous versions of this chapter were presented at Amherst College's Department of Law, Jurisprudence, and Social Thought, Northwestern University's Interdisciplinary Program in Theatre and Drama, Simon Fraser University's Institute of Performance Studies, the Royal Holloway University of London's conference "Sequins, Self & Struggle: Performance, Pageants and Publics in South Africa" Symposium, and the "Conflux" Symposium in the Department of Theater, Dance and Performance Studies at UC Berkeley. I am indebted to colleagues, including this book's editors and anonymous readers, who have provided such thoughtful and provocative feedback. All remaining shortcomings of the essay are entirely my own.

1. Julie Stone Peters, "Law, Literature, and the Vanishing Real: On the Future of an Interdisciplinary Illusion," *PMLA* 120, no. 2 (2005): 442–53, at 451.

2. See Dennis Kezar's introduction to his edited volume *Solon and Thespis: Law and Theater in the English Renaissance* (Notre Dame: University of Notre Dame Press, 2007), 1–16.

3. Peters, "Law, Literature" and also "Legal Performance Good and Bad," *Law, Culture and the Humanities* 4 (2008): 179–200, at 181.

4. Kezar, *Solon and Thespis*, 2–3.

5. Henning Grunwald, "Justice as 'Performance'? The Historiography of Legal Procedure and Political Criminal Justice in Weimar Germany," *InterDisciplines* 2 (2012): 46–78, at 46.

6. Peters, "Law, Literature" and "Legal Performance Good and Bad." For a further elaboration of the questions of law and performance into human rights and transitional justice questions, see Catherine M. Cole, "Performance Transitional Justice, and the Law," *Theatre Journal* 59, no. 2 (2007): 167–87; and Julie Stone Peters, "'Literature,' the 'Rights of Man,' and Narratives of Atrocity: Historical Backgrounds to the Culture of Testimony," *Yale Journal of Law & the Humanities* 17, no. 2 (2005): 253–83.

7. Peters, "Law, Literature," 449.

8. Peters, "Legal Performance," 198.

9. This disciplinary history is well narrated by Julie Stone Peters as well as Andrew Parker and Eve Kosofsky Sedgwick, eds., *Performativity and Performance* (New York: Routledge, 1995); Marvin Carlson, "The Resistance to Theatricality," *SubStance* 31, nos. 2–3 (2002): 238–50; Tracy C. Davis and Thomas Postlewait, ed., *Theatricality* (Cambridge: Cambridge University Press, 2003); and Shannon Jackson, *Professing Performance: Theatre in the Academy from Philology to Performativity* (New York: Cambridge University Press, 2004).

10. Martha Merrill Umphrey, "Law in Drag: Trials and Legal Performativity," *Columbia Journal of Gender and Law* 22 (2011–2012): 114–29, at 120.

11. Joshua Takano Chambers-Letson, *A Race So Different: Performance and Law in Asian America* (New York: New York University Press, 2013), 16.

12. Ibid., 6. See also Pierre Bourdieu, "The Force of Law: Toward a Sociology of the Juridical Field," translator's introduction by Richard Terdiman, *Hastings Law Journal* 38 (1987): 805–53.

13. I have contributed to this imbalance with my book *Performing South Africa's Truth Commission: Stages of Transition* (Bloomington: Indiana University Press, 2010).

14. Umphrey, "Law in Drag," 522–23.

15. J. L. Austin, *How to Do Things with Words*, 2nd ed. (Cambridge, MA: Harvard University Press, 1975).

16. Louis Althusser, "Ideology and Ideological State Apparatuses (Notes towards an Investigation)," in *Lenin and Philosophy, and Other Essays*, trans. Ben Brewster (New York: Monthly Review Press 1971), 85–126, at 118.

17. Mladen Dolar, "Beyond Interpellation," *Qui Parle* 6, no. 2 (Spring–Summer 1993): 75–96; Judith Butler, *The Psychic Life of Power: Theories in Subjection* (Stanford, CA: Stanford University Press, 1997), esp. chap. 4, "'Conscience Doth Make Subjects of Us All': Althusser's Subjection," 106–31.

18. Dolar, "Beyond Interpellation," 76.

19. Ibid., 87.

20. Butler, *Psychic Life of Power*, 129.

21. Mary Bunch, "The Unbecoming Subject of Sex: Performativity, Interpellation, and the Politics of Queer Theory," *Feminist Theory* 14, no. 1 (2013): 39–55, at 50.

22. Ibid., 53.

23. Alexander G. Weheliye, *Habeas Viscus: Racializing Assemblages, Biopolitics, and Black Feminist Theories of the Human* (Durham, NC: Duke University Press, 2014), 4.

24. Judith Butler, *Precarious Life: The Powers of Mourning and Violence* (London: Verso, 2004), 68.

25. For more on "scenes of subjection," see Saidiya V. Hartman, *Scenes of Subjection: Terror, Slavery, and Self-Making in Nineteenth-Century America* (New York: Oxford University Press, 1997). Hartman's research on nineteenth-century America reveals how operations of terror could be found in quotidian practices where terror could hardly be discerned—self-fashioning, dancing in the slave quarters, or the comic inversions and exaggerated body contortions of the minstrel stage.

26. Athol Fugard, *Notebooks, 1960–1977* (New York: Theatre Communications Group, 1984), 132–33.

27. Athol Fugard, John Kani, and Winston Ntshona, *Statements: [Three Plays]* (Oxford: Oxford University Press, 1974); republished by Theatre Communications Group (New York) in 1986. All citations in this chapter refer this latter republication.

28. Albert Wertheim, *The Dramatic Art of Athol Fugard: From South Africa to the World* (Bloomington: Indiana University Press, 2000), 69.

29. For summary of titles from theatrical reviews of this play in South African press, see *Athol Fugard: A Bibliography*, comp. John Read (Grahamstown, SA: National English Literary Museum, 1991). For instance: Owen Williams, "Honesty, Integrity, but Dullness in Play," *Cape Times*, March 29, 1972, 17.

30. Fugard, *Notebooks*, 196.

31. "Coloured" in apartheid South Africa meant "mixed race." Throughout my essay, South African spelling is used so as to draw attention to this historically and culturally specific usage.

32. Fugard, *Statements*, 81.

33. Papers of Athol Fugard, 1918–1997, at the Lilly Library, Indiana University, Bloomington, Indiana: Fugard mss, Box 1, Folder 28, Notebook 1971 to 1972/10. (All subsequent citations to the Lilly Library holdings are listed as "Fugard mss.")

34. Fugard mss, Box 1, Folder 28, Notebook 1971 to 1972/10, May 7, 1972.

35. See https://en.wikisource.org/wiki/Immorality_Act,_1927.

36. See https://en.wikisource.org/wiki/Immorality_Amendment_Act,_1950.

37. Jeanne Colleran, "Re-situating Fugard; Re-thinking Revolutionary Theatre," *South African Theatre Journal* 9, no. 2 (1995): 39–49, at 43.

38. Fugard mss., Box 1, Folder 30, Notebook 1972/11.

39. Fugard mss., Box 4, Folder 29, Typescript of draft of *Statements after an Arrest* with holograph insertions and changes. Handwritten note appears after page 13.

40. Fugard, *Statements*, 80.

41. Wertheim, *The Dramatic Art of Athol Fugard*, 72.

42. Fugard, *Statements*, 81.

43. Martin Orkin, *Drama and the South African State* (Manchester: Manchester University Press, 1991), 110.

44. Geoffrey V. Davis, *Voices of Justice and Reason: Apartheid and Beyond in South African Literature* (New York: Rodopi, 2003), 150.

45. Fugard, *Statements*, 82.

46. Ibid., 85.

47. Ibid., 93–94.

48. Ibid., 89–90.

49. Ibid., 91.

50. Ibid., 82.

51. Ibid., 84–85.

52. Ibid., 93.

53. Just as Judith Butler rejects Mladen Dolar's claim that love can be beyond interpellation, so too does Errol reject this idea. See Butler, *The Psychic Life of Power*, 127–31. On the relation of love and law, see also Paul W. Kahn, *Law and Love: The Trials of King Lear* (New Haven, CT: Yale University Press, 2000).

54. Fugard, *Statements*, 96.

55. Fugard mss., Box 1, File 30, Notebook 1972/11.

56. Fugard mss.; Box 1, Folder 28, Notebook 1971 to 1972 /10. Entry for 8/8/72.

57. Fugard, *Statements*, 96.

58. Ibid.

59. Ibid.
60. Ibid., 98.
61. Ibid., 99.
62. Ibid., 101–2.
63. Ibid., 102.
64. Ibid., 103.
65. Ibid., 104.
66. Ibid., 101.
67. Ibid., 105.
68. Ibid., 105.
69. Dolar, "Beyond Interpellation," 85.
70. Fugard, *Statements*, 106.
71. Ibid., 107–8.
72. Ibid., 108.
73. Ibid., 130.
74. Elizabeth Maddock Dillon, *New World Drama: The Performative Commons in the Atlantic World, 1649–1849* (Durham, NC: Duke University Press, 2014), 50.
75. Bert O. States, *Great Reckonings in Little Rooms: On the Phenomenology of Theater* (Berkeley: University of California Press, 1985), 20.
76. Joseph Slaughter, *Human Rights, Inc.: The World Novel, Narrative Form, and International Law* (New York: Fordham University Press, 2007), and Elizabeth S. Anker, *Fictions of Dignity: Embodying Human Rights in World Literature* (Ithaca, NY: Cornell University Press, 2012).
77. Davis, *Voices of Justice and Reason*, 145.
78. Quoted in Anne Fuchs, *Playing the Market: The Market Theatre, Johannesburg, 1976–1986* (Amsterdam: Rodopi, 2002), 30.
79. Fugard, *Statements*, 82.
80. Jens Meierhenrich, *The Legacies of Law: Long-Run Consequences of Legal Development in South Africa, 1652–2000* (Cambridge: Cambridge University Press, 2008), 112.
81. The Lilly Library at Indiana University, Bloomington, holds several versions of the play manuscript, and one can trace through these its evolving form.
82. Orkin, *Drama and the South African State*, 165.
83. Fugard, *Notebooks*, 196.
84. Ibid.
85. Fugard, *Statements*, 108.
86. Sara Ahmed, *Willful Subjects* (Durham, NC: Duke University Press, 2014), 11.
87. Ibid., 23.
88. Pieter-Dirk Uys, *No Space on Long Street* (unpublished playscript, 2000), 6–7. Available at http://pdu.co.za/no%20space.html.
89. Ibid., 26.
90. Ibid., 32.
91. Ibid., 33.
92. Ibid., 31.
93. Ibid., 31.
94. Ibid., 32.
95. Ibid., 29–30.

CHAPTER 5

Freedom with Silence

Cryptoanalytics and the Differend *in the Afterlives of Legal Things*

LARA D. NIELSEN

The September 26, 2014, disappearance of forty-three students in the southern state of Guerrero, Mexico, quickly met with fiery public protests against the suspected complicity of the city's mayor and municipal police forces with those initially considered responsible for the attack and abduction of the students from the Rural Teachers College in Ayotzinapa—organized crime industry cartels, or *narcos.* On the night of the disappearance, seven people were killed and more than forty seriously wounded. To date, the attorney general's office is prosecuting the case of the Ayotzinapa 43 for kidnapping, murder, and organized crime. National demonstrations mobilized international and digital actions. Launching the Organization of American States (OAS) Inter-American Commission for Human Rights (IACHR) technical cooperation agreement on November 18, 2014, the president of the Commission, Tracy Robinson, outlined a broader inquiry: "The main objective is to solve the underlying structural problems to these disappearances, not only the cases involving the 43 students from Ayotzinapa, but other cases, which unfortunately are many."[1] Refuting the government's initial claim that the disappeared forty-three students were killed by *narcos* (and only narcos) and incinerated in a trash dump, the 2015 IACHR appointed Interdisciplinary Group of Independent Experts (GIEI) findings instead support widespread public belief that state, federal, and army security forces also played a key role in the tracking, seizure, and forced disappearance of the students.[2] Building on its 2013 Mexican report, in 2015 Amnesty International states, "The Ayotzinapa case is similar to the thousands of cases of disappearances which have taken place across the country since the beginning of the 'war on drugs' initiated in 2006 by the previous administration of President Calderón."[3]

Whereas the Mexican attorney general's office considers the students murdered (a criminal case concerned with the punishment of individuals), the OAS Commission for Human Rights, GIEI, and Amnesty International instead report that they are *disappeared* (a crime against humanity committed by the state that is prosecutable in international law). The distinction is critical. As deputy director Santiago Aguirre, of the Miguel Agustín Pro Juárez Human Rights Center (Centro Prodh) explains, the finding for murder and kidnapping dilutes likely state responsibility, whereas forced disappearance is a state crime.[4] As detailed by the February 2015 Mexico Report from the UN Committee on Forced Disappearances, *enforced disappearances* are those linked to detention or abduction by state agents such as police or security forces, or their allies, who conceal the victim's fate.[5] Although there is no evidence that the students are dead, investigative journalist Anabel Hernández says it is "difficult" to think that they are still alive.[6] As evidence, the attorney general's office offers just one piece of incinerated student DNA—evidence the Argentine Forensic Anthropology Team (EAAF) took pains to reject. Carlos Martín Beristain, Spanish investigator for the OAS Commission, summarizes the GIEI conclusions: "The brutal actions show the extent of impunity in which the state security forces acted along with organized crime."[7] Reiterating the point, the December 2015 OAS Inter-American Commission 232-page report, *The Human Rights Situation in Mexico,* lists "State Actors" first in its list of the main sources of violence.[8] Deferring, the government takes exception to the charge of forced disappearances.

In the context of such stalemate, it appears that the throttle of the state's justice systems chokes and stalls. At the time of this writing, no less than three attorneys general have produced no sentences because they say they have no evidence. What is to be done? A 2016 oral history makes some headway, for one.[9] Similarly, short of changing "*the underlying structural problems to these disappearances,*" as Robinson first emphasized, another response on offer to public anguish, rage, fear, and grieving are data-driven evidence regimes. There can be no doubt that we live in dense data and media environments; crucially, states are not the only agents producing and using data and media. Due to the silences produced by the attorney general's office thus far (the office has been accused of using torture to suppress witness accounts), the EAAF and the Centro

Prodh commissioned Forensic Architecture (a research agency based at Goldsmiths, University of London) to examine and reconstruct what happened in Guerrero. Using digital spatiotemporal mapping technologies, the firm has investigated covert operations surrounding drone warfare in Afghanistan, migrants adrift in the Mediterranean, hospital bombings in Syria, military actions in Gaza, and environmental among other conflict cases. For the Ayotzinapa case, Forensic Architecture created an interactive cartographic platform to map out the events of September 26–27, drawing on GIEI investigations, videos, media stories, photographs, and call logs. Launched in September 2017, and with the Musco Universitario Arte Contemporáneo (MUAC), the project claims to demonstrate, "in a clear graphic and cartographic form, the level of collusion and coordination between state agencies and organized crime throughout the night." For many, it is a much welcome report.

No doubt, publics want to count, and to be counted: to be identified and interpreted as meaningful actors, from Ayotzinapa to the Drug War. Accounts vary, but estimates stipulate 80,000–127,000 people have been killed (not including the estimated 27,000 missing) since the Drug War began in Mexico in 2006, in what was (eight years ago) an estimated $19–$29 billion annual cash enterprise.[10] While identification, verification, and testamentary rituals associated with "information" are intrinsic to independent investigations as well as the law's authority, the case of the Ayotzinapa 43 shows that the systematically asymmetrical application of evidentiary measures has profound limits.

It is something of an understatement to say that evidence regimes are not without trouble. Public and institutional responses to the case of the Ayotzinapa 43 nevertheless demonstrate the ubiquitous and indispensable pitch for information and data-driven techniques that define today's global justice and securitization interests and architectures. Even within the law's procedural terms, the problem is that forensic data collection and the information of other official reports can (and do) obfuscate and conceal crime. Corrupted crime scenes, lost and erased videotape, confiscated cellular data, and forced testimony each point to the precariousness of evidentiary claims and protocols. There are further concerns as well. Identificatory classifications index loaded mandates: they are logistical fields of expression, whoever deploys them. As operational protocols, they are programmed to report what they are directed to detect. The fetish character of "information" distorts. The law, meanwhile, is a logistical field of expression in itself. Still at issue is what Michael Taussig once called *the magic of the state,*[11] and what James C. Scott understands as state efforts to rationalize and enforce legibility in a one-sided way: "The legibility of society provides the capacity for large-scale social engineering."[12] The law's discourses and devices transmit the state's totemic authorities—as do corollary systems of communication (medias); mechanisms for the storage and transmission of data (archives and institutions); and the tricky interpolations of mediated spectatorship and witness that legal evidence demands.[13] Considering the prevalence of evidentiary logics governing the protocols of the state and other agents, it is thus rather remarkable that teams of forensic experts called in to examine the case of the Ayotzinapa 43 instead struggle for the right to establish *inconclusive* (as opposed to conclusive) evidence—in other words, to hold out for the ambiguous markers of the case, against pressure to draw definitive conclusions from questionable "evidence."

Be that as it may, what the attorney general's office *has* produced is silence—and make no mistake about it, that is not nothing. Notwithstanding the advances of media architecture, the efforts of international human rights advocates who continue to broadly condemn "a context of generalized disappearances in a great part of the territory (of Mexico)," and the persistence of regional and national communities exhorting lawmakers to recognize *enforced disappearances* as a crime, the powers of silence show no signs of diminishing. In April 2016, the GIEI closed its work and issued its second report, citing efforts to pry into, delegitimize, and obstruct its inquiry. Record numbers of journalists working in nearly every state in Mexico continue to be assassinated for their investigations into corruption[14]—to date, at least 108 since 2006, as well as at least 25 disappeared, from Michoacán, Guerrero, Veracruz, and Oaxaca to Sinaloa, Chihuahua, and the Distrito Federal (DF).[15] Striking out on their own, local communities maintain independent searches for traces of the Ayotzinapa 43 long after the rest have gone.[16]

¤ ¤ ¤

The idea that silence is a resource guides this essay. I look to artists and publics whose strategies for appropriating both the law's verification rituals and its discrepant silences aim to repurpose the fetish character of evidence, at the same time that they seek to more fully recognize and credit the syntax of silences in reticent modes of social agency. Wounded and wary of the failures of the modern law state, an array of social actors presented here grapple with the afterlives of violence, of social death, by activating the glossolalia of "scriptive things": or, genres of data organization that in this essay include commissions, borders, mug shots, cemeteries, hashtags, and bureaucratic strings. Doing so brings into focus the durability of the law's administrative and bureaucratic operations as things that are hidden in plain sight, even as they are rerouted; calls up the specter of object-oriented juridical culture; and retains (as aftereffect) the prolific presence of silences which course through all living things. Because performance (like the law) incurs the haptic encounter, because they share the business of touching lives, both mimetically and methexially agential, in the sense that both summon modes of saying and doing;[17] and because the law indeed remains grounded not just in the rhetoric of the image,[18] but in the performance, combines, and afterlives of things, too, in this essay I look to "scriptive" things that wander and move in some kind of break, to their disquiet digressions and phrasings. In tension with and as opposed to normative "sentences," it's a matter of showing up a panoply of ruses with yet more cryptoanalytic gambits.

It is well known that in Kafka's literature the bureaucratic apparatus of the law rather famously "speaks" (as in *The Trial* [1925]). In performance (and thing) theory, the focus is usually on what a thing asks its users to do, or to perform.[19] Robin Bernstein clarifies: "The term script denotes not a rigid dictation of performed action, but rather a set of invitations that necessarily remain open to resistance, interpretation, and improvisation."[20] Linking scriptive things with their evidentiary deployments across institutional (social) fields—"object-oriented" as well as systems- and network-oriented regimes (even as they pose conflicting fetishisms)—suggests that media, performance, and cultural research can and must examine the dynamics of organizations, infrastructures, and flows that, while socially derived and purposed, nevertheless also (and at the same time) march to their own tune.[21] Relations of production cannot be reduced either to relations between humans or machines alone.[22] Many more assemblages of labor and machines "act" and "speak," fortifying critical repertoires old and new for surviving social enginery that have been put into motion and cannot be easily be mended or retrieved.[23]

Considering law "a thing of this world," as legal scholar David Delaney suggests, critics do well to consider the field of *nomoscapes,* or the "cultural-material environs of the legal and the legal signification of the socio-spatial, and the practical, performative engagements through such constitutive moments happen and unfold."[24] Following Arjun Appadurai's shorthand for global exchange practices (such as mediascapes, ethnoscapes, technoscapes, finanscapes, ideoscapes),[25] the term *nomoscapes* describes legal modes of exchange that are always in flux. Following another anthropologist, Aihwa Ong,[26] they are "archipelagic," as Delaney once described it, and denote diverse *assemblages,* or *agencements,*[27] uneven and highly site-specific designs, or arrangements: commotions of patterns, convergences, dispersals, and refusals that rationalize and distribute sovereignty. The idea that law is a thing in this world has been anticipated by theorists of postcolonial modernities,[28] whose interventions suggest the field of the political is, as Dipesh Chakrabarty puts it, split into "distinct logics which get braided together all the time—the logic of formal-legal and secular frameworks of governance and that of relationships of direct domination and subordination that derive their legitimation from a different set of institutions and practices."[29] What this means is that the production of domination and subordination mobilizes several more social and cultural institutions than the rule of law alone can account.[30] In the Ayotzinapa 43's Mexico—better said, in the Ayotzinapa 43's *Americas*—the field of the political is marked by violence, death, and silence.[31]

In the pages that follow, I take up works that emanate from places where the interpenetrations of intensifying violences mobilize the call of justice claims: in Guerrero, Juárez, Mexico City, Michoacán—and in the transnational imaginary.[32] My selection of case studies reflects a geography and a cartography of violences and silences.[33] I treat with caution (if not skepticism) demands to make art mediate social witness, and to the predilections of "evidence" and witness alike—what Avital Ronell calls "the testamentary whimper," as I soon discuss.[34] Following Guha, Chakrabarty, and Ronell, I think it's worth asking whether the contemporary is marked by too simple an attitude about the verifiability, legibility, and, perhaps most crucially, *the transparency* of political struggles, as if the digital proliferations of information, the technological apparati for making "transparent" and "universal" claims, were enough to interpret the history of the present, in all its fields of struggle—whereas the law's performativity suggests otherwise, social conflict and distress are not so easily dispatched or translated, and data itself is ever changeable. In other words, it's worth asking whether such forms of recognition can even begin to account for the survival repertoires of living with duress.

Just as securitization agents debate the porousness and malleability of data encryption in high-stakes games of ambiguity, it seems, publics cling to norms of perceptibility, penetrability, documentability, and identification.

As two sides of the same coin, it will be said that the latter demands accountability precisely because the former refuses it. By now, it is safe to say that scholars are less convinced that publics are not already so compromised by forms of control that identificatory technologies and discourses remain unassailable.[35] As a performance and media theorist, I am wary of exhibition and spectacle as *what is made to be seen*:[36] of performance as one among brethren techniques in the certifications of presence that deploy intermedial bodies of evidence as agential subjects and objects of transmission.[37]

Likewise, there is a long line of artists and critics who have not taken up the identificatory routines of depositions, testimony, or other evidentiary techniques to theorize the social, but who instead respond to documentary and database "pervertability" as dubious if persistent information pools, where "dark" pools indicate information asymmetry. In an era of metricization, that sense of reserve could not be more important.[38] Driven by digital technologies, the scene of "the contemporary" is intently tuned into evidentiary regimes and rhetorics, to identification, certification, and witness techniques and technologies, building expectations for unassailable data and "documentation" medias. To be sure, if there are hopes about documentary accessibility, it shows political strategy: the desire to make known what might otherwise be repressed. Formulations about active citizens and/as public and creative artists, for instance, proscribe norms for the model cultural agent, a sometimes therapeutic designation that is as intent on forging social change as it authorizes cathartic justice processes.[39] Yet profound questions persist around the status of "information," and of "freedom," particularly in an era of data overload, expanding digital information capture capacities, and machinic (algorithmic) vision. Today, as tracking, seeing, and witness practices involve technologies made by networked and computational agents of all kinds, the fetish character of information (and/as freedom) is ever subject to bureaucratic repurposing, as well. Critics ask, what are its impacts on subject-oriented witness practices?[40]

As performance theorist Sarah Jane Cervanak points out, adherence to the logics of verification regimes index distinctive fault lines in performance theory, too.[41] For Peggy Phelan, visibility routines have long been suspect.[42] Focusing on aesthetic strategies of *surreal presence in unreal time* ("in the break"), Fred Moten's research in blackness and fugitivity ripples across disciplines.[43] For José Esteban Muñoz, it is to the feints of *dis*identifications that performance research attends;[44] more recently, for Branislav Jaklovjević, it is to the subversion and appropriation of self-organization management strategies in a rapidly changing political economy.[45] With such interlocutors in mind, taking up paradigms of verifiability to rethink law and/as performance necessarily incurs the question: How do artists and publics treat the threat and allure of evidentiary regimes and rationales (data, deposition, and documentation) specifically pertaining to the law's masquerade, ornament, and crime?[46] Folded within that question lies another: How are they (and we) simultaneously imbued with the abundances of silence?

Diverting focus from the signs and ornamentations of the law's usually heralded totemic powers (staging laws, courts, judges, juries, depositions, witnesses, perpetrators, and victims), I look toward less celebrated aspects of the law's instrumental remains. Call it the fragmented and fragmentary phrasings of everyday and material ephemera: the haptic, tactic, and strategic materials of those disposable or "leftover" images, objects, people, and things that, for all their quietly unimportant miscellanea, indeed perform, and persist. As the Chilean writer Diamela Eltit explains regarding surviving the Pinochet years in Chile (1973–1990), "To speak of fragments in fragments, by means of fragments [is] not only a methodology but also a recognition that reality was already fragmented. It was fragmented because public life had collapsed and was hemmed in by severe inhibitions that hemmed in the heterogeneous formation of a citizenship."[47] While the cases of Chile and Mexico differ historically, crises of public life are not limited to them, either. Attention to the minor key reflects deliberate strategy: looking awry, the law is less the domain of "truth and beauty" than it is an expression of reason's irrational bends.[48] Looking awry, the fragmentations of social death haunt public life. For legal scholar Robert Cover, the banality of the law (its raw conceit as authorized agent of violence) is to be seen in "the violence of legal acts" that by definition "takes place in a field of pain and death."[49] The law's administrative processes, gaffes, and runarounds seal the argument for law's violences and silences.[50] Not just in the wake of such violences but indeed anteceding it, the rhetorics of wandering and throwaway people and things (papers, photographs, hashtags, and strings) gather their own momentums in another artful drift, another chorus of silences and refusals.[51]

In a sense, granting attention to the minor key is to focus on that which prevents justice from taking place, what Lyotard calls the *differend*. "This is what a wrong (*tort*) would be," Lyotard says: "a damage (*dommage*) accompanied by the loss of the means to prove the damage."[52] Whatever negates the admissibility of suffering, if the positive law tradition grounds its authority in what has been made to be law—according to legal scholar Philippe Nonet, on will, precedent, fallibility, and socially constructed expertise; and if positive law is said to "parade[s] as man's proud affirmation of his creative powers," an emancipation that considers itself secular, man-made, or what is "posited"[53]—then as artifice and artifact, law not only carries the key to the fantasy of the end of law itself, but also to the haptic encounters with its authority (that was always preconditioned by resistances to it): to the murmuring hollows of a prolix silence.

Looking beyond the horizon of "scriptive" things (the material lens), what can performance theory offer to the task of interpreting the legacy of silence and the law (the discursive lens)? To be sure, transnational publics are looking for words, deeds, institutions, systems, and discourses that will do things—and change things (key concerns for performance theorists)—showing that one way that the law "requires to be thought" is in the surplus of effects of the law's silence; or, more specifically, in the sheer breadth and depth of positive law's performativity. Where the law declines to directly "speak" rather forcefully disseminates its powers. As the Ayotzinapa 43 case indicates, that which is generated in the law's deferrals, in its silences, produces fiercely interpenetrating fields of agential activities, controls, and deferrals.

What this means is that whatever the law does and does not do (or say) about the Ayotzinapa 43 participates, first of all, in the production of those silences. Performance theorists typically suggest that language comprises practices that are capable of building norms, realities, and materialities (the illocutionary) as well as deconstructing and producing a set of uncontrolled errancies and effects (the perlocutionary)[54]—generating openings, for instance, in how we can think about the value of certain legal effects. Because the speech act is "a reiterated form of discourse," the alignments of performativity with law suggest that law is no less a discursive and generative site than language, image, or matter itself.[55] But like the law's evidence, performance itself offers no guarantee. Verification rituals of evidentiary regimes and routines (the repetitions of establishment procedures) answer to the demands of protocol, but they may also foreclose the possibility of justice, muting it.

In Marianne Constable's analysis, the signature of positive law lies specifically in its silence *about* justice.[56] I take that to mean that one of the places that the struggle for justice is to be found is in the archival babel of many different kinds of silences. That the archive itself will *out* the effects of its organizational controls, within and beyond the law's silence, that this is the legacy of the 'modern' positive law state, points toward an understanding of the law's equivocal performativity, in which silence emanates not only the violences of positive law, but also, as I insist in this essay, a kind of silence that transmits the resources of an uncontrollable and companion compendium, a loquacious account that warrants many more indices than it appears to command.[57] Before and after the silences and violences of the law, social agents deploy a proliferation of strategic and tactical techniques to enact and articulate that auxiliary compendium that was never merely supplementary but instead principal, *a freedom with silence.*

In other words, if the opposite of the law's silence is not veridiction (Foucault's term), not speech—not words and acts and records and depositions, not legibility, not identification, not testimony, not materially recognizable administrative procedures, not any kind of attempt to repeat or reinstate governing or representational norms, not amnesty, and not memory—but if the opposite of the law's silence is instead what's steadfastly unruly, a genealogy of what is ungovernable, a genealogy of fury, and rage, then it is to the plenitudes, the suspensions, and postponements of the ungovernabilities of silence, to the abeyant and aberrant dormancies of silence, that we must also look.[58] Not just to the law's silence, but to all those other deployments, moratoriums, and adjournments. Recognizing the law's silence as equivocal, and the social life of antagonistic silences as no less polysemous, I want to read legacies of silence as yielding their own kinds of unassimilable and tenebrous archive. An open set of accumulations and assemblages, mapping and producing the effects of silence (including law, language; including cryptography) are also spatially networked and material ones. A surfeit of evidence, matter, and remittances emerge in the swarm of things within, and left out of, the letter of the law; in the material fields of its glossolalia, which can (must) also be phrased as fragments in relation *with* silence.

Looking to artists and publics for whom, like Eltit, the cover of silence itself is an ambivalent resource, I begin with the story of a small town mayor, María Santos Gorrostieta Salazar, who appropriates the authority of standard procedure photographic images—how the eponymous mug shot "speaks"—toward the promise of individualized entrepreneurial citizenship, in the hope of renewing a lease on witness practices. I show that the photograph summons and performs the gaze of state authority, reinvigorating the use of "evidence" for the rewriting of local history, in a bid to reject abjection. Prompting ambivalence, and the im/possibility of restorative justice, however, the strategy finally confirms the status of the photograph as historical rather than evidentiary.[59] Next, Sabina Berman's dramatic feature *Backyard* (a play, and its adaptation into film) presents a postnational historiography of Juárez border economies, including migrant indigenous maquiladora workers for whom the silence of the law is again deadly.[60] The transnational borderlands evince a cartography of dispossession that speaks: in Juárez, "evidence" is disappeared into the desert even as nation and narration rhetorics continue to deny a surfeit hum of relations in the *nomoscape* and *narcoscape* of things.

That surfeit emphatically returns in the installation *127 Cuerpos,* by Teresa Margolles (2011), who offers fragments of forensic evidence in depositions of the real pertaining not only to the dead, but also to the state's bureaucratic apparati. Margolles's study of morgue cataloging practices cannily apprehends the archivizational stages of justice. Doubling the limits of evidentiary regimes with a genealogy of errancy, *127 Cuerpos* studies the string, and the line, as an apparatus of repetition and seriality, showing too that the bid for forensic evidence offers not the same authority as justice, as monolingual call, but as polyphonic and polymorphic, requiring all due reflection on the suspending interpenetrations of its meager traces. In the end I argue that Margolles's silent strings posit an errant cryptoanalytics, working between thing and infinity.

To close the essay, I turn to the baroque glossolalia of so many coded silences deferring the status of witness and testimony alike, in the documentary film by Natalia Almada, about a cemetery in Michoacán. In Almada's *El Velador/The Nightwatchman* (2001), a city of mausoleums maps what could be called the prophetic poetics of statelessness, and, the outlaw state—in concert with the scripted protocols of a ghostly silence that everyone understands. In the end, I return to the Ayotzinapa 43 case to consider the hashtags (#TodosSomosAyotzinapa and #YaMeCansé) as scriptive things chanting an indexical chorus of silence, a pool of remittances from a crowd of signs. In the mugshot, the dramatic features, the installation, the documentary film, and the hashtag, law and/as performance are constitutively intertwined within a multitudinous array of resonant things, producing silence as profusion and polyvocal sign.

"María Santos" and the Mug Shot: *Freedom brings with it responsibilities and I don't dare fall behind*

Photography theorist John Tagg explains the visual realism of the photograph as an evidentiary operation: evidence does not work transparently but reroutes a thing's constitution for its own purposes. Despite the drive to keep photographic evidence inert and inanimate, the camera's technical appropriations draw attention to the instability of subjects, objects, and things—to their ontological heterogeneity, a disturbing fluidity—and thus to the historical status of the photograph.[61] It is with these equivocal ambivalences in mind that I turn to the media-archived story of María Santos Gorrostieta Salazar, former mayor of Tiquicheo (2008–2011), a small town in Michoacán, whose performances of the eponymous mug shot in 2010 are part of the story of her assassination, in 2012. Accounts vary, but newspapers report that Gorrostieta was taken from her car as she was driving her daughter to school around 8:30 in the morning of November 12, 2012. People who saw her on the road that day were terrified as they watched men pull Gorrosieta from her car and beat her, before she "willingly" stepped into the assailants' vehicle; in exchange, they did not take her daughter. Initially thinking that the seizure was a kidnapping, her family waited until November 14 to report Gorrostieta missing. Almost a week later, when she was found by the side of a road in another part of Michoacán, newspapers reported that her body showed evidence of torture.[62] The official cause of death was determined as blunt force trauma to the head, including severe traumatic brain injury. *María Santos,* as the Mexican press sometimes refers to her, was thirty-six. The *Los Angeles Times* headline of November 20 drily announced, "Former Mexico mayor survives 2 assassination attempts but not third," but other sources say there were other attacks, which Gorrostieta never reported.[63]

Journalistic and social media hagiographies agree that Gorrostieta's vocal opposition to drug cartel powers in Michoacán led to the assassination attempts and eventual murder. When President Felipe Calderón declared the War on Drugs in December 2006, the Mexican Armed Forces first went to his home state, Michocán; Gorrostieta's Tiquicheo is located on the roads between Michoacan's West coast and its capital city, Morelia. In 2009, the first attack killed her husband, when gunman ambushed their gun-proof SUV. The second attack, involving a masked gunman with assault rifles, left her seriously wounded by bullets, in January 2010. Thereafter she lived with pain, including the difficulties of a colostomy bag. Refusing to capitulate to the attack, Gossostieta said, "Me levantaré las veces que Dios me lo permita, para continuar buscando, arañando, gestionando planes, proyectos y acciones en beneficio de toda la sociedad, pero más en particular de los desprotegidos" (I will rise up again as many times as God allows me to so that I can keep on seeking, fighting for, and working out plans, projects and actions for the benefit of the people, especially the unprotected, those most in need).

After the January 2010 attack, Gorrostieta did not resign or retreat from the public eye but went very public with her injuries, publishing photographs of her bullet torn body (and the colostomy bag) in the city's newsletter. Widely considered a political maneuver of defiance, and at the same time a public act of supplication, the photos look like and appropriate the classic mug shot. With a frontal view and side shots that encourage, authorize, and in a sense demand the assessing view and judgment of the law, the photos display an injured body, scarred, torn, and punctured. They aren't officially mug shots; to my knowledge, the police did not compel this act of recording, and Gorrostieta is nowhere implicated as a suspect but most pointedly as a victim of crime. Demanding a more effective police state, Gorrostieta mobilizes the rhetoric of the mug shot, to suggest that the police *should* view her "evidence," and record the crime: that the police and by extension, the state, *should* be safeguarding, surveilling, and documenting the welfare of its people; that her assailants *should* be sentenced and brought to justice; that her neighbors *should* be her witness. The photographs thus seek legibility within the common rituals of crime procedures associated with modern law—and in the arts of witness. In so doing, Gorrestieta implores the state to follow its own legal protocols, to enact the promises of law and order that President Enrique Peña Nieto has also been keen to effect in his message-change for transnational communities after his election in 2012, one that highlights an orderly and business-friendly Mexico.[64]

Gorrostieta insists on writing and being written into the records of local and national history. Like the social media that memorialize Gorrostieta, she renounces the right to privacy in the name of an imaginary public good. Posing for the mug shot, public servant Gorrostieta counters everyday public dramaturgies associated with the War on Drugs—publicly performed disappearances and seizures, publicly displayed corpses—with the portrait of the citizen soldier, survivor. In 2010 Gorrostieta said, "I wanted to show them my wounded, mutilated, humiliated body, because I'm not ashamed of it, because it is the product of the great misfortunes that have scarred my life, that of my children and my family."[65] The photographs reproduce a nationalist rhetoric, *¡Que Viva México!,* a timeless and yet historically specific plea for national justice again made urgent in cinema's moving images (in Eisenstein's film of 1932). Trading in the status of official documents and evidentiary regimes, Gorrostieta's photographs recruit publics to the discourse of the nation state.[66]

Folding Gorrostieta's injured body into the political body, the photograph thus "collapses space between public and private lives." In so doing, as cultural theorist Allen Feldman suggests, the deployment of everyday visual surveillance practices also "authorizes other forms of bodily invasion."[67] The photograph invokes the theatrical problem of the spectator, not just as seedy voyeur,[68] but from the no less suspect vantage point of seeing like a state. "Certain forms of knowledge and control require," Scott says, "a narrowing vision":

> The great advantage of such tunnel vision is that it brings into sharp focus certain limited aspects of an otherwise far more complex and unwieldy reality. This very simplification, in turn, makes the phenomenon a center of field of vision more legible and hence more susceptible to careful measurement and calculation. Combined with similar operations, an overall, aggregate, synoptic view of a selective reality is achieved, making possible a high degree of schematic knowledge, control, and manipulation.[69]

As subject and object of investigation, the photos summon the authority of exhibition (to be made into an object), and a very particular one, at that: an elected official, and a woman with rights, for whom portraiture and the inscription of social identity generate value.[70] Crucially, the images thus also produce the achievement of citizenship as conditional property that the law is obliged to serve.[71] Reclaiming the photograph from early documentary traditions that used photographs to record the "degenerate urban poor," as photography theorist Allan Sekula has shown, Gorrostieta's mugshot pointedly plays with desire and the desire to measure; desire and the desire to look. Offering herself as a pictorial statistic reinstates Sekula's thesis on the history of the photograph that has its roots in "scientific policing and eugenics" as well as policing.[72] But Gorrostieta's mug shot inverts the paradigm: *she* is not the social disease, *they* are.

Cultural historians suggest that in Mexico, a print culture tradition in sensationalist photographic images also produces a powerful cross between documentary print and visual public cultures in the popular presses. Arguing it is important to understand Mexican crime media and tabloids today as veering between a nostalgia for the excitements of mid-century law and order documentation (when scooping the most sensationalist images possible first was the main selling point) on the one hand, and on the other hand today's contemporary journalism of censorship and public security, Will Straw also notes that today the presses eschew the big scoop for fear of retaliation. In a sign of neoliberal securitization logics, photojournalists no longer want to be the first ones on the scene, because it is too risky; "journalists have learned to arrive last."[73] While the Committee to Protect Journalists keeps a record of the journalists who have been killed around the world, and Mexico ranks high on the list of dangerous places to practice journalism, scholars suggest that the representation of violence in the Mexican presses primarily functions to commodify securitization rhetorics, selling terror to justify the demand for more police and military powers, without strong analysis of the role that the marketization of security forces play in the law's silences on the war on drugs.[74] Publics clearly revive that optic, and not without its hazards—but what is important here is that Straw's historical observations about documentary cultures encourage law and performance theorists not to force fact from fiction, as if they were oppositional objects of analysis, but rather to rejoin their effects, collating photographic fantasias with "facts."

For instance, when the *Daily Mail* published the mugshots, Gorrostieta is quoted as saying, "*Freedom brings with it responsibilities and I don't dare fall behind.* My long road is not yet finished—the footprint that we leave behind in our country depends on the battle that we lose and the loyalty we put into it" (emphasis added). On the one hand, Gorrostieta's affective deployment of "freedom" summons the privileges and responsibilities of individual citizenship, and performs the authority of her position as a mayor, the duty-bound subject of neoliberal citizenship. It may also be a display of what Lauren Berlant calls cruel optimism, or an affective attachment to principles, beliefs, and ideologies that fail to deliver—such as freedom, the rule of law, democracy, and citizenship. Critics like Berlant look to what the valences of everyday affects can offer towards thinking "lived history," as always fluid, in flux (rather than the fixed material of a set past). Thus (and on the other hand), Gorrostieta's mug shots can indeed be seen to facilitate a "callback," like Bill Brown's reified cultural artifacts that repeat and explode its cultural logics.[75] In a sense, the photos provide valuable "information" to transnational compatriots who have been made into vulnerable "foreigners" in their own towns.

In Latin American performance contexts, the phrase *information for foreigners* carries immediate reference to the 1987 play by that name, written by Griselda Gambaro about Argentina during the Dirty War (1979–1983), when some 30,000 people were killed and disappeared.[76] While Gambaro's play makes palpable the performative and spatial violences of the junta's silencing disinformation campaigns, denouncing state controls, what Gorrostieta's photographs do is activate the regulatory regimes of a talkative archive, an institutional and institutionalizing production in the everyday order of national things. In short, Gorrostieta's pitch authorizes a legal verification and curatorial process that Gambaro, by contrast, reveals as farcically corrupted by power.

What's striking is that both cases recall Eltit's description of violence as "rhizomatic, in the sense that it reproduces itself without beginning or end"[77]—or, in *The Wire*'s Baltimore parlance, "You can't even call this shit war; wars end."[78] For Maurice Blanchot, the *effervescence* of the everyday (that which is most difficult, he says) is explicitly not to be mistaken for the noise of *information,* but rather a question of "opening the everyday onto history" such that the everyday, he says, "allows no hold. It escapes."[79] In Gorrostieta's mug shots, the contest between information and effervescence leads to the question of what is it that escapes (and what colludes) in the law's silence, and, in witness practices; in other words, the equivocality of law and/as performance. Perhaps Gorrostieta's mugshots can be read as an anticipatory call, or deposition, one announcing her own demise, as though she were preparing her own file for a Mexican *Nunca Más*—before such a project could be said to have come into existence.[80] Nearly a month after Gorrostieta's murder, rumors surfaced about a Truth Commission when the *Washington Post* broke a story about an unpublished government list of (what was then) some 25,000 disappearances in Mexico.[81] As yet, critics are not impressed. "*Problema ignorado*" (problem ignored).[82]

Sabina Berman's Border Spaces: *Backyard*

Sabina Berman's play *Backyard* was first published in 2005 by *Gestos,* a multilingual journal devoted to Spanish, Latin American, and U.S. Latino theater, retaining the playwright's pointedly English language title. Set in what Berman carefully calls "the cosmopolitan" border city of Juárez, Chihuahua, it was adapted for Mexican film production in 2009 as *Backyard/El Traspatio.* Immediately, Berman's stubborn and yet very ordinary word, *backyard,* alerts readers to a set of concerns about how the state produces space, and narrates and performs national sovereignty through spatial articulations.[83] What Berman first insists is that the thing that she writes a play about has to be framed by its (American) English moniker: the *backyard.* Historical ambivalences in the term *backyard* go to the crux of Mexican and U.S. national responses to their border territories (and cultures) as both peripheral and central to national concerns, at once an inside and an outside of national and transnational things.

It is perhaps no less important that Berman's use of the word *backyard* deftly points, no less, to elite national habits attempting to narrate and make Mexico (and Mexicans) modern. With *Backyard,* Berman subtly stages *the naming* of Mexico's rural and markedly indigenous border spaces as physically and symbolically remote, cast out from the cultural and political centers of power in Mexico City—even if the urbanization of cities like Juárez is a global phenomenon—and thus Berman offers Juárez as a sign for what the subaltern studies critic Ranajit Guha explains as the "*failure of the bourgeoisie to speak for the nation.*"[84] Against past modes of writing national history establishing dominant institutions (including the law and its elites), for Guha the realm of the political lies instead in the heterogeneous expressions of the experience of exploitation and labor, forms of expression that have "many idioms, norms, and values which put it in a category apart." Hence Guha's objective is to expand the boundaries of historical analysis beyond the state's official instruments, laws, languages, and sites of administration—its evidentiary regimes. With the stories in *Backyard,* Berman floats the possibility of the border's postnational historiography, while avoiding the reductive binary of fiction and nonfiction, making it particularly interesting that *Backyard* was Mexico's official national submission to the Academy Award's Foreign Language Film category in 2009.

The Internet Movie Database sells the work as a "crime/drama/mystery," telling "the true story of the border town of Juárez, Mexico where since the mid-90's thousands of women have gone missing or turned up as sun-burnt corpses in the desert. Can new police captain Blanca Bravo stop the savagery?" More nuanced, the Human Rights Watch Film Festival promotes it is as "An astonishing fictional account of the unending series of murders of young women in Ciudad Juárez, Mexico, which began in 1996. Most of the victims are low-paid laborers who have been drawn to the town by the possibility of work at American-owned factories. In the film Mexican police officer Blanca Bravo is sent to Cuidad Juárez to investigate and comes to learn realities of these [maquila] women's lives, as well as the truth about a police force and local power structure embodied by entrepreneur Mickey Santos that has ceased to care."[85] It is not just that complicity rules the borderlands; it is that something else too binds publics to place.

Berman's drama takes as its point of departure the understanding that the state produces space; space is hierarchical; and that the state's violences are not exceptional but indeed ratified as a technique of governance.[86]

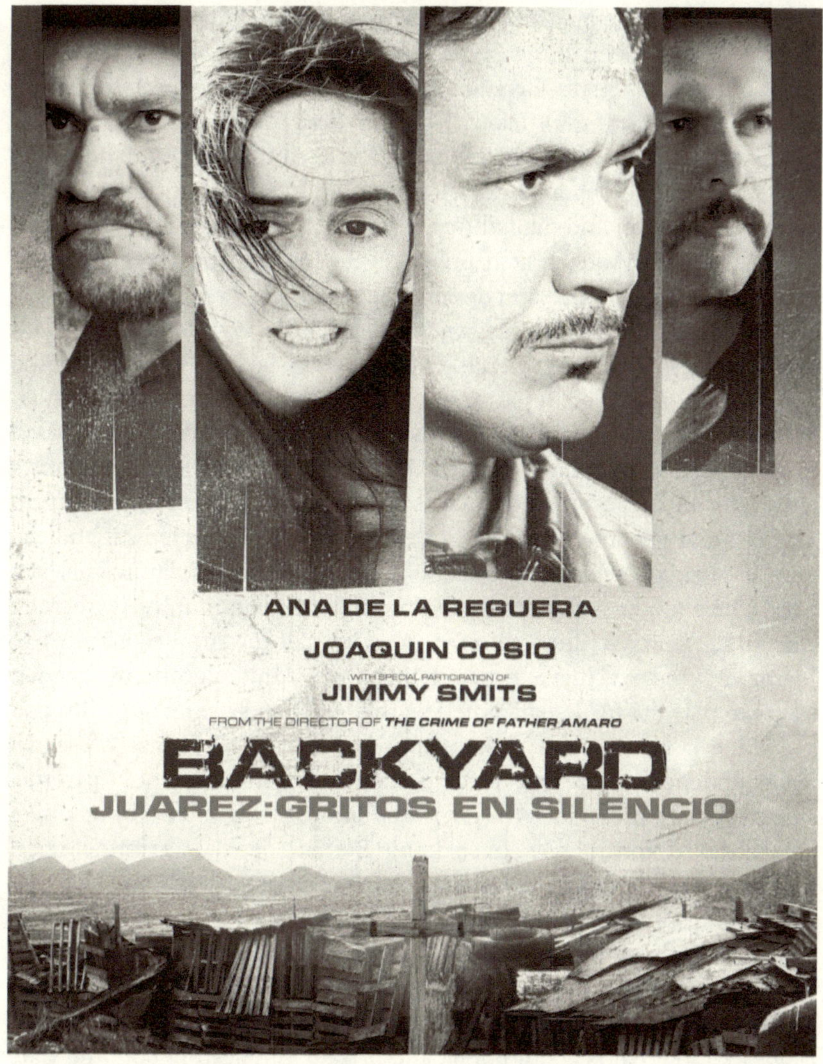

FIGURE 6. Sabina Berman, *Backyard/El Traspatio* (2009). Courtesy of IMCINE.

As if to prove the point in the film production process itself, *Backyard* was shot with some difficulty in Juárez. Berman told the *Los Angeles Times* that "state and municipal authorities 'would have given anything for us not to make the movie in Juárez.'"[87] As crime drama, *Backyard* is explicit about predatory exploitation that is the "bad" stuff of individual men depicted in the play, whether elite or dirt poor—including everyone's most despised villain in gangster films, the corrupt police, prototypical agent of the law's sham. Berman makes an example of an ethical Juárez police officer, explaining, "Blanca's actions were consistent with a law that is superior to the written law," the archetypal Antigone. Dramatic works like *Backyard* use character development and storytelling to reveal the powers of a nation and the failures of its laws to deliver justice, in which the focus on 'story' deliberately privileges the individual to foreground the gaps between experience and democratic ideals.

It is a difficult play to read, and a hard movie to watch, as *Backyard* finally suggests young women like Juana (from Tabasco)—especially the indigenous—are killed in Juárez because they can be killed, not necessarily by the index of exceptionality involving specialists and experts (such as sadists), but by what's normal, the everyday, the wannabe. Juana's encounter with a bewildered Chiapas "compatriot," another migrant from Mexico's indigenous South, turns deadly when she rejects him and the proprietal rights of the traditional boyfriend he tries to claim. This is a man who momentarily locates the promise of "community" with men who find agency in the transient, predatory, throwaway economies of Juárez. By contrast, Juana, experiencing a new kind of economic agency, wants to play the field, exhilarated by the "freedoms" of maquila life that include cell phones and consumer culture; by the promise of sexual "independence," expressed in the pleasures of dancing without parental supervision; by the right to the city;[88] and (more ambiguously) by maquila-enforced birth control pills. In so doing, Berman deploys a criminological narrative structure to depict violence as simultaneously rationalized and irrational disorders.

The casting of Jimmy Smits as closet snuff lord, a rich Mexican expat who regularly crosses the border to cruise maquila towns for preteen girls, is chilling, but the point is that Juana's murder is a story of *feminicidio:* a killing that is "both public and private, implicating both the state (directly or indirectly) and individual perpetrators (private or state actors); it thus encompasses systematic, widespread, and everyday interpersonal violence."[89] Understood as systemic, *feminicidio* signals a complex set of governing regimes which must also be understood as producing legal, social, political, and economic vulnerabilities—systematic dominations and submissions—which make life disposable. Here, the reign of interpenetrating governing regimes makes audible the terrible silence of the law vis-à-vis justice, in its performative effects and its spatial hierarchies.

At the same time, in the *maquila* sector, the hierarchical and predatory labor exploitation that is perfectly "clean," in its white collar and legal institutionalizations (also systemic), remains narratively *implicit* in the drama. The film's visual panoramas of spatial contrasts (and desert affinities) conjoining suburbs of El Paso, Texas, and the toxic industrial camps of the *maquiladora* landscape in Mexico confirm *Backyard* as an investigation into the material productions of transnational border spaces.

As expected, there is no "outside" to border spaces conceived in this way, legal or otherwise, and that is part of Berman's critique. The Chilean critic Nelly Richard observes:

> That there is no exteriority to the system, that nothing is left outside, does not mean that the interior of the institutions does not present dislocations of frames and breakages of diagrams that stimulate and dynamize the game of forces between uniformity and disuniformity. That there is no exteriority to the system, that everything is inside, does not mean that all the regions of the map share the same index of economical capitalist saturation, as if the relation between centers (accumulation) and peripheries (dissemination) gives no place for the unevenly historicized and symbolized textures and materials and, for that reason, is heterogeneous in its capacity to partition oppositional frames and distribute forces that are not centralizing.[90]

Likewise addressing the collusions and joint ventures in state and capital, in a 2009 interview, Berman suggests that critics (particularly in the United States) need to confront the issues, contrasting Mexican with U.S. attitudes: "All the problems that we have today we think are about power. Instead you think it's about ideas." Berman's rebuke points her compatriots, too, back toward national administrations of power and its dispersals, nomoscapes that have already always governed what critical race theorists in the United States call "premature death," the systematic expendability of life within disinterested states.[91]

Usually, responses to the kinds of scenes that Berman writes in *Backyard* involve the mobilization of transnational human rights frameworks, as its billing with the Human Rights Watch Film Festival suggests. Crucially, *Backyard* takes up "the Other Mexicans," for whom "intersectionality" (a term meant to produce antidiscrimination legal doctrine), and the effects of racial difference as a property concern, "in which white racial identity provided the basis for allocating societal benefits both private and public in character,"[92] produce lethal sites for struggle for indigenous communities throughout the Americas. Independent of global human rights organization apparatchiks, the 1994 Zapatista movement (like the grassroots

Idle No More, for instance, in 2012), takes up key concerns dating to the emergence of a transitional justice consensus in the 1990s: advocacy for the restoration of the rule of law, the execution of justice for victims of state crime, and the end to cultures of impunity. As legal scholar Adam Sitze counsels, however, "beware of the trade of amnesty for truth."[93] Likewise concerned with the liability strategies of the bureaucratic state, Berman's *Backyard* points to the persistence of coloniality in transnational American modernities.

More, *Backyard* shows the law as a tool of the state no less busy with material strategies of spatial production, yielding a contested body of spatial representation, of nomoscapes and narcoscapes. In sum, Berman's *Backyard* presents the law and its agents as equivocal in its silence: as a tool for exposing abuses of power from within, as well as "a tool to obfuscate and legitimate it."[94] By directly taking up power in the way Giorgio Agamben describes it, "the state of exception" is to be understood as a "permanent exercise or technique of government rather than a temporary suspension of the rule of law."[95] Berman's *Backyard* presents transnational border spaces that have come to be defined by several regimes of governance techniques showing a proliferation of heterogeneous violences, interlocking policing and maquila tactics.[96] While economists recognize the business rationales of free trade zones and entrepreneurial "narconomics,"[97] the result, *Latin American Research Review* critics increasingly suggest, are apartheid formations and dispossession.[98]

Forensic Lines, Archival Inventory: Teresa Margolles, *127 Cuerpos*

Well represented at global bienniales featuring live art, Teresa Margolles was born in the northwest state of Sinaloa, in Culiacán, where she studied art before moving to Mexico City. Presenting a cryptic poetics, Margolles is a founding member of an artists' collective, SEMEFO (acronym for the *Servicio Médico Forense,* Forensic Medical Service), which was active as a Death Metal Rock Band, and opened its first exhibition in the year of NAFTA, 1994.[99] Remembering the 1994 SEMEFO installation in Mexico City, Coco Fusco observes that it "offered a prescient commentary on Mexico's condition at the onset of the country's entry into the global economic order."[100] True to her art, Margolles went on to earn a diploma in forensic medicine at UNAM in 1995. She and the SEMEFO collective are best known for their work with materials found in morgues: bodies, wash water, blood. This is no whimsy. Resources are scarce for forensic medical services, and, because many bodies (*cuerpos*) continue to go unidentified, the full number of the missing and the disappeared is unverifiable.[101] For most critics, Margolles operates as a kind of forensic archaeologist to Mexican *narcoscapes,* excavating the remains of those who are not identified, or claimed, entire communities conscripted to silence—but may nevertheless have been found at (for instance) execution sites, tagged with threats of retribution (*Narcomensajes,* 2009). Margolles's works include visual, sound, and, most notably, what I would call *olfactory* installations, ones that vaporize cadaver wash water in exhibition spaces; she is sometimes also approached as a textile artist, for her work with various "fabrics," a kind of "borderwork" that doubles the hand wrought work of embroidery with the feminizations of labor after NAFTA.[102]

Rejecting "masochism as metaphor" live art strategies that "create situations of suffering"[103] in favor of working with the forensic remains of those who have actually suffered and died, Margolles uses found materials that *are* leftovers: from the organic fluids, fats, and remainders of corpses that have been found, processed, and assessed by state morgues (in a 2003/2004 interview, Margolles says she was radicalized by Joseph Beuys, who once wrapped his body in animal fat and felt);[104] to the dusty rubble of abandoned housing projects in Juárez (*La Promesa,* 2012). Works have exhibited damp impressions of the dead across institutional sheets, impressing ghostly remainders (*Dermis/Derm,* 1996); a fish task filled with water that was used to wash cadavers (*Fluidos*/Fluids, 1996); cement mixed with wash water (*Untitled,* 2004); and clothes of the dead, *ofrendas* to the ordinary (*Estudio de la ropa de cadaver*/study of a corpse's clothes, 1997).

As the Mexican representative at the 2009 Venice Bienniale, Margolles flew a Mexican flag stained with blood collected from a Sinaloa crime scene, publishing a pointedly phrased exhibition catalog, *¿De qué otra cosa podríamos hablar?* (*What Else Could We Talk About?*). Inside the Mexican pavilion, Margolles brought in relatives of the dead to mop the pavilion floors with wash water and blood, a repetitive domestic chore that staged controversial participatory, or metonymically *relational* techniques.[105] Over time, the work built up sedimented layers of residue throughout the rooms of the pavilion, the daily mopping leaving behind an invisible film of matter that also evaporated and dried on the surfaces it encountered: from Mexican morgue, and the quotidian mop, to Venetian marble, tourists' shoes, hands, mouths, tongues, noses, lungs. The work penetrates and permeates all matter of material surfaces, signaling that surfeit of material relations in the narcoscape of things. Though UNAM (National Autonomous University of Mexico) scholar Frederico Navarrete notes that "the visibility of the corpse in SEMEFO's work began to disappear as Mexico's experience with violent death in the everyday increased in the 1990s," international scholarly focus on Margolles as a solo artist has grown around the themes of corporeal morbidity and the macabre, literalism, and visceralism, and about crime scenes and *narcomensajes,* what the legal scholar R. Scott Bray refers to as summary "funereal dream."[106]

I am more interested in one particular Margolles installation, *127 Cuerpos* (2006), which threads a minimalist approach to the violences of seriality, by way of the material apparatus of the file, as fragment, and inventory. Once perceived, the work produces a sense of nausea and vertigo, enacting encounters with an immanent administrative paradigm that makes *logos* and *nomos,* and the art of government, not separate from the body but unnervingly laces and orders it, materially. The way Margolles so forcefully illuminates the depths of this administrative paradigm is through her attentions to its singular and strikingly bureaucratic detail: the string. Conceived for her exhibition at the 2006 Düsseldorf *Quadrienniale, 127 Cuerpos* is made up of one very long thread (thirty-five meters)—or rather, a series of threads or strings that are tied together and give the appearance of being one string (a thread of things).

It's just a long string of strings, that has 127 parts, one for each of the 127 corpses that the threads were used to respectively sew up, after autopsy. Greater than the sum of its parts, the compendium shrieks and moans in a sound and fury, an inventory not just of morbidity *but of inventory itself.* Arranged formally and in a repetitive structure, it is a thing that prompts "linear" reading, but only insofar as that chronological practice is denounced and dismembered. Literally tearing apart and suturing the body of the archive—in addition to the bodies of the missing—Margolles's "materials" are the cutting and recording processes of administration; the registering, the listing, the evidentiary rituals and regimes themselves. *127 Cuerpos* presents an "original" inventory in a doubling, reeling sense: of and for the dead, of and for an always living archive, a materiality that is corporeal as well as citational, serial, and cryptic. Oscillating between thread and protocol, from the mortuary archive arises that polysemous silence, simultaneously constitutive and antagonistic to the law's silence. In forensics there arises, too, the fetishisms of information database.

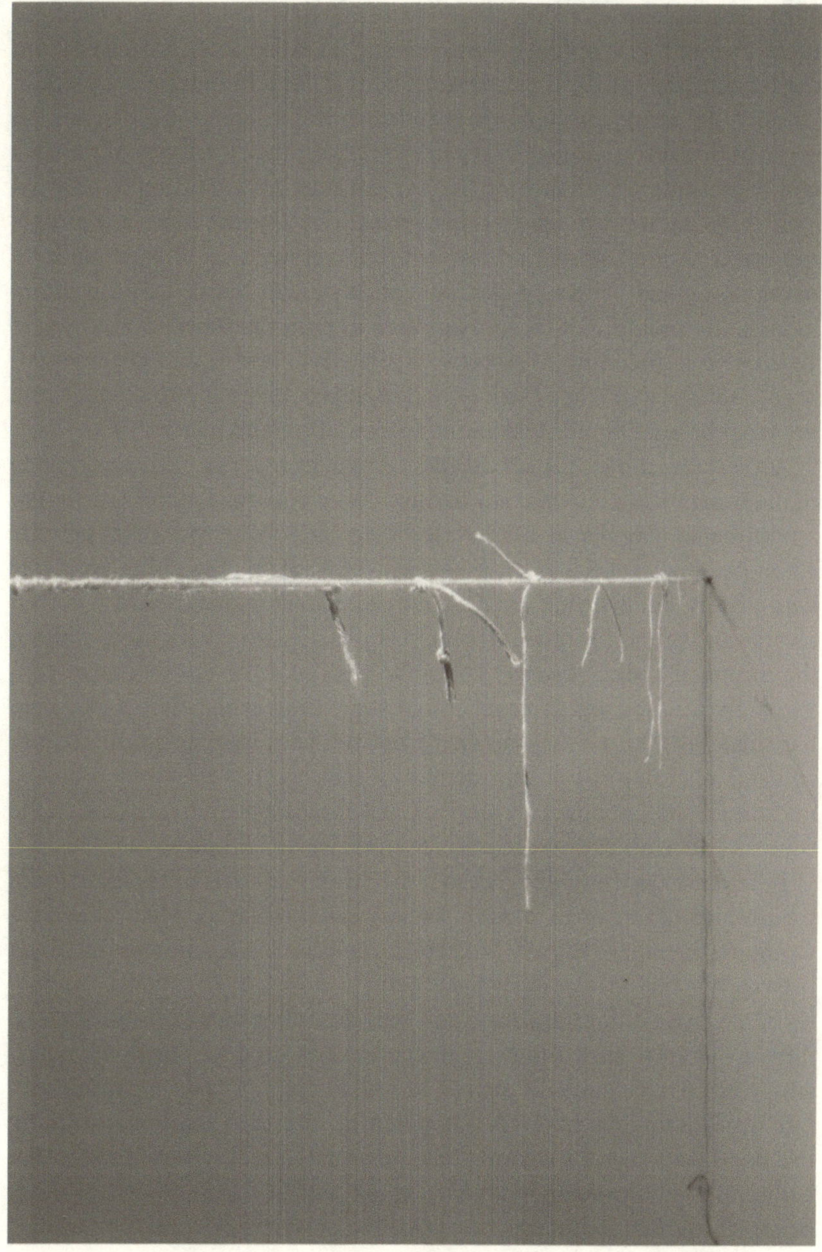

FIGURE 7. Teresa Margolles, *127 Cuerpos* (2006). Courtesy of Teresa Margolles.

In Sven Spieker's reading, "the 'stringing up' of objects was one of the most ancient forms of filing—and the English word, 'file,' is derived from the French (string). Originally meant 'to line something up on a piece of string,'" the string presents an ordering and cataloging mechanism, an organizational technique.[107] This line of 127 strings, then, actually enacts and represents an archive at the same time. In mounting a national archive, to paraphrase Spieker, Margolles's *127 Cuerpos* "does not simply reconnect us with what we have lost [but] reminds us of what we have never possessed."[108] Keeping a studied distance, Margolles's inventory indexes the moment of its subsumption as administrative production. If an archive is made up of paperwork that has "lapsed and become garbage," Spieker says, then "strings, labels, ropes, knots all function to tame the trash by turning it into documents of culture and history."[109]

At the same time, with *127 Cuerpos,* Margolles reduces the heterogeneity of the murmuring bureaucratic archive (law's equivocal performativity) to a minimalist singular line, a focused singularity of purpose that permits an angle into a genealogy of the state's apparatus that is rather pointedly *not* a history, but instead a critique that dramatizes the failures of historical records and proofs to account for the writings of history, within and without the corporeal body. Following Foucault, it is "an archive whose rules constitute themselves together and at that same time as that which they help formulate."[110] The *127 Cuerpos* are "filed" not because they are important, vulnerable, or in any way representative—but because they were ordinary, unclaimed and unnamed: in Mexico City's forensic medical services, in the country's administrative machineries, in the order of things.

In addition to the soiled threads, the other materials of the exhibit are wash water (water used to wash the corpses in Forensic Medical Service Centers); the smell, slightly antiseptic; the colors, a range of dried blood browns; the threads variously used, torn, and frayed. Reportedly, the bodies come from different places; and they are never named. Nevertheless, differences in texture and color in the threads produce a sense of unassimilable tactilicity and difference, as well as the *differend*'s incommensurability. The threads have been handled by forensic examiners, working needle and thread; the threads have penetrated and woven through the bodies of the unknown; the threads speak with and through what cannot be heard in court, but nevertheless exert a powerful force in the negative spaces of the unified threads, as a line.

Wherever it is mapped, the idea of the border also projects a line, as an apparatus of separation that is also porous. The space of the installation allows for movement around the line(s) those threads conjoin and create; and the time, or duration of the work, is open. In the long thread of threads, suspended waist height through a long room, audiences are made to encounter with "forensic" clarity not just the usual absented subject, but in this case, the seriality of its production and cataloging. In its repetition and seriality, the dissimilar is made similar, the organic made machine, the human made non-human—it is disturbing, this juxtaposition of differences that makes for its own classification as well as its own unraveling. The logic of the series demands a lock, tie, or knot, an ordering regime, at the same time that the doxological function generates dispersals.

With *127 Cuerpos,* Margolles stages a meditation about the profoundly material and tactile presence of state apparati that penetrate, manage, classify, identify, and distort the allegorical social body, evincing haunting autopsies of public welfare as a whole. Thus the work also produces a haptic encounter with the symbolic. In the governing and suturing of citizen experience through accounting processes that, in *127 Cuerpos,* are finally made to "speak," the state is conjured as witness to that which it otherwise negates. At the same time, Margolles's forensic attentions to the encryptments of seriality take note of what it is that yet "speaks" in the spaces that have been apparently emptied of those who have been found, or who once were there and whose ontological force remains, noticing too that in her work, those who are usually made to count as passive "evidence" for state archives instead put the state to work.

Yet the thread, a throwaway thing that transforms and confirms the living into the processed matter of the legally dead—inventory—cannot fully claim its quarry. Confronted by the usurpation of the legally codified being (the "human subject," the citizen) and by its status as another kind of thing, in the thread the many is made into the singular, even as the one sears the thread that binds it, giving it color, changing its texture, altering its recording device. Whatever it is, this serial thing calls out a citational commons of the *127.* Minimalist at a glance, the exhibit stages a saturated compendium and a commotion of people and things; a quavering kind of seeing through the looking glass. The moment of recognition is fraught, a seizure of interrupting incompletions swarming forensic catalogs at the peripheries of life everywhere.

Transforming the image and properties of the spectral body in a stroke, the allegorical and material public body (the political, or, *tremulous* private body, as Francis Barker has it) has again been made to appear and to disappear. Reflecting back on the viewer with the uncanny, Margolles subverts colonial empathy: the threads bespeak common verification rituals, the omnipresent signature of bureaucracy and its cagings, procedures and rationales apparently universal in their applications to, and on the behalf of, legal subjects. In Eltit's view, Margolles could be said to be dealing with "the total or partial suspension of the rule of law penetrated, circulated, and lodged in the body of the subject, interrupting thought and altering the energy and direction of everyday life,"[111] a suspension that defines law as the domain of sovereign exception that establishes the line of its reign. As such, the threads simultaneously and sickeningly incur a cryptoanalytic poetics of statelessness: a heterogeneous line of negations, a freedom with silence.

It thus allows too a kind of ontological roaming, what Cervenak calls a wandering in the philosophy of fugitivity. Whatever hails from these threads repeats and exceeds instruments of severance and suture, whether medical or legal, of forensic identifications. Conjuring the line of those who have been cast out, Margolles offers none of the traditional corporeal organs, no cadaver, no mouth, no ears, no eyes to speak of—no text, no words—just an eternal call. Following Briony Fer, the seriality that remains always incurs more: "Invoking infinity, the line cannot be a thing—it is precisely what escapes being a thing."[112] The piece, the strings, dispatch with authorities like language, and law as the ties that bind—even as we are left with the archival surplus of its flimsy apparatus. In *127 Cuerpos,* Margolles presents a formidable principle of serial encryptment. Threads make a line, a border, a logic, an infinity—embedded in clinical exhibition, an immanent story; a silence. As the Chinese dissident artist Ai Wei Wei insists, "Show its detail, that's how you make a critique,"[113] and in Margolles that detail turns on the production line of those cast out, cataloging as seriality and as cryptic taciturnicity, "the silence of something that can speak," whereas, as Derrida explains, "we call mutism the silence of a thing that can't speak."[114]

More prosaically, the autopsy recalls and repeats the work of the butcher, with industrial assembly lines of cadavers. Because Margolles herself physically performs this work and stages fragmentary remains as a critical poetics, I take this to mean that *127 Cuerpos* issues a challenge to the violences of surrogacy, what it is to be used as a shell, a replacement, a substitution, a statistic, a sign; *a subject;* which is to say that by focusing on the absented materiality of the body, on the matter of things, Margolles challenges not only arts discourses (and performance theory) focusing on the uses of surrogacy as a way of talking about the inalienability (and repeatability, or disposability) of the human subject in space and time;[115] but also legal concepts installing the series as systemic, denouncing each in the name of what and who shall not be named (the dispossessed), finally coding the body as "an infinitely expansive site of exchange."[116]

With *127 Cuerpos,* encryptment (meaning to hide, disguise, embed, code) simultaneously constellates a sense of the burial, the tomb, the vault, and the mausoleum. As opposed to the rise of participatory rhetorics in a global performance environment that establish norms for the recognition of arts publics insofar as they demonstrate sufficient entrepreneurial initiative, including the quantifiability of national and municipal creative place-making agendas, Margolles does not waver in looking to the wa(i)vering of archives. What speaks in *127 Cuerpos* makes a demand: as Fred Moten reflects in another context, "critique is part of its repertoire, but it is cryptoanalytic."[117] In *127 Cuerpos,* Margolles shows an operation that binds and is bound up with the cryptoanalytic line, one that can't be simply reduced to "driving the body to abstraction" as the complaint goes, but on the contrary hews to the relentless contingency of its constitution—providing, in Spieker's words, a critique that lies "at the center of every effort to record and measure time,"[118] a minimalist work that apprehends the logics of seriality as bound up in the violences of administration.[119]

Silence as Sign and Resource: Natalia Almada's *El Velador/The Nightwatchman*

Born in Mexico City, with roots in Sinaloa and Sonora, documentary filmmaker Natalia Almada is a dual citizen of Mexico and the United States who studied photography at the Rhode Island School of Design (RISD). In October 2012 she was named a MacArthur Fellow, reportedly the first Latina filmmaker to win the prestigious "genius" grant. Almada works with Mexican national histories that are also family histories; *El General,* for instance, examines the memory of Almada's great-grandfather, General Plutarco Elías Calles.[120] Almada went back to Sinaloa for her 2011 documentary *El Velador/The Nightwatchman,* to film the great *Cementerio of Culiacán,* the *Jardines de Humaya.* Established in 1969, the cemetery is a monumental city of the dead, *Una Necrópolis de Gran Tradición,* and (small surprise) has swiftly grown in size since 2006. *El Velador* asks how it is possible to witness and perceive the intensifications of violent conflict irrupting Mexico's internal borderlands. The film strikes subtle chords of disquiet: Almada's aesthetic refuses voyeuristic approximation of *nacotraficantes, jefes,* or *víctimas* made spectacle; she permits no *narcocapitalist* speed or adventure, or even the elaborate demands of *justicia.* After all, Almada would appear to concur, the camera, documentary, and ethnographic imperative are each bound up with colonial enterprise,[121] and often as "shows of violence we can safely watch," as the Latin Americanist Jean Franco concludes.[122] Almada shows there are better ways.

In Almada's documentary, the camera offers a medium for the performance of something other than what has been imposed upon it, proposing instead an ethics of listening, a kind of aural witness, there in those places where everyday resistance can be "quiet." I saw the film (and met Almada) a week before the MacArthur prize news, at the Minneapolis Walker Art Center, in October 2012. At the audience Q&A, Almada registered her dissatisfaction with mainstream cinematic and documentary economies flashing the usual spectacular displays of *narcocultura* dystopias, anecdotally recounting the claim of major (male) filmmakers who say *women just can't get the pacing right, they can't make a good film.* Instead, it is rather in her deliberate crafting of repetition and rhythm that Almada's camera makes room for the nuances of everyday life.[123]

As the film begins, it is not that we are looking through a glass darkly, no, nothing so melodramatic; it is just that with the camera looking out from the passenger seat of an old baby blue Chevy, we are looking at and through sedimentations of matter—a dirty and dusty windshield of an old chugging truck, a kind of seeing-glass whose truck is Almada's aperture. It dusts our vision. Throughout, a grainy film imposes its own texture on seeing, a tactile mediation. Driving to and from the *cementerio,* watching dust and truck and character and scene, Almada's audiences are first looking at and through a series of framing devices: things that organize and obfuscate their objects of study, and viewers who do the same. The driver, Martín, is the *velador,* the nightwatchman. Now and again he reaches out to rub the dust and dirt off the windshield interior with a worn red cloth, as he drives into the necropolis where miles of city blocks composed of two- and three-story architectural wonders (mausoleums) glow gently in the light of the setting sun. Almada seeks to do the same with her camera, clearing its glass eye of the grime that has accumulated there in national habits of seeing *nomoscapes* and *narcoscapes.* By association, we are all readied to see (and hear) more clearly, more slowly; but of course that grainy dusty dirt will have its sway. Emphatically guests in the *cementerio,* visitors are party to the gritty monumentalizations of memory, and other decompositions.

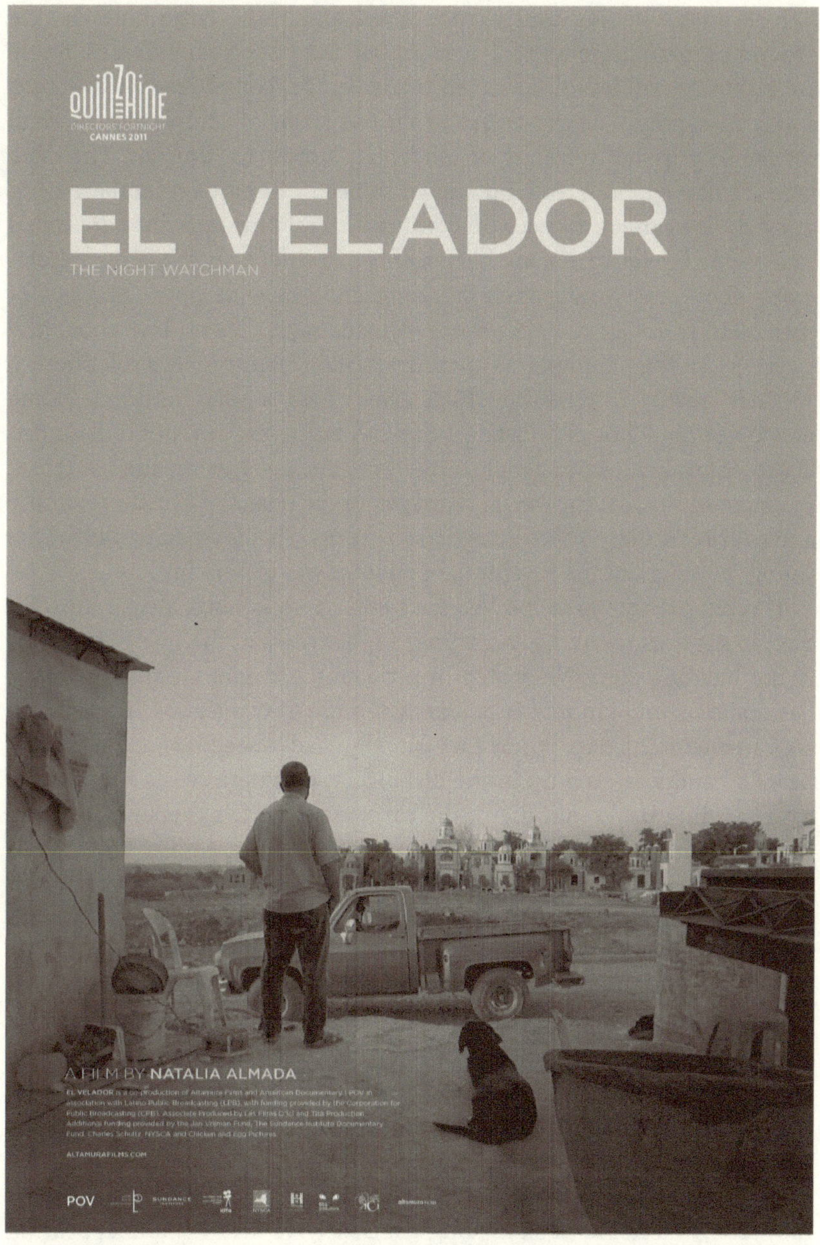

FIGURE 8. Natalia Almada, *El Velador/The Night Watchman* (2011). Courtesy of Natalia Almada.

It is dusk. We see construction sites, small and large holes in the ground preparing the way for new graves, flat 60 × 80cm singles. Some are elaborate, tall buildings called mausoleums, complete with rotundas and landscaping. The graves are in various states of completion, or shall we say in grip and mimicry of modernity's promise, *progress.* The dead here are named, honored, and known subjects, they are remembered and grieved. The camera focuses on a printed bright blue tarp, they are called *lonas,* which covers the shared grave of two brothers; on it, a digital photograph shows two young men laughing, mouths wide open, two sets of even teeth an image of better times. Almada says, "What I love about [the tarps] is that the photographs are mostly taken from people's cell phones, so their quality is terrible, which gives them a very innocent 'home movie' feeling—not the nostalgic Super-8 home movies, but today's pixelated equivalent. Also, people make fantastic collages on the *lonas* that are incredibly revealing visual homages to the dead."[124] The dates on the graves are arresting: 1978–2009; 1990–2009. This is a necropolis for the young, plotting out the inventory of another war generation.

The camera moves to the Velador's still hand, holding a cigarette; and then to his eyes watching (scanning) for activities of the living, hubbubs in the bustling dusk. We watch him watch the rumbling quiet; Almada has made us into kindred *veladores.* A minute or two passes. The camera sees an oncoming dog, floppy ears friendly, glad to see Martín; the camera hears a band warming up in the distance; the camera sees a man with a tuba catching up to join them; the camera sees a food vendor bicycling his three wheeled store slowly down the street. We are given the time to reflect: this is an economy, an entrepreneurial market economy, an urban economy. Like cemeteries everywhere it is an exchange economy, a rationalization of the order of things.[125] Audiences cannot claim to know what it is that Martín sees, except that the practice of seeing, no less documenting, is itself a thing to be watched, a thing that he, the *velador,* also watches. Almada comments, "I've always thought of my camera not as a documentary device, and myself not as a documentarian, but rather that there is a triangular relationship between myself, the camera, and the subject. I thought of Martín as my accomplice: that he was watching me as much as I was watching him." For Martín, perhaps, the task is to carefully look, and not be seen looking too closely; to hear without appearing to be listening. In the *Jardines de Humaya,* the living and the dead speak. What, Almada seems to ask, might audiences learn from this nightwatchman ethics?

The first time Martín speaks, and he doesn't speak often, Martín says, "There are lots of shootouts / they throw parties at night / they bring their bands and they shoot their guns / at night you can't walk around the cemetery." Repetition suggests Martín always arrives at dusk, and leaves in the morning. The camera shows Martín listening to the parties in the distance, and in his shelter, to the television. Almada's camera records snippets of the local evening news report: "An unidentified body was found in a black bag, shot / authorities picked up the corpse and two more bodies outside a nightclub / Culiacán has become a war zone / Los Tígres del Norte cancelled their concert because of all the bloodshed / a week earlier, the body of a young woman was found chopped to pieces, it appears this was a vendetta against one of the cartels." We know nothing else of the night, other than what Martín tells us, the vague sounds in the distance, and the no less vague echo bouncing off the incessant noise of *information*, via televised reports.

In the day shift, a trim and well-dressed young woman mops the marble of a mausoleum, and washes its glass doors. A widow, perhaps. The building is elaborately lit, there are chandeliers, furniture; some have fully functioning air conditioning and stereo systems. The traditional *votivos* and the gladiola make the case that this is a grave, and many of the people buried here were murdered. It's hard to reconcile the scene: morning activities versus night; the quiet of the place with the imminent, the inaudible (though the dog hears more); the humble and the elaborate burial grounds. Back on Martín's modest watch, his rough station is furnished with nothing but a plastic chair and a bare lightbulb. Almada films the ten-inch TV, broadcasting news of "an oncoming thunderstorm / The government makes pledges to preserve the peace and fight any kind of organized delinquency / Calderón declares an economic crisis." Almada records Martín assembling a makeshift camp, he pulls a board and some bedding over four pillars of buckets, spaced in that rectangle we call bed. It seems as if the dead rest with more accommodations. In the morning, the *velador* wakes to a landscape of burning trash, a makeshift landfill at the cemetery's edge. The camera spies a dog with newborn puppies beneath a pile of trash. In a way, the living are all born buried in matter.

Cut to another night. Everything repeats, dusk and dawn; the sounds, and the routine; the truck, the washing, the watering. The television broadcast reports, "Ex-drug Czar Barry McCaffrey said the US is not paying attention / he asks Obama to pay more attention to Mexico's War on Drugs / agreeing with Secretary of Homeland Security Janet Napolitano /

who said that in Ciudad Juárez, civil order has been lost." Against the distant noise of law and order talk, the camera cuts to construction workers plying wood, cement, and rods. It is regular work, it is a working day; every part of the narcoeconomy is, shall we say, *a living*. The sound of a mother's eternal lament at a nearby funeral makes it familiar, "*Ay mi hijo*." The trim young widow, finished with her washing, gets into her white Audi and goes. In a poem inspired by the film, Dolores Dorantes writes, "Someone is building a city," and she's right. For those who bother to look, it's a city for the undead. The narcoeconomy supplies the only factory that's still open, the bank that's still lending, the construction company that keeps on building, the city that never sleeps, the municipal public interest gone private. The story of this living necropolis is ghostly in the sense that it refashions social relations, as sociologist Avery Gordon says: as not only repairing representational mistakes, but also as an effort to understand "the conditions under which a memory was produced in the first place, toward a countermemory, for the future."[126]

"When I started," Almada says, "my idea was to make a film about violence" in a way that was contrary to everything that's been filmed about narcoscapes, focusing instead on the people at the cemetery, the widows, the bricklayers, "*que son gente como los demás* (who are people like everyone else)." Almada remembers wondering, "Can I make a film staying in one place with as few elements as possible? Then being there, I thought, well is it possible for me to make a film in the corner of the cemetery? Because it actually takes place all in one little corner." Unlike her previous films, which have taken on the polyphonous plays of sound (the corridos and narcocorridos, in *Al Otro Lado*) and of peripatetic place (the archival spreads of memory in *El General*), the idiom of *El Velador* is repetition, stillness, and a certain kind of audible silence. Typically, activists and journalists refer to silence as a form of death, of complicity. But as Eltit suggests, there is to be found in silence "a politics of survival and even resistance. For how can one speak when the forums for speech have been taken over or threatened? Silence as a resource can become a sign."[127]

Rather than submit to that old thesis about violence as a thing beyond language that irrevocably removes the subject from history—and because it is rather a question of how language and violence each transmit the other (Pratt)—Almada's *Velador* detects another errant cryptoanalytics of freedom with silence. In a cemetery, of course, there is a ritual *code of silence*. There will be no interviewing here, do not disrespect mourners, so forget depositions, interviews, "testimony," and other verification regimes. Watch instead the repetitions, learn how to hear the iterations of quiet, and above all, show respect. Reflecting, Almada corrects herself, "I set out to answer the question of how to look at violence . . . where it has just occurred, where it is immanent." In the film, nothing much happens. But it is always on the verge of happening; it is happening somewhere; and, it has just happened. *Tiene su proprio ritmo.* (It has its own rhythm.) The *cementerio* is powered by the persistence of everyday life, of the ordinary amidst the extraordinary: money for food, water, and some kind of dwelling; a place to rest, to belong, and to grieve. By setting her camera on the cementerio's materially transformative qualities, Almada offers El Velador's haunting witness as a way of "putting life back in where only a vague memory or a bare trace was visible to those who bothered to look."[128] Something other than the modern law subject, duly legible, presides here.

Eltit's argument about silence as a resource suggests it's not just that the main character in the film, Martín, doesn't talk much. Those phrasings of silence, every part of it, the ritual quiet of the cementerio tucked around the peripheries of the social relations of violence (and night time big bands)—they constitute a refusal to disappear. As Eltit reflects, "To maintain one's silence implied an attitude and a form of negation. It was precisely in silence and from silence that the reorganization of the social text could come about."[129] The silences recall Lyotard's *differend,* in that they are performative, and transmit an ancient tune of statelessness. "There must be some kind of way out of here / Said the joker to the thief"—and the refrain, "So let us not talk falsely now, the hour is getting late."[130] For Almada, those refusals to disappear are in the sun rising and the sun setting; the song of cicadas; a ride in a dusty old Chevy; in hours spent watering the earth, to keep the dust down. It's in a dog yawning and napping, in a widow, mopping; in a daughter's game of hopscotch; and it's in a man, watching. In the end, this is not a documentary film about the state, or the narco state, about Mexico qua some kind of impossibly other, distant terror. This is not about reproducing or censoring violence, two strategies that fetishize killing fields. This is not even about producing *a* voice, or a report, a litany of the what and the who, the where and the when, that "needs" individual representation. It is not about the police, *narcos,* public protest, human rights, citizenship, border spaces, migration, morgues, forensics, or the production of seriality (at least not explicitly). It is not about a hearing, or a legal hearing, it is not about the law; it is not about law's stories; not about recording, documenting, testifying, judging. Not about "justice," not exactly, no. But also, yes, it is about these things, all of them, because there in the polyphonies of silence of unassimilability and incommensurability, it is about that fulsome abandon, a space of release from the testamentary whimper: the eloquence of the *differend*, labors that are inseparable from performance.

#TodosSomosAyotzinapa: *It was the state*

The search for the missing Ayotzinapa 43 reveals a nation haunted by many more disappearances, hidden mass graves, and everyday violences than can be verified as unique to the Guerrero students. That the *normalistas* may have been attacked by the police on their way to the annual commemoration of the 1968 Tlatleloco student massacre, in Mexico City—at the same that they were tracked by federal, army, and state forces (watched)—emphasizes the historical repetition of social struggles radicalized by neoliberal securitization and surveillance horizons.[131] As the inaugural statement of 2014 IACHR objectives suggest, the breadth and depth of factors involved in the disappearances far exceed in scope, for instance, the detention of one Iguala Mayor, José Luis Abarca, and his wife, María de los Ángeles Pineda Villa, for criminal prosecution for their stipulated part in the disappearance of the Ayotzinapa 43, by ordering the attack on the students. What's happening in the Ayotzinapa 43's Mexico forcefully eludes the usual attempts to take individual testimony, evidence, or the police procedural as discrete objects of knowledge. Law and order rhetorics only go so far.

The hashtag *#SomosTodosAyotzinapa* ("We are all Ayotzinapa") expresses popular national and transnational defiance against the compromised authorities of city, state, and federal governments—and specifically against the failures of the law, as the sign and signature of socially produced executive, legislative, judicial, and military authorities to ensure social justice: "*La justicia no va a llegar, aunque busquemos*" (Justice isn't coming, but we're looking for it).[132] In the discourse of narrative, *#SomosTodosAyotzinapa* bespeaks a conjunction of interlocking silences and governing regimes that simultaneously produces and is signified in the multiplication of stories about *narcos* who kill in police uniforms, and vice versa; about an army and other state security forces that may not be any different; about community militias taking matters into their own hands; and about the proliferation of transnational contract, or private security forces that are immune from national and international prosecution. The glare of impunity frames rising concerns about the interpenetrations of law and lawlessness that many stripes of security experts suggest are not exceptional in today's world, but rather characterize it, including forms of control and dispossession—injustices—that are hard to pin down in the rituals of a deposition, a crime report, or a court of law.

#SomosTodosAyotzinapa is a sign for who and what has gone missing as a result of economic neoliberal restructuring: a sign for lacerating fields of struggle associated not only with the 2013 Education Reform Bill pertinent to the *normalistas,* but more generally with the Pact for Mexico's changing regulatory horizons that also include banking, fiscal, energy, and telecommunications reforms. "Since the ratification of NAFTA," Irmgard Emmelhainz explains, Mexicans "have been converted into maquiladora workers (virtually as slaves, because they earn below the minimum living wage), *sicarios* [hit men], entrepreneurs, consumers (or handicapped, indebted consumers), criminals, dead bodies, prisoners, and members of the permanently unemployed underclass. A term has even been coined to the describe the eight million youths excluded from education and work: *ninis* (*ni trabajan ni estudian*), a category of young people who neither work nor study, and depend on their families to support them."[133] As publics issue the specific accusation, *Ayotzinapa: Fue el Estado* ("it was the state"), the affective declaration, *#YaMeCansé,* generalizes the political sentiment of an unhappy commons, "I'm sick of it": sick of fear, violence, repression, and collusion; sick of the failure of a modern law state to deliver justice for its people; sick of the surveillance state; sick of economic exploitation and inequality.

On the one hand, it is precisely within the space of the law's silence, and to its aprorias, that the hashtag *#SomosTodosAyotzinapa* "speaks," which is to say that societies bound by modern law contain within them the capacity to cut and be bound up in the eclipse and containment of justice. If positive law is said to exclude "justice" from its purview, or if the norms of positive law can be said to be silent on the matter of justice, public response to the case of the *normalistas* show publics which nevertheless continue to forge collective languages toward justice: with and without the corroborations of state or legal authorities; international human rights organizations; or modes of governance reconciling human rights and transnational security interests in the name of economic prosperity.[134] Demonstrations for the Ayotzinapa 43, whatever the media, show that one of the ways that the appeal to justice happens is indeed through language, as Constable points out.[135] In so doing, they show that profound dissonances and incommensurabilities in the systems of legal judgment continue to make "justice" scarce, the exercise of authority ever quiescent to the silence of the modern law state.

On the other hand, it can also be said that *#SomosTodosAyotzinapa* and *#YaMeCansé* issue a chorus of another and no less important kind of scriptive thing, an *infrarrealista* sign that also functions as an index. As Rosalind Krauss explains, the index "operates to substitute the registration of sheer physical presence" with the language of more discursive codes.[136] Rather than any one singly profiled voice, a hashtag is a number sign, a symbol that names groups and topics without registering or controlling them. In and as social media, the hashtag enables a following and a uniform camouflage at the same time. Used for unmoderated ad-hoc discussion, it is also a metadata tag. As media theorists Finn Brunton and Helen Nissenbaum explain, the function of the sign's chorus of silence is to hide like a spy in a crowd of signals. For Foucault, the spy, as parrhesiac messenger, is the paradigmatic outsider in the very old cynic tradition, the one "who roams, who is not integrated into society."[137] Evading detailed deposition, *#SomosTodosAyotzinapa* and *#YaMeCansé* are contingent and cryptographic things, channeling an indexical chorus of silence (a syntax) that issues protest and deferral at the same time.

The art of writing and solving codes, it becomes more and more clear, is a worldly discipline, not only for information security markets, but for publics seeking annulment, cover, and obfuscation. Cryptography cultivates silence as a resource and a screen, as affective and strategic cipher in the theaters of refuge and subterfuge. For the Chilean novelist Roberto Bolaño, who found exile in Mexico City in 1968 when he was fifteen, in *infrarrealismo* style the writing of this wily silence (as opposed to the law's abstentious silence) is by definition lawless; like *#SomosTodosAyotzinapa* and *#YaMeCansé,* Bolaño's oeuvre eviscerates the noise and notion of "information," wracking against the pretense of "investigation," and the ostentatious institutionalizations of memory.[138] Wary of memorializing narratives, I am again reminded of Adam Sitze's argument about transitional justice processes, that amnesty is designed to unravel the enmity that is the essence of war—not to deliver justice.[139] As I have written elsewhere, transitional justice processes ensure the futurity of the state.[140] But in the chorus of hashtag signals, in *#SomosTodosAyotzinapa* and *#YaMeCansé,* it is the futurity of the craft and cunning of collective enmity that rises. The sound and the fury of silence function as sign, index, and signal; guile is its molten resource. Even if "modern law fails to acknowledge any debt to what is unsayable," as Constable argues,[141] it is because of and into the forked tongues and gobbling gaps of many kinds of silence that law and enmity—antagonism's dissent—is to be thought.

Conclusion: *Infrarrealista* Tecnics

Writing from and about Mexico, political theorist Pilar Calveiro suggests that established modes of legal and political analysis simply fail to grasp the complexities at hand:

> It could be argued that we are not facing a war against drug trafficking, as is often affirmed, for such a war would presuppose two sides: the government and the drug dealers fighting to the death. On the contrary, the involvement of different state and nonstate actors demonstrates the interpenetrations between government, society, and organized crime which comprises a massive network that disseminates atrocious forms of violence in a struggle for market control amongst its internal factions. Officials from different departments are part of this confrontation and favour one of the sides in order to gain profit. This network affects with its violence large sectors of society that end up being its victims, although they may also be involved with it. Kidnapped for ransom, murdered for revenge or by mistake, or extorted for money, owners of small or medium businesses or merchants, displaced farmers and villagers, and abused immigrants are the most common victims.[142]

Like Guha and Chakrabarty, Calveiro's attentions to networks of reciprocal and relational formations direct analysis toward the material webs producing everyday life. The thick interplay of transnational state, legal, market, and other forces and flows map the violence of neoliberalism and the securitization state beyond national borders. Policing as a mode of governance proliferates. Asymmetrical deployments of evidence and silence annex and rivet the world. In the United States, trading the War on Poverty (Johnson) for the War on Drugs (Nixon) suggests an ideological shift in North American attitudes that turns resources away from the governance of public welfare, making the War on Drugs a creature of neoliberalism.[143] American *narcolandias* follow close on the heels of fallen Fordlandias everywhere.[144] The result is what economists call a "dual economy," high and low wage sectors that meet to volatile effect in the transnational War on Drugs. Everywhere, forensic analysis and criminal law—to identify the remains of the missing and to insist on accountability; less optimistically, to fund the war machine, to exorcise the parrhesic threat—appears to both anchor and delimit ideas about what modern law processes may and may not do about a field of conflict that's killing so many people across the Americas. Can Forensic Architecture map that?

Intervening, Avital Ronell supplies a trenchant critique of verification routines that command the logics of forensics, criminal procedure, and speech acts alike. Defining "the testamentary whimper" as the failing drive to test and prove within the bounds of legal protocols, and in an era when so much value is placed on the powers of documentary evidence, Ronell indicates the urgent need to instead reconsider the "pervertability" of evidentiary testing.[145] What happens, Ronell asks, "to those among us who make existence claims that, according to the rules of cognitive discourse, cannot be validated? What about those whose distress has not been proven, whose rights have not been recognized, and whose pain has yet to be legally seared into our living memories?"[146] Ronell's lithe argument anticipates the stacked powers of one-way evidentiary protocols, and responds to what Lyotard's *differend* seeks to recognize: the principle of incommensurability, in which the one(s) who refuse and are denied recognition, *in addition to* the violences of the law's silence, must be interpreted as deploying silence as a "possibility of phrasing" toward justice.

Building on scholarship about scriptive things and the law's silence, while holding close certain criticisms of evidentiary rhetorics and techniques, it is striking how artists and publics amplify the no less intransigent silence found in the multitudinous elsewheres and afterlives of legal things. Again, it is instructive that Bolaño's *infrarrealista* style, a pulp-fiction mock-documentary that rails against official national culture and all its aspects and reports, *mimics* in order to subvert the nonfiction genre of forensic report, and its failing investigative premises and procedures, returning instead to the perspicacious melee of signs. As tenebrous proxy, equivocal silence transmits the resources of an uncontrollable and companion compendium, a cryptoanalytic that is also and at the same time a genealogy of fury, rage—a tacit ungovernability. It is to the plenitudes and the suspensions of this clamoring silence, to the abeyant and aberrant dormancies of a sage and shrewd silence, to an adroit commons, and to its polysemous antagonisms that we must also look.

As an artist for whom "silence as resource can become a sign," Eltit recounts strategies that express floods of disquiet without surrendering to the demands of legibility. Poets emphasize the difference between a thing said and unsaid; and oral historians cultivate the arts of listening (to rhythms and to gaps), as distinctive from the records of transcription. Heidegger knows the score: "Language, by naming beings for the first time, first brings beings *to* word and to appearance. Only this naming nominates beings to their being *from out* of their being. Such saying is a projecting of the clearing, in which announcement is made of what it is that beings come into the Open *as*."[147] Gorrostieta, Berman, Margolles, Almada, and the Ayotzinapa hashtags suggest strategies for responding to what Ayotzinapa and the "war on drugs" in Mexico seem to stand for (and stand in for), *as*, and as *a projection of the clearing*. They reject, in other words, their announcements *as such*. In different ways, each shows that with respect to the sheer heterogeneity of social fields, the prevalence of documentary "information," and the "cult of immediately ascertainable fact," as Ernest Bloch has it, generate serious dilemmas about the reach and limits of law and performance alike.[148]

I owe the phrasing of this essay's title to Chandan Reddy's 2011 *Freedom with Violence*, where he argues that liberal rights discourses and war go together as two sides of the same coin.[149] The cavalcade of rights struggles, with its constitutive evidentiary controls, is reconfirmed in its disavowals and in its silences. To wit, U.S. congressional reports estimate Mexican cartels control 90 percent of the drugs entering the United States; and Mexican reports suggest at least 70 percent of seized guns (and 100 percent of all assault weapons) originate in the United States. Nobody disputes that 90 percent of maquila production is for U.S. consumption. As Ronell insists (in other contexts), there is a history of non-relation here, and a history to the denial of relationship between what happens in Mexico and the United States—including the denial of profit, or advantage.[150] It is to this and other collusions in rationality that artists, publics, and scholars address legacies of silence, violence, and the law.

Ronell, too, demands a practice and a philosophy (praxis) that quits its complicity with normative demands for intelligibility. In a situation where "everything is staked on the plight of a phrase whose regimen excludes cognitive verification"—and by "everything" Ronell means human distress, including the distress of having *to account* for distress, to offer proof of a distress that others do not know—then she says that reliance on verification has to go. In its stead, Ronell recommends "untested new regions of new idioms, new addresses, new referents"; recognizing silence as a syntax that "runs counter to the traditional adducement of proof."[151] Ronell's thinking is congruent with Bolaño, Guha, and Chakrabarty: that the political is elucidated through other idioms. Focusing on works that struggle with the implications of Ronell's observation, that "language and proof have met their reciprocal limits," we have arrived at a series of thresholds that both do and do not bespeak codes of conduct, refusals that do and do not comply with standard procedures of certification: the public servant Gorrostieta produces a photographic file for the police, Berman narrates a criminological border historiography, Margolles installs a cryptoanalytics in the inventories of the archival string (the line), and in different ways both Almada and the Ayotzinapa 43 hashtags score the phrasings of silence as a sign. They do so through formal engagements with the "grammars" of production and performance (through photography, dramatic feature, installation, documentary film, and social media). Moving between the one and the many, they mount critiques that have no easy or immediate answer. Here, the police, the state, the border, the morgue, the cemetery, and social media present archivizing sites that are as bound up with the protocols of legal regulation as they discard its rituals of verifiability. They do and do not "perform."

Even before the Ayotzinapa 43, Rodrigo Parrini frankly suggests publics can no longer assume they will not be disappeared or tortured in the volatile dynamics of transnational *nomoscapes* and *narcoscapes,* due to the problems Guha and Berman prioritize (domination and subordination). Reporters say that places like Juárez are not to be dismissed as an anomaly, or as a breakdown of the social order. Word is that "Juárez is the new order."[152] In response to such distress, our interlocutors hold out for the reserves of an apposite incommensurability—the silences of encryptments, "idioms," and referents in which, Ronell and Guha imply, arrests against distress might hold. Because the *differend* is a site of absolute incommensurability, in Ronell, releasing language (and thought) from instrumentalizing limitations can also be seen as a move to relinquish the mandate to perform. As we have seen, when the arts deliberately work as active and allied agents in the field of rights witness projects, they not only step in where the official apparati of the modern law state fail to address the demands of human suffering; they seek relief from the constraints of its protocols. Rejecting the inadequacies of verifiability logics, they do not limit themselves to the task of proof, in the narrow sense of the term, but respond to and with the loquaciousness of things, as Eltit affirms: the eloquence of freedom with silence.

NOTES

1. A principal, autonomous body of the Organization of American States (OAS), the IACHR derives its mandate from the OAS Charter and the American Convention on Human Rights. The Inter-American Commission has a mandate to promote respect for human rights in the region and acts as a consultative body to the OAS in this area. The

Commission is composed of seven independent members who are elected in an individual capacity by the OAS General Assembly and who do not represent their countries of origin or residence.

2. The IACHR Interdisciplinary Group of Independent Experts (GIEI) reporting on Ayotzinapa first met in February 2015: Carlos Martín Beristain, a Spanish doctor; Angela Buitrago, a Colombian lawyer; Francisco Cox Vial, a Chilean lawyer; Claudia Paz y Paz, former Attorney General of Guatemala; and Alejandro Valencia Villa, a Colombian human rights lawyer.

3. Amnesty International, *Mexico: Submission to the UN Committee on Enforced Disappearances, 8th Session, 2–13 February* (London: Amnesty International Publications, 2015), 4.

4. Fernando Servín Camacho, "PGR avala que en el caso Iguala se libere de responsabilidad Fernando Servín al Estado," *La Jornada,* 25 Enero 2015: 5, http://www.jornada.unam.mx/2015/01/25/politica/005n1pol; Organization of American States, "OAS Presents Report on Evaluation of Drug Policies in the Countries of the Hemisphere," http://www.oas.org/en/media_center/PReleases/2015/.

5. The third GIEI Report, of May 11, 2015, states: "The Group previously pointed out that the crimes to investigate are of enforced disappearance, not of kidnapping, but stresses that also there were other serious violations of human rights, and crimes, among them: 1) torture (e.g. in the case of Julio César Mondragón Fontes); 2) attempts of murder; 3) concealment, obstruction of justice and abuse of authority; 4) inadequate use of the force; 5) battery and threats suffered by the normalistas that survived the attack. These crimes should also be adequately investigated."

6. Marcela Turati, "Ayotzinapa: sus propios informes comprometen al Ejército," *Proceso,* March 21, 2015, http://www.proceso.com.mx/399067; Anabel Hernández and Steve Fisher, "Ayotzinapa: las aberraciones de la investigacion," *Proceso,* May 16, 2015, http://www.proceso.com.mx/404492/ayotzinapa-prefabricada-la-verdad-historica-de-la-pgr.

7. Paulina Villegas, "Experts Reject Official Account of How 43 Mexican Students Were Killed," *New York Times,* September 6, 2015, 4.

8. "The spiral of violence and impunity brings severe consequences for the Rule of Law in the country. . . . The great challenge for the Mexican State is to close the existing gap between its normative framework and the reality facing a large number of inhabitants who seek access to a prompt and effective justice," said IACHR member James L. Cavallaro.

9. John Gibler, *Una historia oral de la infamia: los ataques a los normalistas de Ayotzinapa* (Ciudad Autónoma de Buenos Aires: Tinta Limón, 2016).

10. U.S. Department of Homeland Security, "The U.S.-Mexico Bi-national Criminal Proceeds Study," June 2010.

11. Michael Taussig, *The Magic of the State* (New York: Routledge, 1997).

12. James C. Scott, *Seeing Like a State: How Certain Schemes to Improve the Human Condition Have Failed* (New Haven, CT: Yale University Press, 1999), 5.

13. Elena Shtromberg, *Art Systems: Brazil and the 1970s* (Austin: University of Texas Press, 2016).

14. Azam Ahmed, "In Mexico, 'It's Easy to Kill a Journalist,'" *New York Times,* April 19, 2017.

15. Citing the murder of the Chihuahua-based *La Jornada* reporter Miraslova Breach in March 2017, as well as fiscal challenges, the daily *El Norte* closed (Gustavo Castillo Garcia, "El día del crimen, tres hombres acechaban a Miroslava Breach," *La Jornada,* 27 Marzo 2017, http://www.jornada.unam.mx/2017/03/27/politica/003n1pol).

16. Screened alongside 136 other works at *Ambulante Cinema Documental Itinerante 2017* in cities throughout Mexico, Ludovic Bouleux's *Guerrero* (2017) is a

documentary portrait of people who have become activists after the 2014 disappearance of the Ayontzinapa 43 (Marién Kadner, "'*Guerrero*', un retrato de la violencia en el Estado más convulso de México," *El Pais,* 1 Abril 2017, http://cultura.elpais.com/cultura/2017/04/01/actualidad/1491014622_323363.html).

17. Robert Cover, "Nomos and Narrative," *Harvard Law Review* (1983): 4–68.

18. Piyel Haldar, "The Function of the Ornament in Quintilian, Alberti, and Court Architecture," in *Law and the Image: The Authority of Art and the Aesthetics of Law,* ed. Costas Douzinas and Lynda Nead, (Chicago: University of Chicago Press, 1999), 117–36; Peter Goodrich, "Specters of Law: Why The History of Legal Spectacle Has Not Been Written," *UC Irvine Law Review* 1, no. 3 (2011): 773–812.

19. Arjun Appadurai, "Introduction: Commodities and the Politics of Value," in *The Social Life of Things: Commodities in Cultural Perspective* (Cambridge: Cambridge University Press, 1986); Bill Brown, "Thing Theory," *Critical Inquiry* 28, no. 1 (Autumn 2001): 1–22.

20. Bernstein continues, "Items of material culture script in much the same sense as literary texts mean: neither a thing nor a poem (for example) is conscious or agential, but a thing can invite behaviors that its maker did and did not envision. . . . To describe elements of material culture as 'scripting' actions is not to suggest that things possess agency or that people lack it, but instead to propose that agency emerges in the constant engagement with the stuff of our lives" (Robin Bernstein, *Racial Innocence: Performing American Childhood, from Slavery to Civil Rights* [New York: New York University Press, 2011], 11–12). See also Marlis Schweitzer and Joanne Zerdy, *Performing Objects and Theatrical Things* (Basingstoke: Palgrave Macmillan, 2014); Penny Harvey, Eleanor Conlin Casella, Gillian Evans, Hannah Knox, Christine McLean, Elizabeth B. Silva, Nicholas Thoburn, and Kath Woodward, *Objects and Materials: A Routledge Companion* (New York: Routledge Press, 2014).

21. Lara D. Nielsen, "This Kinetic World: Rethinking the Grid (Neo-Baroque Calls)," *Performance Philosophy* 3, no. 1 (2017): 285–309, http://dx.doi.org/10.21476/PP.2017.31127.

22. Karl Marx, *A Contribution to the Critique of Political Economy* (Moscow: Progress Publishers, 1977); Raymond Williams, "Base and Superstructure in Marxist Cultural Theory," *New Left Review* 82 (November–December 1973): 48–52.

23. New approaches to realism and materialism are too complex and contradictory to detail quickly, but it can be said that they tend to challenge discursive methods of analysis by positing a *realism* independent of human beliefs and desires, and a *materialism* constituted purely in terms of physical processes and matter, raising big questions about citizenship, spectatorship, witness, authorship, and representation. See Christoph Cox, Jenny Jaskey, and Suhail Malik, *Realism Materialism Art* (Annandale-on-Hudson, NY: Sternberg Press, 2015).

24. David Delaney, "Beyond the Word: Law as a Thing of This World," in *Law and Geography,* ed. J. Holders and C. Harrison (Oxford: Oxford University Press, 2006); David Delaney, *Nomospheric Investigations: The Spatial, the Legal, and the Pragmatics of World-Making* (New York: Routledge, 2010), 25.

25. Arjun Appadurai, "Disjuncture and Difference in the Global Cultural Economy," *Theory, Culture, and Society* 7 (1990): 295–310.

26. Aihwa Ong, *Neoliberalism as Exception: Mutations in Citizenship and Sovereignty* (Durham, NC: Duke University Press, 2006).

27. Jasbir K. Puar explains, "*Assemblage* is actually an awkward translation—the original term in Deleuze and Guattari's work is not the French word *assemblage,* but actually *Agencement,* a term which means design, layout, organization, arrangement, and relations—the focus being not on content but on relations, relations of patterns" (Jasbir K. Puar, "'I Would Rather Be a Cyborg than a Goddess': Intersectionality, Assemblage, and

Affective Politics," European Institute for Progressive Cultural Policies, 2011, http://eipcp.net/transversal/0811/puar/en.

28. Ranajit Guha, "On Some Aspects of the Historiography of Colonial India," in *Subaltern Studies I: Writings on South Asian History and Society,* ed. Ranajit Guha (Delhi: Oxford University Press, 1982), 403–9.

29. Dipesh Chakrabarty, "Subaltern Studies and Postcolonial Historiography," *Nepantla: Views from South* 1, no. 1 (2000): 19.

30. Guha, "On Some Aspects."

31. The "negative relay between thingness and nothingness" that can be detected in the afterlives of slavery rebounding from, in, and toward scenes of subjection (to borrow Saidiya Hartman's phrase) brings Fred Moten to the idea of "nonperformance": or what it is that constitutes the refusal of individuation on offer from the delimitations of legal contracts (Fred Moten, "Blackness and Nonperformance," Museum of Modern Art, 2015; Saidiya Hartman, *Scenes of Subjection: Terror, Slavery, and Self-Making in Nineteenth Century America* [Oxford: Oxford University Press, 1997]).

32. Critics indicate that in Mexico today, "the most violent and recognizable impacts of NAFTA's policies are registered at the capital city's periphery, along the border between Mexico and the United States, and in south-eastern States like Michoacán, Guerro, and Chiapas" (Irmgard Emmelhainz, Jane Hutton, and Marcin Kedzior, "Editorial," *Scapegoat: Architecture/Landscape/Political Economy: Mexico DF/NAFTA* [2013], 7).

33. Lara D. Nielsen, "The Time after NAFTA: (Border) Time and the Other in *Post Tenebras Lux,*" *Scapegoat: Architecture/Landscape/Political Economy: Mexico DF/NAFTA* (2013): 123–30.

34. Avital Ronell, "The Testamentary Whimper," *South Atlantic Quarterly* 102, no. 2/3, (Spring/Summer 2004): 489–99.

35. Patricia Ticineto Clough and Craig Willse, *Beyond Biopolitics: The Governance of Technology and Death* (Durham, NC: Duke University Press, 2011).

36. Guy Debord, *The Society of the Spectacle* (Berkeley, CA: Bureau of Public Secrets, 2014).

37. As I have written elsewhere, "What I mean to call attention to here is Derrida's challenge to studies in performance, for whom performance's ruptures and breaks make it clear that the body is an experience of frames and dislocations. 'Skeptical of discourses of absence and negativity,' Derrida suggests attention be paid instead to the dissonances of intermedia apertures" (Lara D. Nielsen, "So Close to Burning: Intermedia and Documentary Solo Performance in Juan and John [1965]," *Text and Performance Quarterly* 34, no. 3 [2014]: 295). In another lively intervention in the debate about whether documentary media and corporeal performance make the absent body real and present (or make its subjects even more absent, the document as a shroud), Amelia Jones (like Derrida) suggests that the body and the document subtly reinstate the authority of each in the other, as the body is never an unmediated event (Amelia Jones, "'Presence' in Absentia: Experiencing Performance as Documentation," *Art Journal* 56, no. 4 [1997]: 11–18).

38. "The persistent demand now being made for the study of social and economic impact imposes methodologies of metricisation and measurement on artistic and academic endeavors in order to secure dubious notion of 'quality control' and generate trustworthiness in nebulous notions of authenticity" (Jason Bowman, Suhail Malik, and Andrea Phillips, "The Value of Contemporary Art," *PARSE* [2015]: 7).

39. See, for instance, John Dewey, *Art as Experience* (1934; reprint, New York: Perigree Books, 2005); Lucy Lippard, *The Social Turn: Performing Art, Supporting Publics* (New York: Routledge, 1977); Mary Schmidt Campbell and Randy Martin, *Artistic Citizenship: A Public Voice for the Arts* (New York: Routledge, 2006); Doris Sommer, *The Work of Art*

in the World: Civic Agency and the Public Humanities (Durham, NC: Duke University Press, 2014).

40. Art historian Jane Blocker probes the ethics of spectatorship amid the technological mediation of witness (Jane Blocker, *Seeing Witness: Visuality and the Ethics of Testimony* [Minneapolis: University of Minnesota Press, 2009]).

41. Those fault lines are also to be detected in critiques of the 'social turn,' transforming artists from object makers to trisectoral service providers. See Claire Doherty, *The Social Turn: Performing Art, Supporting Publics* (New York: Routledge, 2004); Claire Bishop, *Double Agent* (London: Institute of Contemporary Art, 2009); Claire Bishop, *Artificial Hells: Participatory Art and the Politics of Spectatorship* (New York: Verso Press, 2012); Shannon Jackson, *The Social Turn: Performing Art, Supporting Publics* (New York: Routledge, 2011).

42. Phelan comments, "Institutions whose only function is to preserve and honor objects—traditional museums, archives, banks, and to some degree, universities—are intimately involved in the reproduction of the sterilizing binaries of self/other, possession/dispossession, men/women which are increasingly inadequate formulas for representation. These binaries and their institutional upholders fail to account for that which cannot appear between these tight 'equations' but which nonetheless inform them" (Peggy Phelan, *Unmarked: The Politics of Performance* [New York: Routledge, 1993], 165).

43. See Moten, "Blackness"; Fred Moten, *In the Break: The Aesthetics of the Black Radical Tradition* (Minneapolis: University of Minnesota Press, 2003); Stefano Harney and Fred Moten, *The Undercommons: Fugitive Planning and Black Study* (New York: Autonomedia, 2013); Avery Gordon, "Blackboard Conversation," Walker Art Center, April 20, 2013; James C. Scott, *The Art of Not Being Governed: An Anarchist History of Upland Southeast Asia* (New Haven, CT: Yale University Press, 2009).

44. José Esteban Muñoz, *Disidentifications: Queers of Color and the Performance of Politics* (Durham, NC: Duke University Press, 1999).

45. Branislav Jaklovjević, *Alienation Effects: Performance and Self-Management in Yugoslavia, 1945–91* (Ann Arbor: University of Michigan Press, 2016).

46. Alfred Loos, "Ornament and Crime," *The Industrial Design Reader*, ed. Carma Gorman (1910; reprint, New York: Allworth Press, 2003).

47. Diamela Eltit, "Public Domain," *PMLA* 124, no. 5 (October 2009): 1802.

48. Theodor Adorno, *Negative Dialectics* (New York: Continuum, 1966).

49. Robert Cover, "Violence and the Word," Faculty Scholarship Series, Paper 2708 (New Haven, CT: Yale Law School, 1985), 1.

50. Austin Sarat, *When the State Kills: Capital Punishment and the American Condition* (Princeton, NJ: Princeton University Press, 2012).

51. Lara D. Nielsen, "Garbage, Gone," *Women & Performance* (2002): 105–31.

52. Jean-François Lyotard, *Differend: Phrases in Dispute* (Minneapolis: University of Minnesota Press, 1988), 5.

53. Philippe Nonet, "What Is Positive Law?" *Yale Law Journal* 100 (1990): 699.

54. J. L. Austin, *How to Do Things with Words: The William James Lectures Delivered at Harvard University in 195*, ed. J. O. Urmson and Marina Sbisà (Oxford: Clarendon Press, 1962).

55. Judith Butler, "Performative Agency," *Journal of Cultural Economy* 3, no. 2 (2010): 148, 157.

56. Marianne Constable, *Just Silences: The Limits and Possibilities of Modern Law* (Princeton, NJ: Princeton University Press, 2007), 43.

57. There is a deep body of work that addresses the challenges of the archive, including the genealogy of archival mediations in performance and media studies. See Walter Benjamin, "The Work of Art in the Age of Mechanical Reproduction," 1936, https://

www.marxists.org/reference/subject/philosophy/works/ge/benjamin.htm; Antonin Artaud, *The Theatre and Its Double* (1938; reprint, New York: Grove Press, 1994); Rosalind Krauss, "Notes on the Index: Seventies Art in America," *October* 3 (1977); Rosalind Krauss, *The Originality of the Avant Garde and Other Myths* (Cambridge, MA: MIT Press, 1985); John Tagg, *The Burden of Representation: Essays on Photographies and Histories* (Minneapolis: University of Minnesota Press, 1993); Peggy Phelan, *Unmarked: The Politics of Performance* (New York: Routledge, 1993); Michel Foucault, *Archaeology of Knowledge* (London: Travistock Publications Ltd., 1972); Michel Foucault, *The Order of Things: An Archaeology of the Human Sciences* (New York: Vintage, 1994); Michel de Certeau, *The Practice of Everyday Life*, trans. S. Rendall (Berkeley: University of California Press, 1984); Jacques Derrida, *Writing and Difference*, trans. Alan Bass (Chicago: University of Chicago Press, 1978); Jacques Derrida, *Cinders*, trans. Ned Lukacher (Lincoln: University of Nebraska Press, 1991); Jacques Derrida, *Archive Fever: A Freudian Impression*, trans. Eric Prenowitz (Chicago: University of Chicago Press, 1995); Amelia Jones, "'Presence' in Absentia"; Allen Feldman, *"Violence and Vision: The Prosthetics and Aesthetics of Terror," Public Culture* 10, no. 1 (Fall 1997); Friedrich Kittler, *Gramophone, Film, Typewriter* (1986; reprint, Stanford, CA: Stanford University Press, 1999); Michal Kobialka, *This Is My Body: Representational Practices in the Early Middle Ages* (Ann Arbor: University of Michigan Press, 1999); Michal Kobialka, "Historical Archives, Events and Facts: History Writing as Fragmentary Performance," *Performance Research* 7, no. 4 (2002); Diana Taylor, *The Archive and the Repertoire: Performing Cultural Memory in the Americas* (Durham, NC: Duke University Press, 2003); Sven Spieker, *The Big Archive: Art from Bureaucracy* (Cambridge, MA: MIT Press, 2008); W. J. T. Mitchell, *What Do Pictures Want? The Lives and Loves of Images* (Chicago: University of Chicago Press, 2010).

58. Moten, *In the Break;* Adam Sitze, *Impossible Machine: A Genealogy of South Africa's Truth and Reconciliation Commission* (Ann Arbor: University of Michigan Press, 2013).

59. Tagg, *The Burden of Representation*, 65.

60. Sabina Berman, "Backyard," *Gestos* 39 (April 2005): 107–81; Carlos Carrera, *El Traspatio*, Argos Comunicación, 2009.

61. Tagg, *The Burden of Representation*, 54.

62. Ernesto Martínez, "Asesinan al ex alcaldesa de Tiquicheo, Michoacán," *La Jornada*, November 18, 2012; Proceso, "Exalcaldesa de Tiquicheo: cuando la muerte ronda," November 19, 2012, http://www.proceso.com.mx/; Malcolm Beith, "Paying the Price for Resisting Corruption," *New Statesman*, November 29, 2012, http://www.new statesman.com/.

63. Tracy Wilkinson, "Former Mexico Mayor Survives 2 Assassination Attempts but Not Third," *Los Angeles Times*, November 20, 2012.

64. Enrique Peña Nieto, "U.S., Mexico Should Develop Their Economic Bond," *Washington Post*, November 23, 2012.

65. Sam Webb, "'Please Spare My Little Girl': How Mexico's Fearless Female Mayor Sacrificed Herself to Save Her Daughter's Life as She Was Abducted by Drug Gang, Tortured and Executed," *Daily Mail*, November 26, 2012.

66. Tagg, *The Burden of Representation*, 12.

67. Feldman, "Violence and Vision," 27.

68. Nicholas Ridout, "Regarding Theatre: Thoughts on Recent Work by Simon Vicenzi and Romeo Castellucci," *Theatre Journal* 66, no. 3 (2014): 427–36.

69. Scott, *Seeing Like a State*, 11.

70. Tagg, *The Burden of Representation*, 85.

71. Nicholas Blomley, "Making Private Property: Enclosure, Common Right and the Work of Hedges," *Rural History* 18, no. 1 (2007): 1–21.

72. Sekula explains that photography has its roots in "scientific policing and eugenics [which] mapped out general parameters for the bureaucratic handling of visual documents. It is quite extraordinary that histories of photography have been written thus far with little more than passing reference to their work. I suspect that this has something to do with a certain bourgeois scholarly discretion concerning the dirty work of modernization, especially when the status of photography as a fine art is at stake. . . . It is even more extraordinary that histories of social documentary photography have been written without taking the police into account. Here the issue is the maintenance of a certain liberal humanist myth of the wholly benign origins of socially concerned photography" (Allen Sekula, *Photography against the Grain: Essays and Photo Works, 1973–1983* [Halifax: Press of the Nova Scotia College of Art and Design, 1984], 88, 55–56).

73. Will Straw, "Pulling Back from Apocalypse," *Scapegoat: Architecture/Landscape/ Political Economy,* Mexico DF/NAFTA (2013): 118; Andrea Noble, "Introduction: Visual Culture and Violence in Contemporary Mexico," *Journal of Latin American Cultural Studies* 24, no. 4 (2015): 417–33.

74. Héctor Domínguez Ruvalcaba and Ingnacio Corona, eds., *Gender Violence at the U.S.–Mexico Border: Media Representation and Public Response* (Tucson: University of Arizona Press, 2010).

75. Bill Brown examines reification and the uncanny in minstrelsy artifacts of U.S. popular culture, things which seek to reinstate the exile of people from personhood, as property, as object, as commodity—and which nevertheless also talk back to such intended consolidations. "Objects stare back" (Bill Brown, "Open Relations in an Expanded Field," *differences* 17, no. 3 [2006]: 104).

76. See Griselda Gambaro, *Information for Foreigners: Three Plays* (Evanston, IL: North- western University Press, 1992). In Argentina's Dirty War (1978–1983) about 30,000 people were killed and disappeared. A project in restorative justice, the National Commission on the Disappearance of Persons (*Comisión Nacional sobre la Desaparición de Personas,* CONADEP), with a preface written by Ernesto Sábato in 1984, offers some 50,000 pages of depositions from the survivors of the disappearances, in addition to the photographs of those who remain missing.

77. Eltit, "Public Domain," 1801.

78. David Simon, *The Wire: Season 1,* HBO Video, 2008.

79. Maurice Blanchot, *The Space of Literature* (Lincoln: University of Nebraska Press, 1989), 35.

80. Argentina Comisión Nacional sobre la Desaparición de Personas, CONADEP, *Nunca Más: National Commission on Disappeared People* (Buenos Aires: EUDEBA, 1984).

81. The list details "the dates they disappeared, their ages, the clothes they were wearing, their jobs" with descriptive entries as follows: "His wife went to buy medicine and disappeared; The son was addicted to drugs; Her daughter was forced into a car; The father was arrested by men wearing uniforms and never seen again" (William Booth, "Mexico's Crime Wave Has Left about 25,000 Missing, Government Documents Show," *Washington Post,* November 29, 2012).

82. Ibid.

83. E. W. Soja, *Thirdspace: Journeys to Los Angeles and Other Real-and-Imagined Places* (Oxford: Blackwell, 1996), and *Seeking Spatial Justice* (Minneapolis: University of Minnesota Press), 2010.

84. Guha, "On Some Aspects," 5–6. As community activist Aldo Gonzales Rojas comments, "The liberal state was constructed as an agreement between French and North American perspectives. No one turned to see that indigenous towns also had their proposals" (Renata Bessi and Santiago Navarro F., "Mexico: Electoral Reform Threatens the Self-Determination of Indigenous Peoples," trans. Miriam Taylor, *Truthout,* August 4,

2014, http://www.truth-out.org/news/item/25358-mexico-electoral-reform-threatens-the-self-determination-of-indigenous-peoples).

85. The film was distributed by Paramount in Mexico for its only theatrical release in 2009, and was made available by DVD distribution in Argentina the same year, while Canadian and U.S. DVD distributors picked it up in 2010. At the 2010 Ariel Awards in Mexico, it won five Silver Ariel Awards, for Best Actress, Best Art Direction, Best Cinematography, Best Direction, and Best Sound; in addition to awards at the Havana Film Festival, the Chicago International Film Festival, and Imagen Foundation Awards. Distributed abroad by Mongrel Media and Maya Entertainments, respectively.

86. Pierre Bourdieu, *Language and Symbolic Power* (Cambridge: Polity Press, 1991).

87. Wilkinson, "Former Mexico Mayor."

88. Lefebvre, *The Production of Space*, trans. D. Nicholson Smith (Oxford: Blackwell, 1991).

89. Rosa-Linda Fregoso and Cynthia Bejarano, *Terrorizing Women: Feminicide in the Americas* (Durham, NC: Duke University Press, 2010), 9.

90. Nelly Richard, "The Language of Criticism: How to Speak Difference?," *Nepantla: Views from South* 1, no. 1 (2000): 261.

91. Kimberle Crenshaw, "Mapping the Margins: Intersectionality, Identity Politics, and Violence against Women of Color," *Stanford Law Review* (1991): 1241–99; Richard Delgado and Jean Stefancic, *Critical Race Theory: An Introduction* (New York: New York University Press, 2001); R. W. Gilmore, *Golden Gulag: Prisons, Surplus, Crisis, and Opposition in Globalizing California* (Berkeley: University of California Press, 2007).

92. Cheryl Harris, "Whiteness as Property," *Harvard Law Review* 106, no. 8 (1993): 1709.

93. Sitze, *Impossible Machine*, 1.

94. Bronwyn Anne Leebaw, "The Irreconcilable Goals of Transitional Justice," *Human Rights Quarterly* 30 (2008): 95–118.

95. Giorgio Agamben, *State of Exception* (Chicago: University of Chicago Press, 2005); W. J. T. Mitchell, *What Do Pictures Want?*.

96. Victor Flores Olea, "Violencia y Respuesta," *La Jornada*, December 1, 2014, 20; Julien Mercille, "Violent Narco-Cartels or US Hegemony? The Political Economy of the 'War on Drugs' in Mexico," *Third World Quarterly* 32, no. 9 (2011): 1637–53.

97. Tom Wainwright, *Narconomics: How to Run a Drug Cartel* (New York: Public Affairs, 2016).

98. Martia Idalia Chew Sánchez, "Feminicide: Theorizing Border Violence," *Latin American Research Review: Journal of the Latin American Studies Association* 49, no. 3 (2014): 263–76.

99. R. Scott Bray, "En Piel Ajena: The Work of Teresa Margolles," *Law Text Culture* 11 (2007): 13–50.

100. Coco Fusco, *The Bodies That Were Not Ours and Other Writings* (New York: Routledge, 2001), 62.

101. Candice Skrapec, "The Morgue Was Really from the Dark Ages: Insights from a Forensic Psychologist," in *Making a Killing: Femicide, Free Trade, and La Frontera (Chicana Matters)*, ed. Alicia Gaspar de Alba and Georgina Guzmán (Austin: University of Texas Press, 2010), 245–54.

102. Angela Hennessy, "Teresa Margolles," *Surface Design Journal* (Fall 2013): 64–65; Amy Sara Carroll, "Muerte Sin Fin, Teresa Margolles's Gendered States of Exception," *TDR/The Drama Review* 54, no. 2 (Summer 2010): 103–25.

103. Kathy O'Dell, *Contract with the Skin: Masochism, Performance Art, and the 1970s* (Minneapolis: University of Minnesota Press, 1998).

104. Teresa Margolles, "Santiago Sierra," *Bomb* 68 (2003/2004): 65.

105. Bishop, *Double Agent;* Nicolas Bourriard, *Relational Aesthetics* (Paris: Les Presse Du Reel, 2002).

106. Federico Navarette, "Semefo: de la transgresión al ocultamiento," *Poliéster* 8, no. 27 (2000): 24–31; Bray, "En Piel Ajena," 24, 16.

107. Sven Spieker, *The Big Archive: Art from Bureaucracy* (Cambridge, MA: MIT Press, 2008), ix.

108. Ibid., 4.

109. Ibid., x.

110. Foucault, *Archaeology of Knowledge,* 130.

111. Eltit, "Public Domain," 1801.

112. Briony Fer, *The Infinite Line* (New Haven, CT: Yale University Press, 2004), 37.

113. A. Klayman, *Ai Weiwei: Never Sorry* (DVD) (Expressions United Media, MUSE Film and TV, 2012).

114. Jacques Derrida, "The Spatial Arts: Derrida Interview," in *Deconstruction and the Visual Arts: Art, Media, Architecture,* ed. Peter Brunette and David Willis (Cambridge: Cambridge University Press, 1994), 12.

115. Joseph Roach, *Cities of the Dead: Circum-Atlantic Performance* (New York: Columbia University Press, 1996).

116. Fer, *The Infinite Line,* 44.

117. Fred Moten, "An Ecology of (Eloquent) Things," Indianapolis Museum of Art, April 8, 2011.

118. Spieker, *The Big Archive,* 14.

119. Lara D. Nielsen, "Heterotopic Transformations, The (Il)Liberal Neoliberal," in *Neoliberalism and Global Theatres: Performance Permutations,* ed. Lara D. Nielsen and Patricia Ybarra (Basingstoke: Palgrave Macmillan, 2012), 2–8.

120. With Altamura Films, Almada produces her own work. http://www.altamura-films.com.

121. Nielsen, "The Time after NAFTA."

122. Jean Franco, *Cruel Modernity* (Durham, NC: Duke University Press, 2012).

123. de Certeau, *The Practice of Everyday Life.*

124. Chris Chang, "Interview: Natalia Almada," *Bomb* 116 (October 2011), www.bombmagazine.org.

125. Nielsen, "Garbage, Gone."

126. Avery Gordon, *Ghostly Matters: Haunting and the Sociological Imagination* (Minneapolis: University of Minnesota Press, 1997), 22.

127. Eltit, "Public Domain," 1801.

128. Gordon, *Ghostly Matters.*

129. Eltit, "Public Domain," 1801.

130. Jimi Hendrix, "All Along the Watchtower," *Electric Ladyland,* 1968.

131. "During the four hours between when they left the school and when the police attacks in Iguala began, at about 10 P.M., Rosales said, the students' movements were being monitored via the C4, a federal command and information-gathering post in Chilpancingo to which, he said, only federal police, the Army, and state police have access. In the case records of the Guerrero state prosecutors, Hernández found documentation of the monitoring, showing that the command post had recorded the identification numbers of the two buses the students were travelling in" (Francisco Goldman, "The Missing 43: The Government's Case Collapses," *New Yorker,* June 8, 2015, http://www.newyorker.com/news/news-desk/the-missing-forty-three-the-governments-case-collapses).

132. Arturo Cano, "La justicia no va a llegar, aunque la busquemos, lamentan en Ayotzinapa," *La Jornada,* 26 Octubre 2014, http://www.jornada.unam.mx/.

133. Irmgard Emmelhainz, Jane Hutton, and Marcin Kedzior, *Scapegoat: Architecture/Landscape/Political Economy: Mexico DF/NAFTA* (2013): 20.

134. Paul Amar, *The Security Archipelago: Human-Security States, Sexuality Politics and the End of Neoliberalism* (Durham, NC: Duke University Press, 2013).

135. Marianne Constable, "Our Word Is Our Bond," in *Speech and Silence in American Law,* ed. Austin Sarat (Cambridge: Cambridge University Press, 2010), 18–38, and *Our Word Is Our Bond: How Legal Speech Acts* (Palo Alto, CA: Stanford University Press, 2014).

136. Krauss, "Notes on the Index," 81.

137. Asking "why is democracy such a difficult, improbable, and dangerous place for the emergence of truth-telling?" Foucault suggests "democracy is not the privileged site of parrhesia." Instead, differentiating between Socratic and other kinds of veridiction, Foucault says truth-telling is *most* difficult to practice in democracy, where the transformation of democratic to autocratic parrhesia means that whoever speaks out about *life* (about the mode of life, Foucault says) does so at risk of retaliation from sovereign power (Michel Foucault, *The Courage of Truth: The Government of Self and Others II): Lectures at the College de France, 1983–1984* [New York: Picador/Palgrave MacMillan, 2012], 57–69).

138. Although Bolaño's family left Chile in 1968, he returned to Chile to support Allende in 1973. After the Pinochet coup, Bolaño was arrested and imprisoned for eight days. He moved to Europe in 1977 and lived in Spain until his death in 2003. Bolaño's use of interview transcripts persistently poses a pun on the verisimilitudes of oral testimony, as reliable source of information. *2666,* his final opus about Mexico, reveals an abundance of data that disguises rather than clarifies, as the violence piles on (Roberto Bolaño, *La Literatura Nazi en América* [Barcelona: Seix Barral, 1996]; *La Literatura Nazi en América* [Barcelona: Seix Barral, 2000]; *2666* [Barcelona: Vintage Español 2004]).

139. Sitze, *Impossible Machine,* 158.

140. Lara D. Nielsen, "Performing South Africa's Truth Commission: Stages of Transition." *TDR/The Drama Review* 56, no. 3 (2012): 183–84.

141. Marianne Constable, *Just Silences: The Limits and Possibilities of Modern Law* (Princeton, NJ: Princeton University Press, 2007), 177.

142. Pilar Calveiro, "Private and State Violence under Neoliberalism," *Scapegoat: Architecture/Landscape/Political Economy: Mexico DF/NAFTA* (2013): 105.

143. In 1971, U.S. president Richard Nixon declared a "War on Drugs" using the rhetorics of securitization, and in 1973 he created the Drug Enforcement Administration (DEA) to coordinate the efforts of agencies targeting drug abuse as a "serious national threat." Acknowledging the growing strengths of the Colombian and Mexican cartels in the early 1970s, the DEA was meant to combat "an all-out global war on the drug menace," with a fortified federal agency that would consolidate and coordinate the government's drug control activities at home and abroad. Every U.S. administration since Nixon (except briefly Carter) has sought to '"win" the war on drug production and consumption, through expensive policing and militarizing tactics that, in turn, have contributed to the growth of securitizing governmental agencies, and the military industrial complex—while drastically divesting the state from public welfare programs.

144. Greg Grandin, *Fordlandia: The Rise and Fall of Henry Ford's Forgotten Jungle City* (New York: Picador, 2009).

145. Ronell, "The Testamentary Whimper," 487.

146. Ibid., 490.

147. Martin Heidegger, *Poetry, Language, Thought,* trans. Albert Hofstadter (New York: Harper, 1971), 696.

148. Cited in Allen Feldman, "On Cultural Anesthesia: From Desert Storm to Rodney King," *American Ethnologist* 21, no. 2 (1994): 406.

149. Reddy's point of departure is October 2009, when President Obama signed into law the 2010 National Defense Authorization Act. Attached to that act is an amendment, "The Matthew Shepard and James Byrd, Jr. Hate Crimes Prevention Act." This bill extends the 1969 Hate Crimes Bill to include crimes motivated by a victim's actual or perceived gender, sexual orientation, gender identity, or disability. The 2010 National Defense Authorization Act thus establishes the annual operating budget for the Department of Defense that has not given up on war, at the same time that the amendment incorporates the protection of homosexuality. Thus Reddy argues the new international of gay rights can be used to supplant the war machines of "the West," at the same time that GBLTQ communities are subject to the intensities of assaults "at home."

150. Avital Ronell, with D. Diane Davis, "Confessions of an Anacoluthon: Avital Ronell on Writing, Technology, Pedagogy, Politics," *jac: A Journal of Composition Theory* 20, no. 2 (2000): 243–81.

151. Ronell, "The Testamentary Whimper," 490–94.

152. Charles Bowden, *Juárez: The Laboratory of Our Future* (New York: Aperture, 1998); Charles Bowden, *Murder City: Ciudad Juárez and the Global Economy's New Killing Fields* (New York: Nation Books, 2010).

CHAPTER 6

Twelve Notes on Ferguson

Black Performance and Police Power

Joshua Chambers-Letson

1. Desiree Harris Is Driving Her Car through Ferguson

Somewhere in Ferguson, Desiree Harris is driving her car through her neighborhood when she catches sight of her grandson running. We can't know if he saw or sensed that she was so close to him in the last terrible minutes of his life. "He was a good kid," she later told a reporter; "he came to visit me."[1] Black women in the United States have been trained to live in fear of this very moment. As Audre Lorde wrote in 1982, describing a difference between white feminist mothers and black feminist mothers, "You fear your children will grow up to join the patriarchy and testify against you, we fear our children will be dragged from a car and shot down in the street, and you will turn your backs upon the reasons they are dying."[2] It was daytime, so even if blue lights were flashing, she might not have noticed them. Did she see Michael's face, which, at eighteen, glowed with the softness exuded by boys locked in the slipstream between being a child and becoming an adult? Just a little bit of fuzz capable of growing around his chin. "He was spending the summer with me," she said, "and they did that to him for no reason."[3] She tried to get to him, to no avail: "He was running this way. When I got there my grandson was lying on the ground. I asked the police what happened. They didn't tell me nothing."[4] At some point, before she reaches him, she hears twelve gunshots.

2. Sundown Town

Things have been tense for some time now. Until the 1960s Ferguson was a "sundown town." Sundown towns are white municipalities that mobilize a mixture of law, policy, policing, and intimidation to exclude, regulate and choreograph the movement of black bodies through (and out) of the city's boundaries. Often, black people couldn't be entirely banned in such places because white residents relied on black labor to reproduce and sustain themselves. A short road connected Ferguson with Kinloch, a working-class black suburb. Into the sixties, the city would block the road off "with a chain and construction materials but kept a second road open during the day so housekeepers and nannies could get from Kinloch to jobs in Ferguson."[5] At the time, it was well known to black people throughout the region that Ferguson was "off-limits."[6]

Ferguson police officer Darren Wilson shot Michael Brown to death on August 9, 2014. In the aftermath of the shooting (and the uprising that came after that) the U.S. Department of Justice's Civil Rights Divisions issued a report on an investigation into the Ferguson Police Department. Addressing Ferguson's history of racial segregation, the report noted, "On its own, Ferguson's historical backdrop as a racially segregated community that did not treat African Americans equally under the law does not demonstrate that law enforcement practices today are motivated by impermissible discriminatory intent. It is one factor to consider, however, especially given the evidence that, among some in Ferguson, these attitudes persist today."[7] How, one wonders, does an "attitude" from the past come to "persist" in material form today? By what means does the past continue to take hold of the body in the present?

In the wake of national efforts at desegregation, Ferguson's demographics began to shift, first steadily, then dramatically. In 1990 a quarter of Ferguson's residents were black, but by 2010 black people made up sixty-seven percent of the population. Twenty-five percent of the city's residents were living below the poverty line.[8] But the city's governing class remained white, including the mayor (James Knowles III, elected in 2011 and again in 2017), the courts, and law enforcement. At the time of the Justice Department's report, of fifty-four police officers sworn to serve and protect Ferguson, only four were black. The Municipal Courts, in turn, were staffed by a judge, court clerk, prosecuting attorney, and a host of assistant court clerks: all white.[9] Black people in Ferguson found themselves *held* by the courts and law enforcement with alarming regularity.

Ferguson has an approximate population of 22,000 people, but by 2014 the municipal courts had issued over 16,000 warrants for arrest, a number that police officials themselves described as "staggering."[10] Reflecting in part on Ferguson's circumstance while dissenting in a U.S. Supreme Court police power case, Justice Sonia Sotomayor noted that "outstanding warrants are surprisingly common" in the United States: "the States and Federal Government maintain databases with over 7.8 million outstanding warrants, the vast majority of which appear to be for minor offenses."[11] The overwhelming majority of arrest warrants in Ferguson were not, as the Justice Department noted, issued in the interests of public safety, "but rather as a routine response to missed court appearances and required fine payments."[12] The result is a regime of arrest and incarceration that overwhelmingly targets Ferguson's black population.

After decades of tax and budget cuts at both the state and federal level, local municipalities, like Ferguson, increasingly rely upon revenue streams generated by tickets, fines and fees.[13] As the DOJ report notes, "City officials have consistently set maximizing revenue as the priority for Ferguson's law enforcement activity" and the municipal courts have primarily functioned as mechanisms to coerce (and extract) payment of fines and fees.[14] As a result, "Ferguson uses its police department in large part as a collection agency for its municipal court," just as "the large number of warrants issued by the court, by any count, is due exclusively to the fact that the court uses arrest warrants and the threat of arrest as its primary tool for collecting outstanding fines for municipal code violations."[15] Despite the fact that most warrants were attached to minor infractions, "officers do arrest individuals for outstanding municipal warrants with considerable frequency."[16] Ferguson police are given significant latitude as to whether to arrest a person with an outstanding warrant, resulting in a shocking disparity among those arrested: "During the roughly six-month period from April to September 2014, 256 people were booked into the Ferguson City Jail after being arrested at least in part for an outstanding warrant—96% of whom were African American. Of these individuals, 28 were held for longer than two days, and 27 of these 28 people were black."[17] For black people in Ferguson, "to have the body" may as well refer to what happens when one is *held*, detained, arrested, and dragged before the court against one's will.

3. To Have the Body

In contemporary U.S. law the *writ of habeas corpus* describes the means through which a person may petition a court for redress from unlawful detention. The phrase translates to "you may have the body." Its provenance: a medieval tradition in which a summons grants a state official custodial possession of another's body: the right to hold, or take, a person ("the body") and bring it before the court. So there is a tension between *the writ of habeas corpus* as the means through which the body seeks release from illegal detention and *habeas corpus* as the legal power through which the state takes hold of the subject's body.

Writing for the high court in *Boumedienne v. Bush,* Justice Anthony Kennedy describes *habeas corpus* as a foundational cornerstone to liberty in the United States: "The Framers viewed freedom from unlawful restraint as a fundamental precept of liberty, and they understood the writ of habeas corpus as a vital instrument to secure that freedom."[18] But this history of liberty only coheres by excluding those people who were excluded from freedom, and excluded from freedom because they were not thought to be people. Indeed, such exclusions were the lines across which legal personhood could be defined within U.S. law *as property,* as remarked upon by Alexander G. Weheliye when he notes that "the writ of habeas corpus—and the law more generally—anoints those individualized subjects who are deemed deserving with bodies even while this assemblage [law] continually enlists new and/or different groups to exclude, banish, or exterminate from the world of Man [i.e., proper personhood]."[19]

While holding that a slave could not be considered a citizen with standing to sue in a U.S. court, the same legal body wrote a century and a half earlier (in *Dred Scott v. Sandford*) that "either the class of persons who had been imported as slaves, nor their descendants, whether they had become free or not, were then acknowledged as a part of the people, nor intended to be included in the general words used in that memorable instrument."[20] As Chief Justice Roger Taney famously declared:

> They had for more than a century before been regarded as beings of an inferior order, and altogether unfit to associate with the white race, either in social or political relations; and so far inferior, that they had no rights which the white man was bound to respect; and that the negro might justly and lawfully be reduced to slavery for his benefit. He was bought and sold, and treated as an ordinary article of merchandise and traffic, whenever a profit could be made by it.[21]

If the black body was "*reduced* to slavery *for his benefit,*" this reduction occurred through the combination of violence, the market, and a proliferating cluster of legal performatives that achieved and maintained the transformation of people into objects to be "bought and sold, and treated as an ordinary article of merchandise and traffic." To *have the body* of the slave meant, literally, to possess another person who now, through trick of law, was not "acknowledged as a part of the people" and was to be considered as private property.

Due in no small part to the legal performative's alchemical power to transform one substance into another through the act of (re)naming, during slavery black bodies were reduced to "the flesh," or what Hortense Spillers describes as "that zero degree of social conceptualization" that exists *before* the body.[22] Even as slavery was legally disestablished with the passage of the thirteenth amendment, the reduction of the black body to flesh continued to reverberate across history and in the bodies of the descendants of both the slaves and their masters. As Spillers notes, of black women in particular, "enslavement relegated them to the marketplace of the flesh, an act of commodification so thoroughgoing that the daughters labor even now under the outcome."[23] Thus, as Christina Sharpe observes, black life in the United States is lived, always, in the wake of black people's *reduction* to slavery: "Living in/the wake of slavery is living 'the afterlife of property' and living the afterlife of *partus sequitur ventrem* (that which is brought forth follows the womb), in which the Black child inherits the non/status, the non/being of the mother. The inheritance of a non/status is everywhere apparent *now* in the ongoing criminalization of black women and their children."[24] To recognize the historical (and legal) transformation of people into commodities, of bodies into flesh, is to recognize that the legacy of slavery remains alive in the flesh of those of us who live in its wake. This is to live in what Saidiya Hartman describes as the "time of slavery," which "negates the common-sense intuition of time as continuity or progression, then and now coexist; we are coeval with the dead."[25] If the past persists today, it does so at the level of the flesh.

Black people in the United States know what it means to be held, used, and owned. We are the descendants of the ones who were *reduced* to private property, chained together in the hold of a slave ship. This reduction was not *for their benefit,* however, but for the benefit of the ruling class and of capital ("wherever a profit could be made from it"). And today, too, great profits continue to be extracted from the bodies of slavery's descendants. Ferguson's "staggering" world of arrest warrants, fines, and fees is a chilling testimony to the "ongoing criminalization of black women and their children" in slavery's wake. The ritual practice and legal habitus through which this occurs (the arrest, jailing, and appearance before the court) is one of the means through which the "attitudes" of slavery's regime "persist today." The theater of law enforcement and court procedure in Ferguson stages and materializes the financial *and* racial ideology of slavery (in which value was extracted *from* the black body, reduced to a possession for use by white people) as it is reproduced (and *persists*) in the present at the point of the body, or of the flesh.

4. To Partially and Porously Persist

My emphasis on the body, and my description of law enforcement as a "theater," is meant to underline the implicit role that performance plays in the mediation and materialization of law. In a previous book, I argued that the law is more than just a series of performative utterances or declarations (i.e., legislation and jurisprudence); it is a complex mesh of legal performatives, embodied action, social ritual, and aesthetic forms.[26] I suggested there that the law is performative (it makes something happen in the world), but only to the extent that it is realized and structured through embodied acts of performance (legal habitus, courtroom rituals, law enforcement, etc.). To briefly restate some of these key contentions in our present context, when I say that the law is performative, I mean to invoke J. L. Austin's conceptualization of the performative as an utterance (or a set of words) that makes something happen, or effects a *doing* in the world. In *Scott v. Sandford,* for example, Taney's opinion remakes, transforms, and *reduces* Dred Scott (a person) to private property, stripping his body to the flesh. But in order for this legal fiction to become a material reality, the legally codified system of slavery had to be sustained and maintained by way of embodied practices—and the embodiment of the law in particular.

Taney's ruling could only maintain the force of law so long as people were willing to perform *as if* slaves were not humans. Through performance, an absurd legal fiction (that a human being is not in fact a human being) could be transformed into reality. Hartman describes this as "the obscene theatricality of the slave trade."[27] The coffle and auction block were the places where slavery's legal fiction (that a man or woman is a subhuman *thing*) is *performed* into reality. They were also the sites at which slaves could mobilize performance to stage resistance to their *reduction* to slavery and objecthood:

> As it turns out, what was being staged in these varied renderings of the coffle and the auction block was nothing less than slavery itself, whether in the effort to mute the extreme domination of slavery and the violence that enabled this sale of the flesh through the simulated jollity of the enslaved or the clownish antics of the auctioneer, reconcile subjugation and natural law,

> document the repressive totality of the institution, or fashion a subject who might triumphantly negotiate her debasements.[28]

"The obscene theatricality of the slave trade" was not only a *result* of legal performatives that *reduced* human beings to being things. Performance was the means through which the body of the slave subjected to this *reduction* could be compelled to submit to this unthinkable ordering of the world. In the act of the slave's embodiment of (violently coerced) submission, the submitting body affirmed (for both the white spectator and to other slaves) the legal fiction that a person is not a person.

The spectacle of slavery, and the juridical order that sustained it, collaborated to achieve the total domination of slaves by their masters. Indeed, "the laws of slavery," writes Hartman, "subjected the enslaved to the absolute control and authority of any and every member of the dominant race."[29] The question raised by the DOJ report is whether it is possible that the laws of slavery continue to assert themselves in the present, in the time after slavery's legal disestablishment ("these attitudes persist today")? And, if so, by what means?

After slavery, legal performatives such as the Black Codes (during Reconstruction) and Jim Crow laws (after it) were primary means through which, as Hartman writes, "the well-arranged world sustained itself."[30] As W.E.B. Du Bois observed of the Black Codes in *Black Reconstruction,* "Although the freedman is no longer considered the property of the individual master, he is considered the slave of society, and all independent state legislation will share the tendency to make him such."[31] Accompanying these laws, "the obscene theatricality of the slave trade" found new form in iterative spectacles of antiblack violence. Diana Taylor describes these repeated social scenes—in which members of a culture repeat behaviors that (re)produce and transmit meaning by way of embodied iteration—as "scenarios."[32] The public spectacle of lynching, the theatrical rituals of the Ku Klux Klan (e.g., burning crosses in public), and the scene of law enforcement are prime examples of performance scenarios.

During Reconstruction, lynching scenarios were rehearsed, developed, and deployed by whites at regular intervals in a (successful) effort to reproduce the "badge of slavery" (the systematic domination of black life) in the wake of slavery's formal abolition. Popular performance forms contributed to this process by mediating and reproducing the logics of white supremacy for general audiences. As Koritha Mitchell argues, spectacles of black death were common on the American stage, which "would prove as suitable for killing African Americans as for portraying them in dehumanizing ways."[33] As a result, "theater and lynching *worked together* to make blacks' conception of themselves as modern citizens irrelevant," although black playwrights ingeniously appropriated and used the stage to push back.[34] Still, through the marriage of theater and extrajuridical violence, the badge of slavery was reproduced by way of the (legally tolerated) *staging* of the devaluation, domination, degradation, and possession of black flesh. And through the continued staging of these violent scenarios, the past comes to persist in the present.

I have been mobilizing three distinct but related concepts of temporality: the time of slavery, the time of the law, and the time of performance. We have encountered the first two explicitly. In the time of slavery "then and now coexist" and in the time of law the past also flashes up to take hold of the present. In the realm of jurisprudence, for example, multiple points in time converge as a jurist laces together, in a single passage, precedents and statutes drawn from a constellation of points in time to authorize an interpretation that now determines the status of the law in the present. A defendant in the present may be convicted under a statute passed two hundred years ago. Through law, the past thus choreographs the present and shapes the future, but with variation and difference. But a contradiction arises insofar as the time of law is sharply differentiated from the time of slavery. As Hartman writes, the time of slavery "negates the common-sense intuition of time as continuity or progression," while (within a *stare decisis,* common law system) the law conceives of itself as, precisely, progression or continuity through time.

Ultimately, the law is only as real as the people that perform it into the flesh, so as a performance form, the law's relationship to time is far less progressive or continuous than some jurists have to believe. A police officer may arrest someone under a previous provision of law, long since rescinded by the proper legislative bodies. But though the law is not formally in effect (and even if the arrest is later nullified by a court), in the moment of the arrest that previous provision of law is very much a flesh and blood reality. As Joseph Roach argues, the "three-sided relationship of memory, performance, and substitution" are the means through which "culture reproduces and re-creates itself by a process that can be best described by the word *surrogation.*"[35] Taylor describes something akin to surrogation when she notes that "performances function as vital acts of transfer, transmitting social knowledge, memory, and a sense of identity through reiterated, or what Richard Schechner has called 'twice-behaved behavior.'"[36] But these acts of transfer, and the process of surrogation, are rarely complete nor their outcomes predetermined. As Rebecca Schneider notes, in the time of performance what we encounter is "one time [that is] almost but not fully passing in and as another time. The past can disrupt the present . . . but so too can the present disrupt the past . . . ; neither are entirely 'over' nor discrete, but partially and porously persist."[37] The past *persists* in the present through performance, but always with a difference. And the actors in a given scenario may not even know what's coursing through their bodies as they perform the social script. In performance, the past may be so coded into our activities, so woven into the flesh, that we may not realize that we are acting under its spell.

5. Your Body Is Subject to Invasion

The choreography of law enforcement scenarios, the theatricality of burning a cross at a KKK rally, and a white audience's rapturous consumption of a lynching (in the flesh or by way of theatrical representation) all function as performance. To borrow language from Erving Goffman, such bloody amusements were often staged with the intention of *influencing* the world, by staging white supremacy's ordering of the world and confirming its hold on the black body.[38] Performance can be pedagogical, and these spectacles of violence taught black people that they were less than white people while teaching white people that they could use black bodies in whatever ways they wanted. And they did and they do.

During and after slavery, these ritual scenes of subjection staged white power *and* reproduced it as a material reality at the point of the black body. It was sometimes literally etched into black skin, leaving scars, which Spillers describes as the "hieroglyphics of the flesh."[39] Presaging performance studies' formulation of surrogation and acts of transfer, Spillers asked "if this phenomenon of marking and branding actually 'transfers' from one generation to another, finding its various *symbolic substitutions* in an efficacy of meanings that repeat the initiating moments?"[40] The violence of "marking and branding" black flesh was interlaced with the law (if not simply a materialization of the law's choreography). The law, in turn, was interlaced with this violence. So even as a legal regime (slavery, segregation) faded from the law books, it could sustain within the embodied rituals of social life, transmitting and transferring the "attitudes" of the past in a fashion that allows them to "persist today."

Describing the law as "choreography" is to recognize that law becomes social reality as a result of what Eve Sedgwick and Andrew Parker describe as a "generalized iterability, a pervasive theatricality common to stage and world alike."[41] The law often acts as a script or, better put, choreography for the actions our bodies play out within the social. Andre Lepecki describes choreography as a "haunting machine, a body snatcher."[42] When a body has choreography, the choreography *has* (or snatches) the body: choreography guides the body and sets its movements. To conceive of law or policy as choreography is thus to gain a sense of the law as that which compels bodies in given social scenarios to behave in quite predetermined ways, embodying the "generalized iterability" that reproduces the social order through its enactment. This happens in any host of mundane, everyday instances, but is often most apparent in the courtroom and in the law enforcement scenario.

Resonating with Lepecki's description of choreography as "a body snatcher," Justice Sotomayor's dissent in the police power case mentioned above invites her reader to inhabit the scenario through which the law allows police power to take hold of, or have, the body. "Although many Americans have been stopped for speeding or jaywalking," she writes, setting up the scenario, "few may realize how degrading a stop can be when the officer is looking for more."[43] She then constructs a hypothetical stop/search scenario, addressed to the reader (as if it were happening *to* the reader), and charting a sequence of events that are lifted directly from the court's own archive. *Whren v. United States,* for example, authorizes an officer "to stop you for whatever reason he wants—so long as he can point to a pretextual justification after the fact," which, as a result of *United States v. Brignoni-Ponce,* "may factor in your ethnicity" or other personal details such as how you are dressed, or where you live.[44] Throughout the passage, each of her examples cite a specific case, underlining the fact that her hypothetical scenario is something that occurs with some degree of "generalized iterability" or regular repetition.

"The indignity of the stop is not limited to an officer telling you that you look like a criminal," she insists, because it extends to the body.[45] The officer may "order you to stand 'helpless, perhaps facing a wall,'" before frisking "you for weapons . . . as onlookers pass by" as the officer feels "with sensitive fingers every portion of your body."[46] By now the law *has* the reader's body, but "the officer's control of you does not end with the stop" as it moves on to handcuffing, perhaps in front of your "3-year-old son and 5-year-old-daughter" because you were driving "without [your] seatbelt fastened."[47] And the law's control of the body (its choreography) may persist well after booking, probing, and public humiliation: "Even if you are innocent, you will now join the 65 million Americans with an arrest record and experience the 'civil death' of discrimination by employers, landlords, and whoever else conducts a background check."[48]

Sotomayor takes a number of risks in her opinion. For example, her second-person address calls upon a tradition of social-justice narratives (especially slave narratives) that invite the reader to enact an empathetic identification that may in fact displace the reality of the suffering carceral subject. Hartman describes such a scenario in her reading of a white abolitionist's account of the auction block in which he imagines that it is himself and his family on sale. Here, empathetic identification "must supplant the black captive in order to give expression to black suffering, and as a consequence, the dilemma—the denial of black sentience and the obscurity of suffering—is not attenuated but instantiated."[49] But Sotomayor's mobilization of the second-person address is split between the formal aspects of a legal norm and its actual (unjust) embodiment. As a matter of law, "anyone's dignity can be violated in this manner," but Sotomayor also notes that (as is the case with Ferguson's archive of arrests) "it is no secret that people of color are disproportionate victims of this type of scrutiny."[50]

This section of her opinion was left unsupported by her white colleagues. Justice Elena Kagan dissented separately, and while Justice Ruth Bader Ginsburg joined Sotomayor in the first three sections, Sotomayor began the fourth (where the passage resides) by noting that she was "writing only for myself."[51] Certainly, one can read this as a declaration that she is writing *on behalf* of herself alone, but the tone in the fourth section (laced with the exigencies of black and brown life in the era of Ferguson) allowed many people of color to feel as if Sotomayor were writing for *us*, to apprehend her opinion as writing *by* us. (*For us, by us*, as Solange would say.) And by "for" I do not mean to say that she was speaking *on behalf* of people of color, but rather *to, with,* and *amongst* other people of color. In the dissent this surfaces as a trail of citations that includes, in addition to U.S. jurisprudence, Du Bois, James Baldwin, Michelle Alexander, Ta-Nahisi Coates, Lani Guinier, and Gerald Torres.[52] Speaking to, with, and for us, Sotomayor insists that many of the people of color who are "targeted by police" remain unheard: "Until their voices matter too, our justice system will continue to be anything but."[53] Through her dissent, Sotomayor mobilized the performative power of the court to affirm, officially, what many of us know and have always known: when you are black or brown "*your body is subject to invasion* while courts excuse the violation of your rights."[54]

6. Everybody Here's Going to Jail

When Desiree Harris got to the body of her grandson, the Ferguson police showed no empathy, offering little information, comfort, or compassion: "I asked the police what happened. They didn't tell me nothing."[55] All too often, as Jennifer Doyle remarks, "police do not participate in conversation, even a conversation that recognizes their presence and affirms that what is happening is happening. Or perhaps especially when a crowd [or person] affirms that what is happening is happening. There is no conversing with the inevitable."[56] Worse than this, the silence of the police officer may be preferable to other possible responses by the police. In May 2014 a man raced to a car accident where his girlfriend was badly injured. When he tried to get to her, Ferguson police arrested him. "EMS and other officers were not on the scene during the arrest," notes the DOJ report, "so the accident victim remained unattended, bleeding from her injuries, while officers were arresting the boyfriend."[57] But while there may be no arguing with the inevitable, the outcome of scenarios like this is anything but.

Performance is marked with indeterminacy, variation, and improvisation, so while the law may prescribe an officer's actions within a given scenario, the actors involved still improvise to a large extent. Indeed, in Ferguson a police officer has a great deal of latitude to determine how and if the law should she be applied (including, most importantly, the use of force). For the FPD officer, armed with a "staggering" number of arrest warrants, "the decision to arrest a person for an outstanding warrant is [according to City Officials] 'highly discretionary.'"[58] But the results compiled by the DOJ report are telling: "[FPD] officers do arrest individuals for outstanding municipal warrants with considerable frequency."[59] Furthermore, "despite making up 67% of the population, African Americans accounted for 85% of FPD's traffic stops, 90% of FPD's citations, and 93% of FPD's arrests from 2012 to 2014."[60]

It is often in the police officer's moment of decision (regarding *when, if,* and *how* to apply the law) that he or she becomes an embodiment of the law. In such scenarios, as Walter Benjamin described it, police perform "violence for legal ends (in the right of disposition), but with the simultaneous authority to decide these ends itself within wide limits (in the right of decree)."[61] The performance of the officer's decision regarding his or her authority to deploy force reveals the amorphous but near-total and troublingly pervasive power of the police in the democratic state: "Unlike law, which acknowledges in the 'decision' determined by place and time a metaphysical category that gives it a claim to critical evaluation, a consideration of the police institution encounters nothing essential at all. Its power is formless, like its nowhere tangible, all-pervasive, ghostly presence in the life of civilized states."[62] This "formless" power, though present within an "absolute monarchy," is, for Benjamin, more "devastating" in democracies, "where their [the police's] existence, elevated by no such relation [i.e., the 'legislative and executive supremacy' of the monarch], bears witness to the greatest conceivable degeneration of violence."[63]

The officer's actions may be quite illegal—either as a result of a defect in training (not being taught the law), will (not caring what the law is), or accident (forgetting or mistaking the law)—but in the law enforcement scenario the officer's actions *are* the law. In the DOJ report, the racial disparities that occur in the FPD's record "occur, at least in part, because Ferguson law enforcement practices are directly shaped and perpetuated by racial bias."[64] The discretionary, sovereign authority of the police officer comes to function as the means through which something that is legally abolished (racial discrimination by the state) takes fleshy, material form. This is often most recognizable in the scenes of subjection that occur during an officer's apprehension and arrest of a black person, particularly when the use of violence or force is involved. In such instances, the spectacle of the officer's violence *stages* white power's *hold* over and *use of* the black body. This may be true, even when it is not the intent of the officer to do so, and even if the officer is also black, because it is the performance scenario (a black body being beaten by a cop) that transfers and "repeat the initiating moments," not necessarily the will or intent or even circumstances of the actors involved.

The notion of violence as performance, and as a form of performance that instructs people about their place *within* the social, is not new. As Yves Winter has argued, for example, for Machiavelli (a foundational theorist and practitioner of modern Western politics), "violence functions as a rhetorical and theatrical element of the first order," so much so that "theatricality, it turns out, is constitutive not only of Machiavelli's politics but also of his understanding of war. In contrast to a long tradition . . . that treats war as brute force and as the crude deployment of violence, Machiavelli insists on war's representational dimension."[65] The "representational dimension" of violence is that which—as Spillers infers—"transfers" or transmits "its various *symbolic substitutions* in an efficacy of meanings that repeat the initiating moments" through embodied action.[66] For Winter's

Machiavelli, as for the slave master, as for the police officer, force can be a means through which the state stages its power over the body—the means through which power takes *hold* of the black body, as much as it functions as a means through which power is forcibly internalized into the body held by the law. As Sotomayor said, *your body is subject to invasion*. Especially when you are a person of color.

To reach that conclusion, Sotomayor draws upon a realm of thought much deeper than the sanctioned tomes of U.S. jurisprudence, turning to a black intellectual tradition that includes James Baldwin's *The Fire Next Time. The Fire Next Time,* first published in 1963, consists of two essays: the first, a letter to Baldwin's nephew; and the second, a meditation on the nature and experience of black life in a pathologically (and self-destructively) racist United States.[67] In the first, Baldwin warns his nephew, "You can only be destroyed by believing that you really are what the white world calls a *nigger,*" and in the second Baldwin shows the reader how it is that one might come to internalize such a belief.[68]

In a few striking passages, early in the second essay, Baldwin illustrates both the theatricality of police force as a means through which the white world takes hold of the black body, and as a means through which a phobic white public projects its own racist fantasies about black people across and into black bodies. In one moment, police power surfaces as a soft method for choreographing the black body's movement through segregated space. "I was thirteen and was crossing Fifth Avenue on my way to the Forty-second street library," he recalls, "and the cop in the middle of the street muttered as I passed him, 'Why don't you niggers stay uptown where you belong?'"[69] Only an utterance, the cop's words would have accumulated some degree of coercive effect for the young Baldwin, already well schooled, through force, in the NYPD's power over and claim to his body: "When I was ten, and didn't look, certainly, any older, two policemen amused themselves with me by frisking me, making comic (and terrifying) speculations concerning my ancestry and probable sexual prowess, and for good measure, leaving me flat on my back in one of Harlem's empty lots."[70] The lesson, here, remains strikingly similar to one taught through the theatricalization of violence during lynch law, or in the scenes of subjection of the transatlantic slave trade: the black body remains a site for "amusement" and objectification at white hands. "It was absolutely clear," Baldwin continues, "that the police would whip you and take you in as long as they could get away with it, and that everyone else—housewives, taxi-drivers, elevator boys, dishwashers, bartenders, lawyers, judges, doctors, and grocers—would never by the operation of any generous human feeling, cease to *use* you as an outlet for his frustration and hostilities."[71]

Ninety percent of the use of force *documented* by the Ferguson Police Department's is used against black people.[72] While cataloging the disparate use of "excessive force" by the FPD, the DOJ report pays particular attention to the movements, gestures, and actions of bodies within the scene of unlawful arrest: "Individuals encountering police under these circumstances are confused and surprised to find themselves being detained. They decline to stop or try to walk away, believing it within their rights to do so. They pull away, incredulously, or respond with anger. Officers tend to respond to these reactions with force."[73] Parts of this passage, with their sensuous description of the body, might as well be a description of dance: "they decline to stop or try to walk away," "they pull away, incredulously." The choreographic power of the law is on full display here, as the report accounts for a string of examples in which the FPD's deployment of force "appeared to be used as punishment for noncompliance with an order that lacked legal authority."[74] In such instances, as the officer performs violence, violence becomes the law. All too often, in Ferguson, the law demands the total submission of the black body to white hands, lawful or otherwise.

In one instance, "an officer stopped a 20-year-old African-American man for dancing in the middle of a residential street."[75] When a warrant check came up empty, the officer released the man, who unleashed a torrent of profanity on the officer. The officer then arrested the man for "Manner of Walking in Roadway."[76] Dancing, or "manner of walking," are potential crimes by which the black body may be subject to the hold of law enforcement, but here, even *talking* results in police coercion and potential force. When a man detained by the FPD wanted to log a complaint against excessive use of force during his arrest, "several different officers refused to let him speak to a sergeant to make a complaint about the incident and threatened to keep him in jail longer if he did not stop asking to make a complaint."[77] The FPD's use of force is given tacit approval by a lax supervisory structure that rarely limits, punishes, or bars officers for the excessive or unlawful use of force, because "supervisors seems to believe that any level of resistance justifies any level of force."[78] As a result, "FPD leadership sends a message that FPD officers *can behave as they like,* regardless of law or policy, and even if caught, that punishment will be light."[79] Which might be more accurately described as *behaving as they like* toward black people (regardless of law or policy), and of *using* black bodies as objects for amusement in any host of violent ways and without real repercussion.

A fourteen-year-old black kid was waiting in an abandoned house for a friend when, in December 2011, Ferguson police officers set a police dog upon him. He was five-foot-five, 140 pounds, and unarmed, and after the dog dragged him to the ground, biting him multiple times, FPD struck him, "one of them putting a boot on the side of his head. He recalled the officers laughing about the incident afterward."[80] Of FPD's use of canines, the report concludes that, "They [often] appear to use canines not to counter a physical threat but to inflict punishment."[81] The resonance between what happened to that little boy and what happened to a ten-year-old Baldwin in the empty Harlem lot is unmistakable. Both incidents conclude, figuratively or literally, with a boot on the side of the head and the punishment is enacted, here, for little more than the crime of being in a black body. Violence, in such instances, stages the state's domination or hold upon the black body, as much as it coerces and compels the black body to perform submission and silence. And it carries with it the echo of the violence of slavery. Remember that Baldwin characterizes his childhood beating at the hands of police officers as a whipping, conjuring the scenario of slavery's scenes of subjection: "The police would whip you and take you in as long as they could get away with it."[82]

On the six-month anniversary of the day that Darren Wilson shot Michael Brown, protestors gathered outside of the Ferguson police station:

> According to protestors, and consistent with several video recordings from that evening, the protestors stood peacefully in the police department's parking lot, on the sidewalks in front of it, and across the street. Video footage shows that two FPD vehicles abruptly accelerated from the police parking lot into the street. An officer announces, "Everybody here's going to jail."[83]

Nonetheless, black people persist in resisting.

7. The Uprising

If the racialization of black people reduces the black body to a kind of living objecthood, to be had and used for white amusement, Moten reminds us that "the history of blackness is testament to the fact that objects can and do resist."[84] The flesh is, after all, a site of struggle. For as Amber Musser writes, "Flesh occupies a fraught position within studies of difference. It oscillates between being a symptom of abjection and objectification and a territory ripe for reclamation. Despite its resonance with objectification and the negation of subjectivity, flesh has become an important political space. To ignore flesh is to ignore how bodies have been made to speak of difference."[85] Just as performance is a means of reducing a body to flesh, performance can be the means through which the flesh speaks, refusing to be ignored.

On August 9, 2014, Michael's body lies in the street in seventy-six-degree heat for four hours as the police investigate the murder. When his body is finally removed, residents spread flowers in the place where he drew his last breath. They march spontaneously, often silent, with arms raised in a symbolic gesture that invokes witness reports that his hands were raised in submission as Wilson shot him to death. Others erupt into violence, largely directed at private property. People burn down a Quick Trip, the equivalent of a 7-Eleven, and the FPD responds with a disproportionate declaration of a suburban ground war: tanks, armor, tear gas, and rubber bullets flow through Ferguson's streets. After days, the police assault and the rebellion simmers down to a tense accord. The tanks withdraw and the people wait for an indictment that will never come.

On November 17, 2014, the week before a grand jury announces its decision in Wilson's case, Governor Jay Nixon of Missouri declares a preemptive state of emergency. He activates the National Guard while placing the FPD under the unified command of the state police. The people are asked, from all quarters, to protest peacefully and remain nonviolent. On November 24, St. Louis county prosecutor Robert McCulloch announces that the grand jury will not indict Wilson for the murder, having failed to find probable cause. Protestors begin to assemble across the country. Protesters take to the streets in Ferguson.

On this night, Michael's mother, Lesley McSpadden, addresses a group of protestors. Her speech is peppered by angry and anguished cries of "Fuck the police" rising up from the crowd. Visibly shaken, she stands surrounded by a flank of family and friends. "I don't do nothing to nobody," she cries, before slipping into a sobbing silence. Her husband and Michael's stepfather, Louis Head, jumps onto the stage and holds her in his arms, rocking her back and forth. And then he explodes as his body spins out toward the crowd and he shouts: "Burn this motherfucker down." He trembles, wrenching his arms toward the ground, over and over and over again. The body explodes in all directions and he repeats the invective: "Burn this bitch down." He *shakes,* as if dancing, embodying Fanon's observation that "in the colonial world, the colonized's affectivity is kept on edge like a running sore flinching from a caustic agent. And the psyche retracts, is obliterated, and finds an outlet through muscular spasms that have caused many an expert to classify the colonized as hysterical."[86] But this is not hysteria; it's grief, which is often (in spite of itself) the most articulate of the emotions. "Give me a mike," he shrieks, and when one doesn't come he raises his fist to his mouth as if it could amplify the sound of his loss throughout the nation. He screams again, "Burn this bitch down." He didn't need to say it: Ferguson was already starting to burn.

Protestors tip over a police vehicle outside of Ferguson City Hall and set it ablaze. Around the country people begin to pour into the streets, hands raised in the air and chanting, "Hands up, don't shoot!" Traffic is shut down along major thoroughfares in urban areas as waves of arrests light up in cities across the republic: St. Louis, Boston, Los Angeles, Atlanta, Minneapolis, New York, DC, Philadelphia, Detroit, Chicago. In Ferguson, and despite heavy police presence, many of the businesses on Ferguson's West Florissant Avenue are left unprotected. The first of twenty-five buildings begins to burn, gutting the economic core of the city. Once again, clouds of smoke and pepper spray engulf the people and streets.

The morning after, CNN plays cellphone footage of Head's outburst on loop, amidst footage of burning buildings. His comments are quickly condemned as "unacceptable." This word, "unacceptable," comes from the mouth of Brown family attorney Daryl Park during an interview with Don Lemons. The video makes its rounds on the web. Missouri's lieutenant governor, Peter Kinder, declares that Head "should be arrested and charged with inciting to riot." Both St. Louis County Police and the Ferguson Police Department announce an investigation into Head's outburst.[87] Given speculation about criminal charges, it's critical for the Brown family lawyers to diffuse his explosion. They convene a press conference in order to mute his scream, describing it as a howl of "desperation and frustration" made in the heat of passion. In the final instance, says family attorney Benjamin Crump, the Brown family "understands we all have a responsibility to protect the community" and that "nobody is going to condone violence."

8. There's Never an Excuse for Violence

Another scenario routine and reportorial: a black family suffering the grief of a loved one murdered by the police is forced to call for nonviolence and calm. In the days following the second Ferguson uprising, a Staten

Island grand jury declines to indict a white police officer for the murder of another unarmed black man. On July 17, 2014, the NYPD claims that Eric Garner was selling untaxed cigarettes, but witnesses argue he was breaking up a fight. The police claim that Garner was resisting arrest. Witnesses insist that there was no need to arrest Garner in the first place. Before he dies, Garner makes a final plea:

> Everyone standing here will tell you I didn't do nothing. I did not sell nothing . . . I'm minding my business, officer, I'm minding my business. Please just leave me alone. I told you the last time, please just leave me alone. Please please, don't touch me. Do not touch me.[88]

This is not a man who is resisting; this is a man who is begging. While wrestling Garner to the ground, the police place him in an illegal chokehold. He chokes to death on the street as he pleads for his life, gasping, eight times, "I can't breathe."[89]

Garner's family performs the same ritualistic call for peace extracted from the Browns. Later, New York mayor Bill de Blasio holds a press conference. In widely praised remarks, the white mayor invokes his mixed-raced black son, Dante, in order to express his identification with the fear and frustration that black people feel toward police: "And for so many of our families, there's a fear. And not just from some of the painful realities—crime and violence in some of our neighborhoods—but are they safe from the very people they want to have faith in as their protectors?"[90] New York City police condemn the mayor's remarks, setting into motion a series of work stoppages and protests. At the same time, like every other leader, de Blasio calls for nonviolent protest, reanimating and ventriloquizing Eric in order to do so: "There can't be violence. [Eric's father, Ben] said Eric would not have wanted violence, violence won't get us anywhere." President Barack Obama also addresses the nation to call for nonviolence: "Those of you who are watching tonight understand there's never an excuse for violence."[91]

Official pleas for nonviolence, though not unexpected, have a bitter edge to them when the uprisings are rising up *against* police violence; violence that, when enacted upon and across black bodies, is sustained and supported through any range of official excuses, including the law. What's at stake here, then, is less the inexusability of *all* forms of violence than the law's claim to what Benjamin described as a monopoly of violence: "The law's interest in a monopoly of violence vis-à-vis individuals is not explained by the intention of preserving legal ends but, rather, by that of preserving the law itself; that violence, when not in the hands of the law, threatens it not by the ends that it may pursue but by its mere existence outside the law."[92] In the United States the law has tolerated, excused, and even encouraged a wide range of violence when it is applied to black bodies. This includes both state-sanctioned violence (e.g., police action, the slave trade) *and* extrajuridical violence (e.g., police action, lynching). Thus, we might conclude, alongside Weheliye, that "in the end, the law, whether bound by national borders or spanning the globe, establishes an international division of humanity, which grants previously excluded subjects limited access to personhood as property at the same time as it fortifies the supremacy of Man."[93]

Blackness becomes a constitutive limit defining the presumed norms of U.S. law and the exterior against which "Man," or white civic personhood, is defined. In *Scott v. Sandford,* or the apportionment compromise of the U.S. Constitution, for example, the black body is the threshold through which personhood and, by extension, citizenship can be defined; violence (state based *and* extrajuridical) polices this line. Violence *toward* the black body is acceptable, violence *from* the black body is intolerable and, as we see in Ferguson, any form of resistance (physical or verbal) may be matched with equal or (usually) greater forms of violence in response.

Baldwin's critique of violence marks this very problem. "In the United States," he writes, "violence and heroism have been made synonymous except when it comes to blacks."[94] Liberal pleas for nonviolent responses to antiblack violence belie the fact that "few liberals have any notion of how long, how costly, and how heartbreaking a task it is to gather the evidence that one can carry into court, or how long such court battles take."[95] And how often such court battles come up nil. But in the United States the most modest measure of reform or formal equality, achieved by way of due process, is often mistaken for success, sometimes papering over the continuation of "the well-established order" of white supremacy. As Baldwin also argued: "White Americans congratulate themselves on the 1954 Supreme Court decision outlawing segregation in the schools; they suppose, in spite of the mountain of evidence that has since accumulated to the contrary, that this was proof of a change of heart—or as they like to say, progress."[96] Thus, he concludes, "The real reason that non-violence is considered to be a virtue in Negroes . . . is that white men do not want their lives, their self-image, or their property threatened."[97] Popular uprisings often target private property, like Ferguson's Quick Trip, making official pleas for nonviolence that much more suspicious.

The official demand that black people in places like Ferguson cohere to dominant standards of nonviolence and protest within the law, while remaining subject to relentless forms of state violence, are manifestly rejected in the scene of an uprising. This negation of the negation also surfaces at the site of a body that pulls away from an officer attempting unlawful detention, or in the sound of a scream coming from a body that refuses to be dominated by the officer's blows. We might think of blackness here not just as constitutive limit, but also as a disruptive, disorganizing presence, which Moten describes thus: "Blackness—the extended movement of a specific upheaval, an ongoing irruption that anarranges every line."[98] This "irruption that anarranges every line" refuses, or exceeds, sovereign control, as reflected in the surge of uprisings in a place like Ferguson, or in Baldwin's own reflections on black people's refusal to accord to the standards set by the white world.

Tellingly, the example Baldwin provides is a legal infraction (black people stealing from white people). Such acts of theft, he argues, reveal the complex matrix of power in which black people are *held.* As he describes it, black people's refusal to submit to white standards, including the law, often results from the hypocritical nature of the standards: "His own condition is overwhelming proof that white people do not live by these standards."[99] But even more importantly, by refusing to submit to the law's compulsion to obey, blackness (and black performance) stands in defiance of the logic through which black bodies remain in the hold of, subjected to, or used by white power:

> In any case, white people, who had robbed black people of their liberty and who profited by this theft every hour that they lived, had no moral ground on which to stand. They had the judges, the juries, the shotguns, the law—in a word, power. But it was a criminal power, to be feared but not respected, and to be outwitted in any way whatever. And those virtues preached but not practiced by the white world were merely another means of *holding* Negroes in subjection.[100]

Blackness surfaces here as the anarrangement, refusal, and disorganization of power under white supremacy, an *outwitting* and evasion of the apparatuses of the law (judges, juries, shotguns, and police) as a means for resisting the *hold* of subjection.

For Moten, "the resistance to enslavement" is similarly "the performative essence of blackness (or, perhaps less controversially, the essence of black performance)."[101] The resistance of the object recurs, in Moten's terms, as "the ontological and historical priority of resistance to power and objection to subjection, the old-new thing, the *freedom drive that animates black performances.*"[102] In this sense, the uprising is not only inevitable, it is an *a priori* requirement for a new and better (dis)ordering of the world after and beyond the one established by and within white supremacy. Black performance is often the site in which this world flickers into being, whether it occurs in the form of a body pulling away from unlawful arrest, a scream, or on a stage, as a performance gives flesh to a prophecy of and claim to historical vengeance.

9. Histoircal Vengeance

The Fire Next Time cemented Baldwin's place in the arts wing of the black radical tradition. As the singer Nina Simone described him, "Jimmy, who had set the Village alight with *The Fire Next Time,* was a wonderful, mischievous child-genius at Langston [Hughes's] side, with his great round eyes which for some reason always made him look slightly sad."[103] This book, which "set the Village alight," ends, appropriately enough, with an incendiary prophecy: "If we do not now dare everything, the fulfillment of that prophecy, re-created from the Bible in song by a slave, is upon us: *God gave Noah the rainbow sign, No more water, the fire next time!*"[104] Rather than drawing authority from scripture, Baldwin gives credit to the creative, improvisatory ingenuity of the slave(s). It was they, he indicates, who appropriated scripture, improvising upon its themes and mediating it through the performance of the song, in order to transform God's covenant into a promise of divine vengeance for the white world's continued use of, and crimes against, black flesh.

Baldwin described this as "historical vengeance," which he feared to be an inevitability:

> I could also see that the intransigence and ignorance of the white world might make that vengeance inevitable—a vengeance that does not really depend on, and cannot really be executed by, any person or organization, and cannot be prevented by any police force or army: historical vengeance, a cosmic vengeance, based on the law that we recognize when we say, "Whatever goes up must come down." And here we are, at the center of the arc, trapped in the gaudiest, most valuable, and most improbable water wheel the world has ever seen.[105]

The "arc" might here be Dr. King's "arc of the moral universe" bending toward justice, where we are stuck "at the center." Not stuck, but "trapped," in which sense the arc might also recall the ark on which Noah survived the flood. To be "trapped" or held in the "center of the arc," in turn conjures those other boats in which our ancestors were held in the hold, "trapped" at the center of the Atlantic en route to a "racial nightmare" that continues to this day.[106]

In 1963, the same year Baldwin published *The Fire Next Time,* Medgar Evers was assassinated in his Jackson, Mississippi, driveway. A few months later, Addie Mae Collins, Carol Denise McNair, Carole Robertson, and Cynthia Wesley were attending bible study when four members of the Klan set off a bomb at the historic Sixteenth Street Baptist Church in Birmingham, Alabama. Infuriated and aggrieved over the murder of Evers and those four little girls, Simone too began to spin a portrait of the coming fire. "The idea of fighting for the rights of my people, killing for them if it came to that, didn't disturb me too much," she later recalled, "even back then I wasn't convinced that non-violence could get us what we wanted."[107] But to express this insurgent conviction Simone didn't take to physical acts of violence, so much as she animated the insurgent capacities of black performance. "I knew nothing about killing," she continued, but "I did know about music. I sat down at my piano. An hour later I came out of my apartment with the sheet music for 'Mississippi Goddam' in my hand. It was my first civil rights song, and it erupted out of me quicker than I could write it down."[108] An indictment of U.S. American apartheid, the song was first performed at the Village Gate before it was recorded live during a 1964 concert at Carnegie Hall, released on vinyl by Phillips later that year under the title *In Concert.*

"Mississippi Goddam" echoes and enacts Moten's description of blackness as an "ongoing irruption that anarranges every line." There, Moten's figuration of blackness is indebted to and bears the resemblance of the formal innovations of jazz, wherein the musician breaks from and disorganizes a melody or rhythm to produce a new sound. Simone herself described this confluence of jazz and blackness, understanding them less as biological or ontologically fixed (essentialist) *things,* than a kind of attitude performed into being at the point of the black body: "To me 'jazz' meant a way of thinking, a way of being, and the black man in America was jazz in everything he did—in the way he walked, talked, thought and acted."[109] Jazz and blackness are described here as a means of outwitting (white) power "in any way whatever," as Baldwin described it. Or as he also wrote, in his description of the critically disruptive and insurgent dimensions of black music, "This is the freedom that one hears in some gospel songs, for example, and in jazz. In all jazz, and especially in the blues, there is something tart and ironic, authoritative and double-edged."[110]

Simone mobilized the "double-edged" power of black performance in songs like "Mississippi Goddam" and, as Shana Redmond describes it, "Simone's radical methods of sound and performance modeled the strategies of revision that structured the transition from the Civil Rights Movement to the militancy of the Black Power Movement."[111] As Simone discovered, performance could be more than just a way of "spurring [student activists] on as best I could from where I sat—on stage, an artist, separate somehow." It became an act of insurgency: "My music was . . . [now] dedicated to the fight for freedom and the historical destiny of my people."[112]

Alongside "Mississippi Goddamn," *In Concert* included Simone's cover of Bertolt Brecht and Kurt Weill's "Pirate Jenny." There, she transposed the song from its location in the fictional landscape of *The Threepenny Opera* to the very real landscape of segregated South Carolina. Pirate Jenny tells the story of a domestic laborer, working in a portside inn, and carrying a deadly secret. A trio of Simone's voice, her piano, and a drum set, the song begins with a direct address to the listener, delivered over a staccato melody erupting from the piano:

> You people can watch while I'm scrubbing these floors
> And I'm scrubbing the floors while you're gawking
> Maybe once you tip me and it makes you feel swell . . .
> In this crummy Southern town
> In this crummy old hotel
> But you'll never guess to who you're talkin'.
> No. You couldn't ever guess to who you're talking.

Like Jenny, watched by the patrons of the inn, Simone was being watched (by a mostly white audience) as she performed in Carnegie Hall.

As she suggests that her audience might not know her true identity ("you'll never guess to who you're talkin"), Simone reveals the insurgent undercurrents flowing beneath her performance. Describing this moment, Malik Gaines argues that "in 'Pirate Jenny,' Simone relies on the authorization of her body to inhabit the role, this time of a beleaguered servant who dreams vividly of revolution, not a far stretch of the imagination in sixties black America."[113] In Ernst Bloch's analysis of this line (reviewing Brecht's original production), he insists that it "would not have its sweet and dangerous overtones, if there was no revolutionary condition in the world and if oppressed humanity was not rising up to fully realize itself."[114] Drawing a similar conclusion (in reference to Simone's version), Daphne Brooks argues, "Without ever mentioning race explicitly, Simone's cover of 'Pirate Jenny' would, in the midst of evolving black enfranchisement struggles, generate all sorts of rich historical allusions to the trajectory of African American forced migration, with a 'Black Freighter' coming and going, making a passage in the middle of the song toward our heroine who prophesies her own reversed stowage of escape on board the ship."[115] A direct address to the audience, "Pirate Jenny" tells a story about the white consumption of the spectacle of black labor/suffering, while rejecting the audience's own cynical self-satisfaction at engaging in this economy of consumption ("maybe once you tip me and it makes you feel swell"). But it is also a foreboding vision of the coming fire.

At the song's conclusion, Jenny takes in the spectacle of her vengeance. The Black Freighter arrives and its crew begins the wholesale destruction of the town. But here, Jenny assumes the insurgent ground, performing the function of sovereign decision: "And they're chainin' up people / And they're bringin' em to me / Askin' me, 'Kill them now, or later?" As she contemplates her response, Simone slows the song to a barely perceptible crawl. Having taken hold of the listener's ear, she takes command of time itself, crawling slowly across each word, giving the listener time to think through her intent in the gaps between the repeatedly broken phrases. She stretches her voice thin and bare across the vowels, and it recedes into raw growls that roll over the consonants (like the ship across the waves) as she issues her verdict: "I'll say, 'Right now.'" All sound stops and she spits the words into the microphone atop a whisper before pausing to utter them again. The second time more air and rasp than tone, an emphatic beat separating the words "right" and "now." The air trails out from behind her lips.

For Simone's Jenny, the violence of vengeance is instructive: "Then they'll pile up the bodies, and I'll say, 'That'll learn ya!'" Violence, as we have seen, is often pedagogical. In the famous primal scene of Frederick Douglass's autobiography, the young Douglass listens to the screams of his Aunt Hester, a slave, while her master, Antony, beats her. Antony, too, is teaching a lesson through violence. "Now, you d—d b—h," he cries in the midst of his amusements, "I'll learn you how to disobey my orders!"[116] The lesson is clear: Hester is Antony's property, to do with as he pleases; she's not a person, she's a thing, to remain always in the hold; her proper place is a state of submission and terror. Like the screams of Aunt Hester, Jenny will not be held in belly of the ship. Indeed, it turns out that she commands it.

Simone's lesson delivered, Jenny boards the boat and "the ship / The Black Freighter / Disappears out to sea." Placing an ocean of time between each word as if to allow the audience to contemplate her meaning, she delivers the final phrase, "and / on / it / is / me" as the gravelly scrape of her voice crawls down into the darkness. Inverting the direction of the middle passage, the black ship moves out across the Atlantic toward the horizon of emancipation. The song sets Jenny free, but the people in that audience in Carnegie Hall are left holding onto little else but the prophecy of coming fire, lingering in their ears like the trace of her growl.

10. Still Life

In the time of grief, there are times when you would, if you could, go back to that moment before someone died—the last minutes when they were alive, before they weren't. C. Riley Snorton describes this as the time of "still life," which is of critical importance for black people, and black trans people in particular, since black (trans) life is often experienced as living *toward* death:

> In the future imperfect . . . [the activist formation of] Black (Trans) Lives Matter provides a conceptual framework to understand the ongoing struggle in the present by way of a future (aspiration) in which black lives *will have* mattered to everyone. For some, including and following Fanon, that future effectively means the end of the world. And perhaps black and trans lives mattering in this way would end the world but worlds end all the time. . . . Even so and as yet, there is still life.[117]

Still life is the time before death. But it's also a name for the way we perform and improvise new forms of existence, new ways of being in the world, and even new worlds in that time in which we are still alive. "Everything now, we must assume," writes Baldwin, "is in our hands."[118] For this reason, we must "not falter in our duty now," which is to "end the racial nightmare . . . and change the history of the world."[119] Even so and as yet, there is still life.

11. Twelve

one two three
four five
six seven eight
nine ten eleven

12.

Somewhere in Ferguson, Desiree Harris is driving her car
through her neighborhood.
Somewhere in Ferguson, Desiree Harris is driving her car
through her neighborhood.
Somewhere in Ferguson, Desiree Harris is driving her car
through her neighborhood.
Somewhere in Ferguson, Desiree Harris is driving her car
through her neighborhood.
Somewhere in Ferguson, Desiree Harris is driving her car
through her neighborhood.
Somewhere in Ferguson, Desiree Harris is driving her car
through her neighborhood.
Somewhere in Ferguson, Desiree Harris is driving her car
through her neighborhood.
Somewhere in Ferguson, Desiree Harris is driving her car
through her neighborhood.
Somewhere in Ferguson, Desiree Harris is driving her car
through her neighborhood.
Somewhere in Ferguson, Desiree Harris is driving her car
through her neighborhood.
Somewhere in Ferguson, Desiree Harris is driving her car
through her neighborhood.
Somewhere in Ferguson, Desiree Harris is driving her car
through her neighborhood.

NOTES

1. A. Greg, "Outraged Crowds Gather after a Police Officer Shot an Unarmed Teenager on the Street in St Louis and His Grandmother Discovers His Body," *Daily Mail*, August 9, 2014, http://www.dailymail.co.uk/news/article-2720924/Missouri-woman-finds-grandson-dead-shot-police.html (accessed April 28, 2017).

2. Audre Lorde, "Age, Race, Class, and Sex: Women Redefining Difference," in *Sister Outsider: Essays and Speeches* (Berkeley, CA: Crossing Press, 2007), 119.

3. A. Greg, "Outraged Crowds."

4. Ibid.

5. Richard Rothstein, "The Making of Ferguson: Public Policies at the Root of Its Troubles," Economic Policy Institutes, http://www.epi.org/publication/making-ferguson/ (accessed April 28, 2017).

6. U.S. Department of Justice Civil Rights Division, "Investigation of the Ferguson Police Department," Department of Justice, 2015: https://www.justice.gov/sites/default/files/opa/press-releases/attachments/2015/03/04/ferguson_police_department_report_1.pdf, 76 (hereafter, DOJ).

7. Ibid.

8. Ibid.

9. Ibid., 7–8.

10. Ibid., 55.

11. *Utah v. Strieff*, 579 U.S., Sotomayor, S., dissenting at 7 (2015).

12. Ibid., 3.

13. Between 2010 and 2015, for example, Ferguson raised its general fund revenue from $11 million to $13 million, annually. In 2010, $1.38 million was generated by court fines and fees and in 2015 the city anticipated this number at 3.09 million: DOJ, 9–10.

14. Ibid., 9.

15. Ibid., 55. Ferguson often set fees within the highest brackets in the region (a "Weeds/Tall Grass" charge in Ferguson ranged between $77 and $102, compared to $5 in a nearby town): ibid., 10. Given the relatively high number of Ferguson residents living at or near the poverty line, it is not uncommon for people to be unable to pay their fines. This problem is compounded by the fact that Ferguson offered no community service option for repayment, and that failure to pay on schedule or to appear before the court regularly resulted in a proliferation of more fees and, ultimately, the issuance of an arrest warrant.

16. Ibid., 56.

17. Ibid.

18. *Boumediene v. Bush*, 553 U.S. 723 (2008), 739.

19. Alexander G. Weheliye, *Habeas Corpus: Racializing Assemblages, Biopolitics, and Black Feminist Theories of the Human* (Durham, NC: Duke University Press, 2014), 79. Weheliye's use of the term "Man" is drawn from the work of Sylvia Wynter, who uses "Man to designate the modern, secular, and western version of the human that differentiates full humans from not-quite-human and nonhumans on the basis of biology and economics": 139n3.

20. *Dred Scott v. Sandford*, 60 U.S. 393 (1856), 739.

21. Ibid.

22. Hortense J. Spillers, "Mama's Baby, Papa's Maybe: An American Grammar Book," in *Black, White, and in Color: Essays on American Literature and Culture* (Chicago: University of Chicago Press, 2003), 206.

23. Spillers, "Interstices: A Small Drama of Words," in ibid., 155.

24. Christina Sharpe, *In the Wake: On Blackness and Being* (Durham, NC: Duke University Press, 2016), 15.

25. Saidiya V. Hartman, "The Time of Slavery," *South Atlantic Quarterly* 101, no. 4 (2002): 759.

26. Joshua Takano Chambers-Letson, *A Race So Different: Performance and Law in Asian America* (New York: New York University Press, 2013).

27. Saidiya V. Hartman, *Scenes of Subjection: Terror, Slavery, and Self-Making in Nineteenth-Century America* (Oxford: Oxford University Press, 1997), 17.

28. Ibid., 41.

29. Ibid., 24.

30. Ibid., 183.

31. W. E. B. Du Bois, *Black Reconstruction in America 1860–1880* (New York: Free Press, 1998), 136.

32. Diana Taylor, *The Archive and the Repertoire: Performing Cultural Memory in the Americas* (Durham, NC: Duke University Press, 2003), 28–33.

33. Koritha Mitchell, "Black-Authored Lynching Drama's Challenge to Theater History," in *Black Performance Theory*, ed. Thomas DeFrantz and Anita Gonzalez (Durham, NC: Duke University Press, 2014), 89.

34. Ibid. See also *Living with Lynching: African American Lynching Plays, Performance, and Citizenship, 1890–1930* (Urbana: University of Illinois Press, 2011).

35. Joseph R. Roach, *Cities of the Dead: Circum-Atlantic Performance* (New York: Columbia University Press, 1996), 2.

36. Taylor, *The Archive and the Repertoire*, 2–3.

37. Rebecca Schneider, *Performing Remains: Art and War in Times of Theatrical Reenactment* (London: Routledge, 2011), 15.

38. Goffman works with an (albeit broad) definition of performance as "all the activity of a given participant on a given occasion which serves to influence in any way any of the other participants" (Erving Goffman, *The Presentation of Self in Everyday Life* [New York: Anchor, 1959], 15).

39. Spillers, "Mama's Baby, Papa's Maybe," 207.

40. Ibid.

41. Andrew Parker and Eve Kosofsky Sedgwick, "Introduction: Performativity and Performance," in *Performativity and Performance* (New York: Routledge, 1995), 4.

42. André Lepecki, *Exhausting Dance: Performance and the Politics of Movement* (London: Routledge, 2006), 63.

43. *Utah v. Strieff*, Sotomayor, S., dissenting at 10.

44. Ibid.

45. Ibid.

46. Ibid.

47. Ibid., 11.

48. Ibid.

49. Hartman, *Scenes of Subjection*, 19.

50. *Utah v. Strieff*, Sotomayor, S., dissenting at 12.

51. Ibid., 10.

52. Ibid., 12.

53. Ibid.

54. Ibid.

55. A. Greg, "Outraged Crowds."

56. Jennifer Doyle, "Campus Security" (Los Angeles: Semiotext(e), 2014), 12.

57. DOJ, 81.

58. Ibid., 63.

59. Ibid., 62. Tellingly, black people in Ferguson were more likely to be subject to vehicular search, being twenty-six percent less likely to have contraband in the car (ibid).

60. Ibid., 62.

61. Walter Benjamin, "Critique of Violence," in *Reflections: Essays, Aphorisms, Autobiographical Writings*, ed. Peter Demetz (New York: Schocken, 1978), 287.

62. Ibid.

63. Ibid.

64. DOJ, 70.

65. Yves Winter, "The Prince and His Art of War: Machiavelli's Military Populism," *Social Research: An International Quarterly* 81, no. 1 (2014): 175, 86.

66. Spillers, "Mama's Baby, Papa's Maybe," 207.

67. James Baldwin, *The Fire Next Time* (1963; reprint, New York: Vintage, 1993).

68. Ibid., 19.

69. Ibid., 4.
70. Ibid., 19–20.
71. Ibid., 21.
72. DOJ, 5, 28.
73. Ibid., 34.
74. Ibid., 34–35.
75. Ibid., 25.
76. Ibid.
77. Ibid., 83.
78. Ibid., 40.
79. Ibid., 86.
80. Ibid., 32.
81. Ibid., 33.
82. Baldwin, *The Fire Next Time,* 21.
83. DOJ, 27.
84. Fred Moten, *In the Break: The Aesthetics of the Black Radical Tradition* (Minneapolis: University of Minnesota Press, 2003), 1.
85. Amber Musser, *Sensational Flesh: Race, Power, and Masochism* (New York: New York University Press, 2014), 20.
86. Frantz Fanon, *The Wretched of the Earth,* trans. Richard Philcox (New York: Grove Press, 2004), 19.
87. Elliot C. McLaughlin and Catherine E. Schoichett, "Police Asking: Did Michael's Browns' Stepfather Intend to Spark Riots," December 3, 2014, http://www.cnn.com/2014/12/02/justice/ferguson-protests-investigation/ (accessed April 28, 2017).
88. Susanna Capulouto, "Eric Garner: The Haunting Last Words of a Dying Man," December 8, 2014, http://www.cnn.com/2014/12/04/us/garner-last-words/ (accessed April 28, 2017).
89. Ibid.
90. Bill De Blasio, "Remarks on Eric Garner Decision," December 3, 2014. The official website of the City of New York: http://www1.nyc.gov/office-of-the-mayor/news/542–14/transcript-mayor-de-blasio-holds-media-availability-mt-sinai-united-christian-church-staten (accessed April 28, 2017).
91. Barack Obama, "Remarks by the President after Announcement of the Decision by the Grand Jury in Ferguson, Missouri," November 24, 2014, http://www.whitehouse.gov/the-press-office/2014/11/24/remarks-president-after-announcement-decision-grand-jury-ferguson-missou (accessed April 28, 2017).
92. Benjamin, "Critique of Violence," 281.
93. Weheliye, *Habeas Corpus,* 79.
94. Baldwin, *The Fire Next Time,* 58.
95. DOJ, 8.
96. Baldwin, *The Fire Next Time,* 86.
97. Ibid., 59.
98. Moten, *In the Break,* 1.
99. Baldwin, *The Fire Next Time,* 22.
100. Ibid., 23 (emphasis added).
101. Moten, *In the Break,* 16.
102. Ibid., 12 (emphasis added).
103. Nina Simone and Stephen Cleary, *I Put a Spell on You: The Autobiography of Nina Simone,* 2nd ed. (New York: Da Capo Press, 2003), 80.
104. Baldwin, *The Fire Next Time,* 105–6.
105. Ibid., 105.

106. Ibid.

107. Simone and Cleary, *I Put a Spell on You,* 89–90.

108. Ibid., 90.

109. Ibid., 68–69.

110. Baldwin, *The Fire Next Time,* 42–43.

111. Shana L. Redmond, *Anthem: Social Movements and the Sound of Solidarity in the African Diaspora* (New York: New York University Press, 2014), 183.

112. Simone and Cleary, *I Put a Spell on You,* 91.

113. Malik Gaines, *Black Performance on the Outskirts of the Left: A History of the Impossible* (New York: New York University Press, 2017), 33

114. Ernst Bloch, "The Song of Pirate Jenny in the *Threepenny Opera,*" in *Literary Essays* (Stanford, CA: Stanford University Press, 1998), 349.

115. Daphne A. Brooks, "Nina Simone's Triple Play," *Callaloo* 34, no. 1 (2011): 181.

116. Frederick Douglass, *Narrative of the Life of Frederick Douglass, an American Slave,* ed. Houston A. Baker (New York: Penguin Books, 1982), 52.

117. C. Riley Snorton, *Black on Both Sides: A Racial History of Trans Identity* (Minneapolis: University of Minnesota Press, 2017), 169.

118. Baldwin, *The Fire Next Time,* 105.

119. Ibid.

Contributors

Joshua Chambers-Letson is Assistant Professor of Performance Studies at Northwestern University.

Catherine M. Cole is Divisional Dean of the Arts at the University of Washington in Seattle, where she also serves as Professor in the School of Drama.

Lawrence Douglas is James J. Grosfeld Professor of Law, Jurisprudence & Social Thought at Amherst College.

Ryan Hartigan is Assistant Professor of Theater at the University of Nebraska.

Lara D. Nielsen is Profesora Associada at IE University Madrid, Spain.

Julie Stone Peters is Professor in the Department of English and Comparative Literature at Columbia University.

Ann Pellegrini is Professor of Social and Cultural Analysis and Performance Studies, and Director of the Center for the Study of Gender and Sexuality at New York University.

Austin Sarat is Associate Dean of the Faculty, the William Nelson Cromwell Professor of Jurisprudence & Political Science, and Professor of Law, Jurisprudence & Social Thought at Amherst College.

Karen Shimakawa is the Chair and Associate Professor of Performance Studies in the New York University Tisch School of the Arts.

Martha Merrill Umphrey is Director of the Center for Humanistic Inquiry and Bertrand H. Snell 1894 Professor in American Government in the Department of Law, Jurisprudence and Social Thought and Class Dean at Amherst College.

Index

www.ingramcontent.com/pod-product-compliance
Lightning Source LLC
LaVergne TN
LVHW091123080826
845145LV00008B/2029

* 9 7 8 1 6 2 5 3 4 3 5 5 0 *